Essential Grammar
for Today's Writers, Students, and Teachers

This innovative and affordable resource is designed for writers, language students, and classroom teachers who need an accessible guide to essential English grammar. Without becoming mired in detailed linguistic definitions, Nancy Sullivan helps writers understand and apply grammatical concepts to develop the skills they need to enhance their own writing. She clearly explains English grammar basics, using a highly practical, hands-on approach to mastering the use of language. While the text focuses on word classifications and how each word class functions in sentences, Sullivan provides examples and exercises that are contextually grounded in engaging discussions of language development. Online instructor materials provide teachers with additional suggestions and activities designed to enhance these basic grammar lessons.

"Nancy Sullivan's *Essential Grammar for Today's Writers, Students and Teachers* achieves what few grammar texts accomplish: it presents its subject in a thorough, yet accessible style and format to vanquish any fears students and teachers may have about learning and teaching this timeless topic. The text includes examples that appeal to a range of audiences and alleviates the traditional assumption that the parts of speech and the way we use them is a mystery to be mastered only by experts. This book will remain a valuable reference for its readers long after a course has ended. In other words, it is indeed essential."
—**Kristine L. Blair, Bowling Green State University**

"Nancy Sullivan's text provides a fresh, clear approach to grammar for students in all disciplines, particularly future language arts teachers. Beginning with and building on the basics and working through verbal phrases and dependent clauses, Sullivan methodically explores the way English works. This reasonably priced book includes virtually all the concepts needed for teaching English grammar. Teachers will appreciate its streamlined approach—less reading and more doing is always good in a grammar class."
—**Elizabeth Ruleman, Tennessee Wesleyan College**

Nancy M. Sullivan teaches grammar and linguistics at Texas A&M University-Corpus Christi, where she has been a member of the English Department for over twenty years. Her research on the intersection of language attitudes and identity has been widely published. Sullivan's keen interest in and avid study of grammar has been inspired by her students, who continue to spark her curiosity with their insights and questions.

Essential Grammar
for Today's Writers, Students, and Teachers

Nancy M. Sullivan

Routledge
Taylor & Francis Group

NEW YORK AND LONDON

First published 2015
by Routledge
711 Third Avenue, New York, NY 10017

Simultaneously published
by Routledge
2 Park Square, Milton Park, Abingdon, Oxon, OX14 4RN

Routledge is an imprint of the Taylor & Francis Group, an informa business

Library of Congress Cataloging in Publication Data
Sullivan, Nancy, 1949–
Essential grammar for today's writers, students, and teachers / by Nancy Sullivan.
pages cm.
Includes index.
ISBN 978-0-7656-4174-8 (pbk.: alk. paper) 1. English language—Grammar. I. Title.
PE1112.S85 2014
428.2—dc23 2014018403

ISBN: 978-1-138-85702-5 (hbk)
ISBN: 978-0-7656-4174-8 (pbk)
ISBN: 978-1-315-71865-1 (ebk)

Online resources for adopting instructors, including additional instructors' materials, are available at:
www.routledge.com/9780765641748

For my mom, who always encouraged me to write a book,
although she was not expecting the main characters to be
nouns, verbs, and dangling participles,

and

for my sister Gail Sullivan Eakright (1947–2009),
a longtime educator, talented artist, and best friend.

Contents

Preface ....*xi*

Acknowledgments ....*xiii*

Introduction ....*xv*

Commonly Used Abbreviations ....*xxi*

Chapter 1 / Word Classes...3
Language Focus: Language and the Brain 3
Nouns 4
Adjectives...7
    Determiners 9
        Articles 9
        Demonstratives 9
        Quantifiers 9
        Possessives 10
        Numbers 10
    Descriptive Adjectives 11
Pronouns...13
    Personal Pronouns 14
    Reflexive Pronouns..15
    Demonstrative Pronouns 16
    Indefinite Pronouns..18
Verbs...21
    Three Simple Verb Tenses 23
    Auxiliary Verbs..23
        The Perfect..23
        The Progressive..24
        The Perfect Progressive 24
        Modals 25

Adverbs 26

    Adverbs Modifying Verbs 27

        Adverbs of Manner..27

        Adverbs of Time, Place, and Frequency 28

    Adverbs Modifying Adjectives and Adverbs 29

Prepositions 31

Conjunctions 33

    Coordinating Conjunctions...33

    Correlative Conjunctions..34

Interjections 36

Chapter Review..36

Chapter 2 / Extending The Basics 41

Language Focus: The Sounds of Language 41

Extending Nouns 42

    The Pronoun Substitution Test 43

    Noun Phrase Appositives..46

Extending Prepositional Phrases 49

    Adjectival Prepositional Phrases 51

    Adverbial Prepositional Phrases...54

    Prepositional Phrases Versus Phrasal Verbs 57

Extending Verbs with Active and Passive Voice 59

Extending Conjunctions with Conjunctive Adverbs 65

Chapter Review..67

Chapter 3 / Sentence Patterns 71

Language Focus: Sociolinguistics...71

Verb Classes 72

    Linking Verbs 72

    Intransitive and Transitive Verbs 76

        Intransitive Verbs 76

        Transitive Verbs...77

Sentence Patterns..80

    Linking Verb Patterns 80

    Intransitive and Transitive Verb Patterns.....................................83

Intransitive Verb Pattern..83

Transitive Verb Patterns..84

Chapter Review 91

Chapter 4 / Verbals: Gerunds, Participles, and Infinitives....................95

Language Focus: Language Acquisition 95

Gerunds 96

Identifying Gerunds...96

Tests for Gerunds..98

Pronoun Substitution Test 98

Possessive Subject Test 100

Verb Conjugation Test..101

Participles 105

Identifying Participles..107

Punctuation of Participles..111

Differences Between Gerunds and Participles 114

Infinitives..116

Identifying Infinitives 117

Infinitives as Nouns 118

Infinitives as Adjectives...119

Infinitives as Adverbs 121

Adverb Infinitives Modifying Verbs...................................121

Adverb Infinitives Modifying Adjectives 122

Chapter Review..124

Chapter 5 / Adjective, Adverb, and Noun Clauses.............................129

Language Focus: The History of English.....................................129

Adjective Clauses..132

Relative Pronouns...132

Adjective Clauses with Relative Pronouns

"Which" and "That" 133

Relative Pronoun "Which"..133

Relative Pronoun "That"..135

Adjective Clauses with Relative Pronouns

"Who," "Whom," and "Whose"..137

Relative Pronoun "Who"..137

x   Contents

Relative Pronoun "Whom" 138

Relative Pronoun "Whose" 140

Punctuation of Adjective Clauses 143

Adjective Clause Quirks 146

Relative Pronoun Deletion 146

Adjective Clauses with Relative Adverbs 148

Adverb Clauses 149

Subordinating Conjunctions 149

Adverb Clauses Modifying Verbs 150

Adverb Clauses Modifying Adjectives and Adverbs 152

Adverb Clauses Introduced by "That" 152

Adverb Clauses Introduced by "Than" 156

Noun Clauses 158

Noun Clause Slots 158

"That Type" Noun Clause 160

"Wh– Type" Noun Clause 164

Chapter Review 169

Answers to Exercises *171*

Hyperlinks *205*

Glossary *207*

Index *219*

About the Author *229*

Preface

The purpose of this book is to make basic grammar concepts and terminology accessible to future teachers who will need this knowledge for their own classrooms. The book is also designed to help students who are not pursuing teaching certification gain more insight into how sentences are structured, along with the important punctuation rules that support those structures and clarify meaning.

Most students start my grammar course with limited instruction in grammar and find the idea of an entire semester of studying grammar rather intimidating. Current textbooks often assume that students already know basic grammatical concepts and terminology; as a result, most books are too advanced and include much more material than can be covered in one semester. *Essential Grammar for Today's Writers, Students, and Teachers* provides a semester-long course book that does not assume a strong background in grammar.

In addition to its focus on the basics, this book adds an intriguing layer to the study of grammar: linguistic topics provide context for the grammar concepts. At the beginning of each chapter, a **Language Focus** box introduces a linguistic topic that supports the grammar examples and exercises. This replaces inane, disconnected examples (e.g., "Sally threw John a ball") with a linguistic thread that connects all of the chapters.

The linguistic topics also provide fodder for further conversations. For example, in Chapter 5 on clauses, the topic is the history of the English language. The exercises and examples span 2,000 years of the formation of our language—it's all about who invaded the big rock and what languages they brought with them.

Additional information about the linguistic topics and links to related websites can be found in **Did you know?** boxes. For example, in Chapter 5, there is a link to a rap version of Geoffrey Chaucer's *Canterbury Tales*, along with a translation into Modern English. In Chapter 3, which discusses the sounds of language, there is a link to a short and funny segment from *CBS Sunday Morning* that gives examples of female celebrities using "vocal fry," a creaky voice affectation heard among some young women.

Some of the **Did you know?** boxes directly support the grammar concepts being discussed. For example, the popular Bruno Mars song "When I Was Your Man" shows how the past form of a verb sometimes is used rather than its past participle form: "I should have gave you all my hours" versus "I should have given you all my hours." Listening to the song to find this usage brings the discussion of verb forms to life.

The additional information in the **Did you know?** boxes can be used to stimulate classroom discussion or it can be ignored, depending on the time and interests of the instructor and students. Of course, as a linguist, I tend to be biased about the linguistic topics, and I am convinced that readers will find them interesting and relevant as well. At the very least, I expect that they will gain a better understanding of language as a by-product of their grammar study.

As speakers of English, students already know a lot about grammar and language, so it is often a matter of helping them connect that knowledge to the structures and terminology used in this book. In fact, the key to understanding grammar is to explore grammatical forms in terms of their function. Therefore, we look at what the words, phrases, and clauses are doing in the sentence (function) rather than what these elements look like (form). By examining words, phrases, and clauses in context, students learn to assess the grammatical functions that these forms perform in a sentence. This helps them understand that grammar concepts are not static entities.

In this book, I provide both traditional and contemporary grammar terminology and definitions. When future teachers enter their own classrooms, they may find the traditional terminology still being used in other textbooks. Therefore, I feel it is important to equip them with the language that they will need to be able to work with a variety of texts.

The instructors' website is a rich resource of creative and engaging activities that support students' learning of grammar, such as grammar bingo. Also included are pedagogical suggestions that can be used to help students connect grammar to their own texts. For example, at the beginning of the semester, I ask students to write a "Grammar Literacy Paper"—a personal essay in which each student reflects on his or her own grammar journey. This paper is used throughout the semester to explore the grammar concepts that we are discussing in class. Activities related to this initial assignment are available on the website.

Finally, I hope you will agree with me that this book offers writers, students, and teachers relevant and interesting insights into language while exploring essential grammar terminology and punctuation. Please feel free to email me with your comments and suggestions. My email address is available on the instructors' website.

Acknowledgments

First of all, I would like to acknowledge and thank Suzanne Phelps Chambers, Executive Editor at M.E. Sharpe, whose belief in and commitment to the project made this book possible. Simply put, it would not have happened without her. I would also like to thank Brianna Ascher, Editorial Coordinator, and the rest of the staff at M.E. Sharpe who participated in the production of this book. I'd particularly like to thank Laura Brengelman, Assistant Managing Editor and Project Editor. As a result of her meticulous editing, she not only made this a better book, she taught me how to be a better editor and writer. Her enthusiasm, guidance, and patience kept me focused throughout the process.

Thank you also to my longtime friend Andreas Jozwiak, whose constructive comments gave important feedback from a student's point of view. Additionally, the Paul and Mary Haas Foundation provided support through a generous fellowship that enabled me to complete this project.

Finally, I would like to acknowledge my husband, Wes Adkison, for his unwavering support during this lengthy project. His absolute belief in the need for this book and his confidence in my writing it kept me steadily moving forward.

Introduction

Most likely, there are a variety of reasons why you are reading this introduction and taking a grammar course. The course may be required for teacher certification or a degree in English, or you may be convinced that a good foundation in grammar is essential for your career. My goal in writing this book is to provide you with the basics of English grammar that you will need to address grammar questions in your own future classroom or workplace. As a result of your grammar study, I promise that you will develop a stronger "metalinguistic" awareness (the ability to reflect on and analyze language) that will support better reading and writing.

I have taught grammar for more than twenty years. When I first started to teach it, the course's goal was to provide a review of grammar for students pursuing primary or secondary teaching certification. But I found that my students, both then and now, often had little or no experience with grammar terminology and concepts prior to taking the class. (So much for the course being a review!) Many students have reported that their primary and secondary school teachers avoided discussions of grammar. If grammar was addressed at all, their teachers appeared to be less than comfortable with the material.

Part of the problem stems from the status of grammar as a classroom subject, which has been controversial over the past forty years. After a report in the 1970s argued that grammar had little to no value in developing writing skills, the subject was dropped from the curriculum in many schools. Now that students of that era are in their own classrooms teaching, they tend to avoid grammar because they do not have the background or confidence to teach it.

I don't want to spend time debating the various viewpoints; however, it is important to note that there is a great deal of new research underscoring the value of grammar in the curriculum to support reading and writing. A rich resource on this debate (and suggestions for teaching grammar) is the website http://teach-grammar.com/topics, which contains articles from some of the top educators in language and writing studies.

I decided to write *Essential Grammar for Today's Writers, Students, and Teachers* with my students in mind. Most are pursuing certification in TESOL (Teaching English to Speakers of Other Languages), elementary language arts, or secondary

English. Knowledge of basic grammar is particularly important for future classroom teachers. Instructors and their students need a shared vocabulary to communicate clearly and effectively about their texts. In addition, based on recent research and my experience as an educator, I am convinced that understanding grammar enhances our ability to both write and read.

Descriptive Versus Prescriptive Grammar

Introductions to grammar books typically describe their approach to the study of grammar as either prescriptive or descriptive. A prescriptive grammar is grounded in rules found in traditional grammar handbooks, such as "Never end a sentence with a preposition" (why not?), "Don't start a sentence with a conjunction" (it's legal!), and "Don't split an infinitive" (what does that mean?). A descriptive grammar aims to describe the system of grammar used by native speakers.

In the field of linguistics, all dialects are considered legitimate forms of communication. In the real world, however, we all know that people judge some dialects as "better" than others. The term "Standard English" generally is applied to the dialect spoken by educated speakers; "Nonstandard English" can be described as dialectical varieties that follow other rules. Some dialects are stigmatized as being "incorrect" or "bad" English, to the point where speaking such a dialect can limit an individual's career opportunities. My South Texas students often talk about how extremely self-conscious they are about their "bad" speech, but generally, it is simply their accent and not their usage of grammar that is being pointed out as "different." Nevertheless, years of criticism have left a mark.

Take, for example, the use of "be" in African American English, as in "I be late." This usage would be considered nonstandard, even though it cleverly expands the Standard English form of "be" ("I am late"), which is also used in African American English. I know a number of highly educated people who use nonstandard forms when they speak (most often unconsciously); however, when they write academic texts, they use Standard English. I soon learned not to mention this inconsistency in usage to friends—they tend to get very defensive (I wasn't criticizing, really).

Some grammar books claim to be purely descriptive and not prescriptive, but the differences between the two approaches are not that clear cut. In this book, I often point out the traditional definitions of terms and prescriptive rules because many of those are still used in language arts books. I also point out that "use" and "rules" can differ; for example, would you use the word "whom" at a party with your friends just because you're educated? Only if you wanted to be referred to as a show-off or a snob—or worse. So, even though I fall into the descriptive camp, I am still describing the rules of the dialect used by educated speakers of English in the United States.

Grammar Terminology

You will find that some of the terminology used in this book is not consistent with that found in other books. In fact, almost no two books use the exact same grammar terminology. (Sorry to break that news to you.) For example, I have found that the number of verb tenses ranges from two to twelve (I chose three), depending on the source.

Not only does terminology vary, but often the analyses of sentence structures does as well. In this book, I strive for consistency and keep to the basics of English language structure. For those of you who plan to teach, you should be able to apply what you learn here to any grammar book that you use in the future.

Even the term "grammar" has a range of definitions. Some books use grammar as a broad term that encompasses punctuation, structural patterns, word formation patterns, sound systems, and more; others books are more restrictive. I use the term "grammar" to cover the terminology associated with grammar concepts, sentence patterns, and punctuation.

Essential Grammar for Today's Writers, Students, and Teachers focuses on the function of the grammatical unit in the sentence, not its form. By contrast, you may have found that some books look primarily at the form, not the function. For example, in school, you probably learned that a noun is a person, place, or thing, right? So you would analyze the word "classroom" as a noun (thing). But what about the sentence "He had a great classroom experience"? Is "classroom" still a noun? If we are examining the function of a word, "classroom" would be labeled an adjective because it is modifying the noun "experience."

What about the word "jogging" in the sentence "Jogging is my hobby"? "Jogging" looks like a verb, but is it functioning as a verb in this sentence? No, it is the subject, and so it functions as a noun (a gerund).

In this book, we will look at words in context, and we will analyze them by their functions within that context. (Your awareness of this approach is so important that I will mention it numerous times.) By studying grammar, you gradually will discover new ways to think about sentence structure. Punctuation plays an important role in clarifying that structure; therefore, I also point out important punctuation rules throughout the book.

Organization of the Book

Let's discuss what lies ahead. The book is organized into five chapters. We start small with word classes (also known as parts of speech) in Chapter 1 and end with larger constructions in Chapter 5—sentences with two or more clauses (each clause having its own subject and verb). Each chapter builds on the content of the previous chapters. Therefore, it is important to make sure that you have a good grasp of the material in each chapter before moving on to the next.

Each chapter begins with the important concepts (in bold) that you are expected to learn. The opening paragraph is followed by a **Language Focus** box, which highlights an area of linguistic studies—that is, the study of language—adding an exciting dimension to the grammar book. (Okay, so I am a little prejudiced about linguistics because I am a linguist.)

The language focus adds context to the examples and exercises. For instance, in Chapter 1, the grammar focus is word classes, but the language focus is language and the brain. A number of the exercises use the topic of Genie, a girl who was locked in a small room until the age of thirteen. She was forbidden to make any noise, and so she grew up without language. Linguists wondered whether Genie would be able to learn language at such an "old" age (supporting or negating the "use it or lose it" argument). Genie's story provides an intriguing language topic for the exercises.

The language focus is reinforced by a number of **Did you know?** boxes. These give you a closer look at some interesting linguistic topics. Many of them have links to websites that provide more detailed information. The story of Genie is reinforced by a **Did you know?** box that provides links to short videos of her and about her.

In Chapter 4, the grammar focus is verbals (gerunds, participles, and infinitives), while the language focus is on language acquisition. To support the learning of verbals, a number of the examples refer to research being conducted on primates. Some researchers believe that primates can learn language—a controversial but fascinating topic. They seek to prove this by showing primates using symbols, sign language, and keyboards (a type of sign language). In a **Did you know?** box, you can follow a link to a well-known primate research lab that shows a chimpanzee communicating with her handlers. Another link shows Koko, a gorilla who lives at the Maui Ape Preserve, signing her sadness over the death of her cat (All Ball became road kill). Interestingly, some researchers argue that if primates are taught language, they may be able to develop other advanced cognitive skills (a Planet of the Apes scenario?).

After the **Language Focus** box, each chapter is divided into sections based on the major grammar concepts being covered (e.g., nouns, verbs, adjectives, gerunds). A short overview of the concepts is followed by an introduction to the organization of the discussions; a number of subheadings break up the concepts into smaller units.

Numerous exercises throughout the chapters help you practice what you are learning. These are followed by summary exercises at the end in the **Chapter Review**. As the material becomes more challenging, there will be more exercises to give you added opportunities to engage with the material and check your comprehension. At the end of the book, you can find the **Answers to Exercises**, which provides answers to the first five in each exercise. Also provided are a list of **Hyperlinks**, a useful **Glossary** of the terminology used in this book, and an **Index** to help you navigate to various subjects. Throughout the book, important terms and major headings are in bold, and examples are in italics.

What You Will Not Find in This Book

Let me briefly address what elements are not included in this book because there are reasons for their elimination. You will not find evidence of the grammar police trying to enforce the prescriptive rules of grammar. I realize that there are many ways of speaking and writing, and we choose the appropriate level of formality or informality based on our audience and communication goals. I am simply providing you with the structures and terminology of English grammar based on native speaker usage.

You will not find a highly academic tone in this text. My goal is to communicate with you as I communicate with my students in the classroom. I may break the rules of formal academic writing, for example, by using a contraction, like I'm doing right now. Contractions are grammatical, but their usage in formal writing is discouraged because they give an informal tone to the text. My goal is to present grammar concepts not as a series of disjointed items but rather as an ongoing discussion that allows you to build on what you already know. With more knowledge, you can make grammatical choices that fit with what you are trying to achieve in your text.

You will not find a comprehensive examination of all grammar concepts, all exceptions to rules, or all of the possible sentence patterns of English. I made some difficult decisions about which grammar concepts to exclude from this book and what exceptions to point out. For instance, you will not diagram a sentence (although I do think there is a place for diagramming in some classrooms). As a result of such decisions, you are not paying for a book that covers too much material for a one-semester course.

Essential Grammar for Today's Writers, Students, and Teachers is designed to give you the basic and most important grammar terms and structures. Providing you with the essential foundation, it empowers you to continue to explore more advanced grammar concepts if needed and according to your interest level.

What I Think About Grammar

Even after twenty-plus years, I am continually amazed at how interesting grammar study can be. I learn something every semester from the questions that students ask and the knowledge and insight that they bring to the discussions. Plus, I can always use the brain massage that I get when I investigate a perplexing grammar problem.

Finally, please take advantage of this book. Use it to build confidence in your own ability to teach or use grammar for professional and personal purposes. I hope you gain a new interest in grammar or at least develop a new respect for it as a topic worthy of intellectual pursuit.

Commonly Used Abbreviations

There are a number of terms abbreviated in this book with acronyms or shortened forms. I provide explanations within the text, but here is another reference point for those terms:

ADJ	adjective/adjectival
ADV	adverb/adverbial
DO	direct object
FANBOYS	coordinating conjunctions—for, and, nor, but, or, yet, so
IO	indirect object
IV	intransitive verb
LV	linking verb
N	noun
NP	noun phrase
OC	object complement
OP	object of preposition
P	preposition
PA	predicate adjective
PN	predicate nominative
PP	prepositional phrase
PRO	pronoun
PST	pronoun substitution test
TV	transitive verb
V	verb
VCT	verb conjugation test
Ved	past tense form of verb (e.g., walked, ate)
Ven	past participle verb form (e.g., walked, eaten)
Ving	present participle verb form (e.g., walking, eating)
VP	verb phrase
*	indicates that the sentence is considered ungrammatical
?	indicates grammaticality is questionable

Essential Grammar
for Today's Writers, Students, and Teachers

1
Word Classes

In case you did not read the introduction (if possible, please go back and do so), let me quickly point out one of the features of this book before you get started. At the beginning of each chapter, you will see a **Language Focus** box, which may seem a little out of place at first glance. However, this box is very important as it sets up the language focus for the chapter. Its purpose is to provide interesting context for the grammar examples and exercises. You will also see a number of **Did you know?** boxes that include relevant and engaging facts (and many links) about language.

The term "linguistics" is used throughout this book to refer to the study of language. As students of grammar, you are budding linguists! Okay, you are now ready to proceed.

This chapter focuses on the major word classifications. These classifications traditionally were referred to as the eight **parts of speech**, but they are now called **word classes**. Understanding these classifications is critical to your success in this course. Important grammatical concepts to learn in this chapter are **noun**, **adjective**, **pronoun**, **verb**, **adverb**, **preposition**, **conjunction**, and **interjection**.

Language Focus: Language and the Brain

Researchers in the fields of psycholinguistics and neurolinguistics investigate how languages are learned, lost, produced, understood, and stored in the brain. Some of the questions that these linguists ask include: How do we learn a first or second language? How do our short- and long-term memories affect language processing? What processes are involved in making the sounds that form words? Where do we store word meaning, and how do we access this information? How do we take a series of words and get meaning from them?

Before we begin our exploration of these individual classes of words, it is important to look at the bigger picture—the sentence. Using traditional terminology, the sentence is divided into two parts: the **subject** and the **predicate**. Sentences need these two parts (the exception being a command with an understood subject, e.g., "Sit down"), and, for the most part, they must be in this order:

Brains   *evolve.*
subject   predicate

Above, the subject is *Brains*, and the predicate is *evolve*. The predicate contains at least a verb. No matter how long it is, a grammatical sentence must have a recognizable subject and predicate:

The complex human brain   *has stimulated much research into its design*.
subject   predicate

In the example above, the subject is *The complex human brain*, and the predicate is *has stimulated much research into its design*, with *has stimulated* as the verb. Following traditional terminology, *brain* would be considered the **simple subject** within the **complete subject** (*The complex human brain*), and *has stimulated* would be the **simple predicate** within the **complete predicate** (*has stimulated much research into its design*).

In more contemporary approaches, the terminology differs slightly. The sentence is divided into the **subject noun phrase** and the **verb phrase**:

• head noun • head verb
↓   ↓

The complex human brain   *has stimulated much research into its design*.
subject noun phrase   verb phrase

A subject noun phrase must have a **head noun** (*brain* in the above sentence), and the verb phrase must contain at least a **head verb**, also referred to as the **main verb** (*stimulated* in the sentence above). In this book, we will use the terms **subject noun phrase**, **head noun**, **verb phrase**, and **head verb**.

As mentioned in the introduction, this book classifies words by their function in a sentence. This means that we will always consider the function rather than the form of the word. To do so, the word must have context. For example, the word "human" has a noun form, but in the subject noun phrase shown above (*The complex human brain*), *human* functions as an adjective describing what kind of *brain* (a human brain, not a monkey brain). You will get a better understanding of function versus form analysis as we move through this chapter.

Nouns

The traditional definition of a **noun** is that it names a person, place, thing, or idea. That definition is sometimes useful, but it eventually will lead you astray. Instead, we will look at some tests that will help you identify nouns. First, let's review some of the terminology associated with nouns.

In traditional grammar, the major classifications of nouns are common and proper, count and noncount. **Common nouns** are not capitalized (language, brain, symbols). **Proper nouns** are capitalized, and they are, for example, names of specific people (Jong, Eduardo, President Obama), places (Budapest, the Vatican, the Center for Applied Linguistics), or events (Hanukkah, Christmas, Mardi Gras).

The terms **count** and **noncount** refer to nouns that can be counted (one brain, two brains) and those that cannot (*one oxygen, *two oxygens; *one ice, *two ices). (The asterisk is used throughout this book to indicate language that would be considered ungrammatical by a native speaker.) Count nouns have both singular forms and plural forms (brain, brains; neuron, neurons; wish, wishes, etc.) and can be used with numbers (two brains; 1,000,000 neurons; three wishes). Noncount nouns (also called **mass nouns**) do not have plural forms and cannot be counted, but they can be used with words such as "little" and "much" (little oxygen, much ice, much fluency, etc.).

How do you know whether a word is a noun? It is easy if the word is a count noun because it will have both singular and plural forms (language/languages), and you can put a determiner (a, an, or the) or a number (one, two, three, etc.) in front of it (a language, the language, two languages). You can ONLY do this to nouns. (Note that there may be one or more adjectives between the determiner or number and the noun—for example, "the difficult comprehensive exams.")

The challenge is that mass nouns and most proper nouns do not have different singular and plural forms, and you cannot always use determiners or numbers with them. For example, you cannot make "milk" or "honesty" plural (*milks, *honesties) or put a determiner (a, an, or the) in front of "honesty" (*the/a honesty is important). But you can put "the" in front of "milk" (The milk turned sour). Even "honesty" could take a determiner in certain contexts: "The honesty of her testimony was questioned."

The ability to change a noun from singular to plural and to use a determiner or number in front of it are just two tests that can be used for recognizing a large number of nouns, but obviously, more noun tests are needed. These will be discussed later in this chapter. In the meantime, let's practice identifying nouns by using the singular/plural and determiner tests.

Exercise 1.1 Getting a Grip on Nouns

Find and underline all of the nouns in the following sentences by using the singular/plural and determiner tests. The number of nouns in the first five sentences is indicated at the end of each sentence.

Example:

Our brains are complex machines. (2)
singular/plural test: brain/brains, machine/machines
determiner test: the brains, the machines

1. The brain has a left hemisphere and a right hemisphere. (3)
2. Some psycholinguists study the organization of the brain. (3)
3. Researchers conduct fascinating experiments on people. (3)
4. Brain scanners have facilitated psycholinguistic studies. (2)
5. Linguists may define language as a set of rules. (4)
6. How do adults learn another language?
7. People process written language rapidly.
8. One psychologist believed errors in speech reveal repressed emotions.
9. Children acquire nouns earlier than verbs.
10. Our mental dictionary is interesting to researchers.

Now that you've underlined all of the nouns, pay attention to where they are found in the sentences. Did you notice that all of the subjects are nouns? (1. *brain*; 2. *psycholinguists*; 3. *Researchers*; 4. *scanners*; 5. *Linguists*; 6. *adults*; 7. *People*; 8. *psychologist*; 9. *Children*; 10. *dictionary*). With few exceptions, subject slots are occupied by nouns or pronouns (pronouns will be discussed later in this chapter after adjectives), and, as subjects, they precede the verb of the sentence (in questions, word order can change, e.g., "Are you going?"). Nouns are also located in other slots in the above sentences, such as the object slot after the verb. We will look more closely at those noun slots in Chapters 2 and 3.

DID YOU KNOW?

Nouns provide insights into our social and cultural history. We are constantly adding new nouns to our vocabulary to reflect present-day realities. For example, look at all of the new social media terminology. We now have the noun "Facebook" (and a lot of verbs that result from it, such as "to friend" someone). The nouns "Twitter" and "tweets" were born in 2006. Can you think of other nouns that recently have been added to our vocabulary because of social media?

Adjectives

In this section, we review the most common terminology associated with **adjectives**. The traditional definition is that an adjective modifies a noun or pronoun. In reality, adjectives do a lot more work than the traditional definition gives them credit for. They can change, expand, qualify, quantify, add to, and enrich the concepts of the nouns and pronouns they modify. There are many types of adjectives. Here, you will learn to recognize words that function as adjectives, and in the following chapters, you will be introduced to other adjective forms.

There are two types of adjectives: **determiners** and **descriptive adjectives**. Determiners include articles (the, an, a), demonstratives (this, that, these, those), numbers (one, two, first, second, etc.), possessives (my, psycholinguist's, your, etc.), and quantifiers (some, few, many, etc.). Descriptive adjectives represent the largest number of adjectives (tall, short, small, gray, sloppy, difficult, etc.). We add new descriptive adjectives to our language all the time and even change the meanings of existing ones. For example,

That dessert was <u>fabulicious</u>!

She is feeling <u>tweepish</u> about the tweet she sent. She regrets sending it.

I got paid to be part of an experiment at school. What a <u>sweet</u> deal!

A noun can have a number of adjectives modifying it, for example,

<u>Severe</u> <u>brain</u> damage can affect <u>some</u> <u>language</u> skills.

In the above sentence, *severe* and *brain* both function as adjectives modifying the noun *damage* (*severe damage, brain damage*), and both *some* and *language* function as adjectives modifying the noun *skills* (*some skills, language skills*). If we examine *brain* and *language* from a traditional perspective (a person, place, or thing), we would label these words as nouns; however, we always look at the function of a word, not what it looks like. These words function as adjectives in this sentence.

Adjectives regularly occupy two slots in relationship to the nouns that they modify (although they can also be found elsewhere). Most often, an adjective precedes the noun it modifies, for example, "<u>slow</u> speech." "Slow" is an adjective modifying the noun "speech." Here are some examples with the adjectives (ADJ) underlined and arrows pointing to the nouns (N) that they modify:

<u>left</u> hemisphere   (<u>ADJ</u> N)

your language   (ADJ N)

two dialects   (ADJ N)

As mentioned above, a noun can have multiple adjectives modifying it:

brain's left hemisphere   (ADJ ADJ N)

your native language   (ADJ ADJ N)

two different dialects   (ADJ ADJ N)

The other slot where adjectives are often found is after a certain type of verb. In this case, the adjective goes back and modifies the subject, as shown in the following sentence:

Language is complex.

This adjective comes after a specific kind a verb called a **linking verb**. We will discuss linking verbs in greater detail in Chapter 3. In short, the typical linking verb is what is known as a "be" verb (is, are, was, were, will be, has been, etc.). In the example above, the adjective *complex* goes back and links to the subject noun *language*. Here are some other examples of sentences with adjectives that come after linking verbs and modify the subjects.

The message was garbled. ←*The* is also an adjective modifying *message*.

Chinese class is interesting. ←*Chinese* is also an adjective modifying *class*.

Some accents can seem different. ←*Some* is also an adjective modifying *accents*.

Now that we know the two slots where adjectives are found, let's look more closely at the two types of adjectives: determiners and descriptive adjectives. We examine determiners first.

Determiners

Adjectives that are determiners generally precede the nouns they modify. These include **articles**, **demonstratives**, **quantifiers**, **possessives**, and **numbers**.

Articles

Some of the most commonly used English words are **articles**. "The" (called a **definite article**) assumes reference to a specific noun, for example, "the speech organism," while "a" and "an" (**indefinite articles**) refer to nonspecific nouns, as in "a speech organism" or "an organism." They are great signal words—they tell us, "Heads up! Here comes a noun or pronoun." They always function as adjectives:

The grammar of a child shows a pattern.

Children learn the rules of grammar in a systematic way.

Demonstratives

Four words can function as **demonstrative adjectives**: this, that, these, those. They are used with nouns to point out a specific person (people) or thing(s):

This brain suffered damage.

That brain suffered severe damage.

The researcher read about these studies.

Language behavior was examined in those studies.

Quantifiers

Adjectives that tell us how much or how many of the following noun are labeled **quantifiers**:

Few children are not able to learn language.

Most children learn language rapidly.

Some children experience language delay.

All normal children have the capacity to learn language.

Children are able to learn several languages at a young age.

Which quantifier is used depends on whether the noun is count or noncount. For example, the quantifier "few" cannot be used with the noncount noun "honesty" (*few honesty), but the quantifier "little" can be used (little honesty). Other common quantifiers are much, several, no, more, enough, less, and many.

Possessives

As the term indicates, these **possessive** adjectives show possession of a noun:

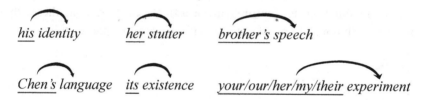

his identity   *her stutter*   *brother's speech*

Chen's language   *its existence*   *your/our/her/my/their experiment*

Possessives can easily be confused with other word classes—especially if you can't let go of the traditional definition of a noun. For example, *Chen's* and *brother's* may be mislabeled as nouns because of their forms, but they function as adjectives above. Possessive adjectives can also be confused with possessive pronouns (his, hers, mine, etc.), which will be discussed in the upcoming section on pronouns.

Numbers

Commonly used as adjectives, **numbers** can also modify nouns:

Behaviorist B.F. Skinner was accused of experimenting on his two children.

Two men, Broca and Wernicke, made major discoveries about brain functions in the 1800s.

Descriptive Adjectives

Adjectives that do not fall into the category of determiners are considered **descriptive adjectives**. Below are examples that show a descriptive adjective in front of the noun that it modifies.

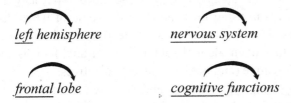

<u>left</u> hemisphere   <u>nervous</u> system

<u>frontal</u> lobe   <u>cognitive</u> functions

Here are examples of descriptive adjectives that come after linking verbs and modify the subjects.

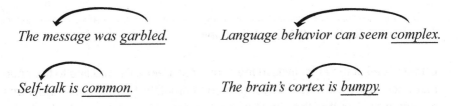

The message was <u>garbled</u>.   Language behavior can seem <u>complex</u>.

Self-talk is <u>common</u>.   The brain's cortex is <u>bumpy</u>.

Many descriptive adjectives have comparative and superlative forms, meaning that they are gradable (e.g., tall, taller, tallest). Most often, this is done by adding the suffixes "–er" and "–est" to descriptive adjectives with one syllable, such as "smart" (smart, smarter, smartest). The comparative and superlative forms of adjectives with two or more syllables (except adjectives ending in "–y," e.g., bumpy, bumpier, bumpiest), are preceded by "more" (comparative) and "most" (superlative):

> She is <u>intelligent</u>.
> She is <u>more intelligent</u> than her roommate.
> She is the <u>most intelligent</u> of all.

One test to find gradable adjectives is the **very test**. If the suspected adjective can be intensified by the adverb "very," then it could be an adjective. Here is an example of the adjective "intelligent" being intensified by the adverb "very":

> She is intelligent. = She is very intelligent.

Not all adjectives are gradable. For example, you are either married or not (although you may hear the expression "She is very married," which indicates something more than a legal commitment, or "She is very pregnant," indicating size rather than status). In addition, many adjectives that can function as another word class (e.g., noun) are not gradable, such as "language" in "language area." Here, "language" functions as a descriptive adjective, and it is not gradable.

WARNING!

You will see that some adverbs can also be preceded by "very." We will discuss these later in this chapter.

Like nouns, descriptive adjectives are continually being added to our language. Young adults are often pioneers in using these new words, some of which have longer life spans than others. Think of some of the adjectives used to describe someone who has imbibed too much alcohol (other than "drunk")—it is most likely a long, colorful list of creative (and not so creative) adjectives.

In sum, adjectives modify nouns and pronouns, and they are often found in two positions in relation to the nouns and pronouns that they modify: preceding the noun or following a linking verb (referring back to the subject).

Exercise 1.2 Getting a Grip on Adjectives

Underline all of the adjectives in the sentences below. Draw a line to the noun that each adjective modifies. To help you complete this exercise, the verbs are set in bold so that they don't distract you from the nouns and adjectives.

Example:

The left hemisphere of the brain **regulates** many language processes.

1. Artificial intelligence **copies** human behavior.
2. New experimental designs **have emerged**.
3. Your left side **is regulated** by the right hemisphere.
4. Dysgraphia **is** a writing disorder.
5. Speech errors **provide** researchers with helpful information.
6. The brain **processes** positive words faster than negative words.
7. Brain activity **can be measured** while a person **is reading**.
8. A brain **processes** ambiguous words more slowly than unambiguous words.
9. Researchers **study** the psycholinguistic mechanisms that **affect** language production.
10. There **is** evidence that young girls **have** better language skills than young boys.

Pronouns

Here we examine four types of **pronouns**: **personal**, **reflexive**, **demonstrative**, and **indefinite**. (Relative pronouns are examined in Chapter 5.) The traditional definition of a pronoun is that it substitutes for a noun:

> *Children* acquire language easily. *They* are amazing learners.
> *The child's grammar* may seem irregular. However, *it* is very normal.

In the first example above, *they* replaces *children*; *children* is called the **antecedent** of the pronoun *they*. Because *children* is a plural noun, the plural pronoun *they* is used. In the second example, *The child's grammar* is the antecedent of *it*. (Note that the pronoun substitutes for the noun and its adjectives.)

The mismatching of pronouns and their antecedents is one place where beginning writers and English language learners often make errors. They may use a plural pronoun when referring to a singular noun, for example, *"The problem was easy to fix, and I took care of them quickly" (in this case, "them" refers back to the singular noun "problem").

Pronouns occupy the same slots as nouns (subject, object, etc.), which makes sense given that they replace nouns. The inventory of pronouns is stable, meaning that we don't add new ones to English as we do with nouns and adjectives. However, we can get creative with pronouns. For example, some dialects have "youse" for the plural form of "you," as in "I saw youse." The Southern plural version is "y'all" or "all y'all." My use of "you guys" as a plural form of "you" reflects my Chicago dialect.

We now examine each type of pronoun starting with personal pronouns. We will also practice differentiating personal pronouns from the adjectives that share the same or similar forms.

DID YOU KNOW?

Research by Professor James W. Pennebaker shows that when someone is lying, he or she tends to avoid the personal pronoun "I." In a short YouTube video, he uses the example of former congressman Anthony Weiner lying about posting sexually explicit photos of himself. You can see the lies multiply in this interesting video. Search for "Language of Truth and Lies: I-Words" or go to www.youtube.com/watch?v=Vc073RlC7_M.

Personal Pronouns

Table 1.1 provides an overview of the **personal** and **reflexive pronouns** of English. If you are familiar with the works of William Shakespeare or the Bible, you know that there used to be another second-person pronoun set (you): thou, ye, thee, thine, and thyself. There are dialects of English in northern England that still retain some of these old forms. Additionally, some Quakers in the United States still use thee and thou.

Table 1.1

Personal and Reflexive Pronouns

	Personal Pronouns			Reflexive Pronouns
	Subject	Object	Possessive	
First Person				
singular	I	me	mine	myself
plural	we	us	ours	ourselves
Second Person				
singular	you	you	yours	yourself
plural				yourselves
Third Person				
singular	she, he, it	her, him, it	hers, his, its	himself, herself, itself
plural	they	them	theirs	themselves

It is important to distinguish the **personal pronoun** forms from the possessive adjectives that have the exact or similar word forms (e.g., his). We know that adjectives must be attached to nouns, whereas pronouns are not (rather, they substitute for nouns). For example, the following sentences have personal pronouns (PRO) as well as possessive adjectives (ADJ). The adjectives that can be confused with personal pronouns (there also are other types of adjectives in the sentences) have arrows pointing to the nouns they modify:

> *One type of brain disorder is called jargon aphasia. My grandfather has*
> *this disorder.*   ADJ
>
> *His is the result of a stroke. His speech is difficult to understand, and I*
> PRO   ADJ   PRO
> *sometimes have trouble communicating with him. He gets frustrated with*
>   PRO PRO
> *his disability.*
> ADJ

His is used three times above—once as a pronoun and twice as an adjective. Note that the adjective is always attached to a noun.

Because pronouns can be confused with adjectives, Exercise 1.3 gives you important practice distinguishing between the two.

Exercise 1.3 Getting a Grip on Personal Pronouns Versus Adjectives

Decide whether the underlined words function as pronouns (P) or adjectives (A). Circle the correct answer. In addition, if the word is functioning as an adjective, draw an arrow to the noun that it modifies.

1. P (A)   Your brain has two hemispheres—the left and the right.
2. P (A)   Sentence context affects our language processing.
3. P (A)   Damage to specific regions of the brain can affect your language.
4. (P) A   Research on aging may help us in the future.
5. P (A)   Research labs are trying to map our neural structures.
6. P (A)   Neuromagnetic imaging can show where your brain processes words.
7. (P) A   Gabby Giffords, the Arizona representative shot at a political rally, relearned speech after her brain injury.
8. P (A)   My grandfather has Alzheimer's disease, a form of brain degeneration.
9. P (A)   He knows that his speech is abnormal.
10. (P) A   We take care of him in our home.

Reflexive Pronouns

Related to personal pronouns, **reflexive pronouns** have the suffixes "–self" (singular) or "–selves" (plural). For the most part, reflexive pronouns are used to refer back to the subject:

> Some linguistic researchers study *themselves*.

> I taught *myself* Chinese (or) I taught Chinese to *myself*.

Reflexive pronouns can also be used for emphasis:

> Einstein *himself* donated his brain to science.

> The decision to have surgery to stop seizures is something
>
> epileptics must decide *themselves*.

Demonstrative Pronouns

There are four **demonstrative pronouns** in English: this, that, these, and those. Below are examples of sentences using these pronouns:

> *Did you see this?*
> *That was a bad experiment.*
> *These came from the bonobo experiment.*
> *I need to examine those.*

Demonstrative pronouns are often confused with demonstrative adjectives. When modifying nouns, they are adjectives; when used alone, they are pronouns:

> *How do we identify those sounds?*   ←Function: ADJECTIVE modifying the noun *sounds*

> *How do we identify those?*   ←Function: PRONOUN (object)

> *This experiment tested word memory.*   ←Function: ADJECTIVE modifying the noun *experiment*

> *This was the first of its kind.*   ←Function: PRONOUN (subject)

A pronoun references a noun, which should be clear from the context:

> *The experiment tested a person's memory. This was the first of its kind.*

It is important to be able to distinguish between a demonstrative pronoun and a demonstrative adjective. Below, a demonstrative pronoun and a demonstrative adjective are shown in context:

> *Researchers studied students' memory of their instructors' lectures.*
>
> *Memories about the main topic stayed intact for two days, but, after five*
>
> *days, those were lost. Instructors may not like this news.*
>   PRO   ADJ

Exercise 1.4 Getting a Grip on Personal, Reflexive, and Demonstrative Pronouns

Underline all of the pronouns in the following sentences and mark them as personal (p), reflexive (r), or demonstrative (d). The number of pronouns in the first five sentences is indicated at the end of the sentence. Be careful not to underline adjectives! (Hint: Not all sentences have pronouns.)

Example:

p   p

The scan showed her brain had healed faster than they thought it would. (2)

1. You cannot stop yourself from processing language. Your brain does it automatically. (3)

2. Have you ever had a word on the tip of your tongue, but you couldn't say it? (3)

3. Psycholinguists study this phenomenon. They call it a "word retrieval" problem. (2)

4. Dysgraphia is a writing disorder. This is also considered a processing disorder. (1)

5. A study found that a patient with dysgraphia could spell words, but he could not spell nonwords, like "plarf." (1)

6. Psycholinguists investigate speech errors. These studies help us understand our brains.

7. Sometimes we flip two sounds. For example, I once said "bare rook" instead of "rare book."

8. This error shows how we plan our speech. It indicates how far in advance our words are chosen.

9. You may understand yourself when you make a speech error, but other people may be clueless.

10. People with Broca's aphasia often get frustrated with their speech.

DID YOU KNOW?

The error of switching sounds is called a **spoonerism**, named for the Reverend William Archibald Spooner (1844–1930), an Anglican priest and an Oxford don who was well known for his tendency to transpose sounds. For example, he extolled to his Oxford congregation that "The Lord is a **sh**oving **l**eopard" rather than "The Lord is a **l**oving **sh**epherd." It is reported that he referred to the "**d**ear old **q**ueen" as the "**q**ueer old **d**ean." There are a number of amusing online sites dedicated to spoonerisms as well as a book entitled *Smart Feller Fart Smeller: And Other Spoonerisms*, by John Agee.

Indefinite Pronouns

There is another large group of pronouns called **indefinite pronouns**. Table 1.2 lists some of the most common ones.

Table 1.2
Common Indefinite Pronouns

all	much
another	neither
any, anyone, anybody, anything	none, no one, nobody, nothing
both	one(s)
each	other, others
every, everyone, everybody, everything	several
few	some, someone, somebody,
many, more, most	something

To better understand indefinite pronouns, examine the difference between the following two sentences:

Four students will be conducting the experiments.
Some will be conducting the experiments.

In the first sentence, we know exactly how many students will be conducting experiments (*Four* functions as an adjective), but the number of student researchers in the second sentence is unclear (*Some* is the indefinite pronoun). Consider how many times you have asked, "How many people will be at the party?" and have received a vague (indefinite pronoun) response: "A few." Often, follow-up questions are needed.

Like demonstratives, indefinite pronouns can be confused with adjectives that have the same forms but different functions. Remember, an <u>adjective must modify a noun or pronoun</u>. Below are examples that contrast indefinite pronouns with adjective quantifiers:

Most children learn the word "no" first. ←Function: ADJECTIVE
                                                            modifying *children*

Most learn the word "no" first. ←Function: PRONOUN (subject)

Both children used sign language. ←Function: ADJECTIVE
                                                            modifying *children*

Both learned sign language from ←Function: PRONOUN (subject)
their deaf parents.

You distinguish the pronoun form from the adjective form by looking at its function in the sentence. Is it modifying a noun or pronoun? If yes, then it is an adjective; if no, then it is a pronoun.

Exercise 1.5 Getting a Grip on Indefinite Pronouns Versus Adjective Quantifiers

How do the underlined words function? Circle P for indefinite pronoun and A for adjective quantifier.

1. P A   <u>One</u> study showed that one shot of alcohol increased some participants' ability to pronounce a foreign language more fluently.
2. P A   <u>Most</u> lost that ability after drinking a second shot of alcohol.
3. P A   Why might <u>some</u> Southerners misunderstand the speech of Northerners (and vice versa)?
4. P A   <u>Many</u> children have not been tested for dyslexia, even though they may be poor readers.
5. P A   How <u>one</u> learns to read may affect attitudes toward reading.
6. P A   Dementia is a brain disease that can impair <u>many</u> cognitive abilities, such as speaking or understanding language.
7. P A   Dementia may cause changes in personality for <u>some</u>.
8. P A   <u>Many</u> believe that language is unique to humans.
9. P A   For <u>most</u> children, the brain is able to rebuild itself after injury.

10. (P / A   <u>Some</u> researchers examined Albert Einstein's brain for
              "clues" after he died.

We have examined four different types of pronouns, and now we will review all of the pronouns together. Below you need to demonstrate that you
are able to recognize words that function as pronouns.

Exercise 1.6 Getting a Grip on Personal, Reflexive, Demonstrative, and Indefinite Pronouns

Underline the personal, reflexive, demonstrative, and indefinite pronouns in
the sentences below. The number of pronouns to find in the first five sentences is indicated in parentheses. (Hint: One sentence has no pronouns.)

1. <u>Nobody</u> understands the brain completely. (1)
2. How many meanings does "bank" have, and how do <u>we</u> choose the
   correct <u>one</u>? (2)
3. <u>Children</u> first learn common words, and many of those can come from
   <u>their</u> storybooks. (2)
4. Do babies teach <u>themselves</u> how to speak, or do <u>they</u> need our
   instruction? (2)
5. Your brain processes ambiguous words more slowly than unambiguous
   <u>ones</u>. (1)
6. One theory argues that our language determines our worldview.
7. Male students made more slips of the tongue when an attractive
   female experimenter asked them to read words than those in a similar
   experiment with no "distractions."
8. Those with the attractive female experimenter often read "past fashion"
   as "fast passion."
9. Slips of the tongue are part of everyone's speech. Don't worry yourself
   over such errors.
10. Some argue that chimpanzees can learn language. This is a very
    controversial viewpoint.

Exercise 1.7 Getting a Grip on Identifying Pronouns

Go back to the first page of this chapter and count all of the personal, reflexive, demonstrative, and indefinite pronouns in the **Language Focus** section. How many pronouns did you find?

Verbs

This section will provide a basic overview of **verbs**. Verbs will be examined in greater detail in Chapters 2 and 3.

Let's start with the traditional definition found in student textbooks: a verb is the word class (part of speech) that shows action or a state of being. However, that definition doesn't explain the full range of jobs that verbs do. For example, the verb "has" in "He has a dictionary" does not show action or a state of being but rather shows possession. Verbs are powerful sentence elements that determine the structure of the verb phrase. This topic will be taken up in greater detail in Chapter 3, where we explore sentence patterns.

The term "verb tense" refers to the way that verbs are classified to indicate the time of action. The problem is that grammar books vary widely in their terminology and the way verbs are categorized into tenses. For example, many books claim that there are only two simple verb tenses (present and past, e.g., walk/walked), which are made more complex by using **auxiliary verbs** (e.g., <u>have</u> walked, <u>had</u> walked, <u>will</u> walk, <u>may</u> walk, <u>might</u> walk). Others start with three verb tenses (present, past, future, e.g., walk/walked/will walk) that are expanded by using auxiliaries. The number of verb tenses claimed in grammar textbooks can range from two to twelve. To add to the confusion, it is arguable that all are legitimate. Here, we will use the three-verb tense system.

Before we examine verb tenses and their expansion through auxiliaries, it is essential for you to know the terminology associated with the different forms that verbs take. You will use this terminology throughout this book, so make sure that you do not purge the information from your brain after you finish this chapter!

Every verb has the following forms: **base, present, past, infinitive, present participle**, and **past participle**. You can see examples of these forms in Table 1.3 below. The present and past forms correspond to present and past tenses. Note that the "s" in parentheses under "Present Form" represents the third-person singular suffix "–s" or "–es," as in "He/She/It looks," versus the other present forms, for example, "I look," "You look," "We look," "They look," "The students look."

Table 1.3

Verb Forms

Base Form	Present Form	Past Form (Ved)	Infinitive Form (to V)	Present Participle Form (Ving)	Past Participle Form (Ven)
look	look(s)	looked	to look	looking	looked
take	take(s)	took	to take	taking	taken
eat	eat(s)	ate	to eat	eating	eaten
be	is, am, are	was, were	to be	being	been

In Table 1.3, the verb "look" is typical of most English verbs, meaning that it follows a regular pattern. The past is formed by adding the suffix "–ed" to the base ("looked"); the infinitive is formed by adding "to" to the base ("to look"); and the present participle is formed by adding the suffix "–ing" to the base ("looking"). The past participle form is often the same as the past tense form (e.g., walked, looked). However, as you can see with the next two verbs, "take" and "eat," the past and past participle forms are different (e.g., took/taken, ate/eaten). There are a number of verbs like "take" that have irregular forms (e.g., go, fly, do, ride, speak). To help find the past participle form, I put "have" in front of the verb, for example, (have) eaten, (have) fallen, and so on.

The verb "be" is the most irregular verb in the English language, as you can see in Table 1.3. Irregular verb forms are drilled into students throughout elementary school, and they are a real challenge for English language learners.

To differentiate these forms in our discussions, I will use the abbreviations **Ved** for the past form, **to V** for the infinitive form, **Ving** for the present participle form, and **Ven** for the past participle form. Make your elementary school teacher proud by filling in the table in the following exercise (correctly)!

Exercise 1.8 Getting a Grip on Verb Forms

Complete the table for these irregular verbs.

Base	Present Form	Past Form (Ved)	Infinitive Form (to V)	Present Participle Form (Ving)	Past Participle Form (Ven)
go	goes	went?	to go	going	gone
beat	beats	beatt	to beat	beating	beaten
do	does	did	to do	doing	did done
ride	rides	rode	to ride	riding	rode ridden

DID YOU KNOW?

Many dialects in the United States have regularized the irregular past participle form, particularly in spoken English. For example, rather than using the irregular Ven form "gone," the past form "went" is used, as in, "I've went there before." Here is another example: "I've ate there before" versus "I've eaten there before." Is this "wrong"? Go to www.youtube.com/watch?v=ekzHlouo8Q4, listen to Bruno Mars sing "When I Was Your Man," and find his substitution of a past form (Ved) for a past participle form (Ven). (Hint: It's in the chorus.)

Now that you understand verb forms, we will examine verbs using the three-tense system and then expand those forms with auxiliary verbs. Tense expresses time in the past, present, and future. Auxiliary verbs also help orient the time of an event (**aspect**) and the speaker's or writer's stance (**modals**).

Three Simple Verb Tenses

The three simple verb tenses are **present, past,** and **future**. Table 1.3 shows the present and past tense forms; the future tense is created by adding "will" to the base form. Below is an example of the verb "study" in context.

Present Tense: *The psycholinguist studies speech errors.*

Past Tense: *The psycholinguist studied speech errors.*

Future Tense: *The psycholinguist will study speech errors.*

Auxiliary Verbs

Verbs are made more complex through the use of auxiliaries. The two main auxiliary verbs are "have" and "be" as in "have studied" and "is studying." The verb "do" can also serve as an auxiliary verb in questions and negatives, for example, "Do you have a project?" "I do not have one yet." Because auxiliary verbs "help" the head verb, they are often referred to as "helping verbs." The auxiliaries situate an event in time and indicate its completion or continuation, which is called **aspect**.

We start by examining how the "have" and "be" auxiliaries form three aspects of verbs: **perfect, progressive,** and **perfect progressive**. There is also a group of auxiliary verbs called modals, which we will explore after aspect.

The Perfect

The **perfect** aspect is formed with the auxiliary verb "have" and the past participle form (Ven) of the head verb. "Have" is used with the head verb (*studied* in the sentence below) to indicate when an event is taking/took/will take place during a specific time period (it also can indicate that the action may continue). Below are examples of the three perfect forms of the verb "study" (have + Ven):

Present Perfect: *The psycholinguist has studied speech errors for twenty years.*

Past Perfect: *The psycholinguist had studied speech errors for twenty years before he retired.*

Future Perfect: *The psycholinguist will have studied speech errors for twenty years when he retires.*

The Progressive

This **progressive** aspect is formed with the auxiliary verb "be" and the present participle form (Ving) of the head verb. It is used to show that an action is/was/will be ongoing. Below are some examples of the use of "be" in the progressive forms of the verb "study" (be + Ving):

Present Progressive: *The psycholinguist is studying speech errors.*

Past Progressive: *The psycholinguist was studying speech errors.*

Future Progressive: *The psycholinguist will be studying speech errors.*

The Perfect Progressive

The **perfect progressive** is formed with the auxiliaries "have" and "be." The auxiliary "have" reflects the verb tense, and "be" is always in the Ven form, "been." The perfect progressive is used to emphasize an ongoing action or the duration of an action:

Present Perfect Progressive: *The psycholinguist has been studying speech errors for twenty years.*

Past Perfect Progressive: *The psycholinguist had been studying speech errors before his retirement.*

Future Perfect Progressive: *The psycholinguist will have been studying speech errors for twenty-five years when he retires.*

We choose the verb form based on the time elements that we want to indicate or contrast. This knowledge of verbs is so important that it is taught as early as the first grade. For English language learners, these verb forms can be particularly challenging.

Exercise 1.9 Getting a Grip on Verb Tenses and Expanded Verb Forms

Take a look at the sentences below and use the "evidence" provided in the completed sentences to fill in the blanks with the correct verb forms:

Present: Our cultural background affects our way of thinking.
Past: Our cultural background ~~has~~ affected our way of thinking.

Future: Our cultural background <u>will affect</u> our way of thinking.

Present Perfect: Our cultural background _has affected_ our way of thinking.

Past Perfect: Our cultural background <u>had affected</u> our way of thinking.

Future Perfect: Our cultural background <u>will have affected</u> our way of thinking.

Present Progressive: Our cultural background <u>is affecting</u> our way of thinking.

Past Progressive: Our cultural background <u>was affecting</u> our way of thinking.

Future Progressive: Our cultural background _will be affecting_ our way of thinking.

Present Perfect Progressive: Our cultural background <u>has been affecting</u> our way of thinking.

Past Perfect Progressive: Our cultural background _had been affecting_ our way of thinking.

Future Perfect Progressive: Our cultural background <u>will have been affecting</u> our way of thinking.

Modals

English has a number of **modals**: can, could, may, might, must, shall, should, would, and will ("ought to" is sometimes included as a modal as well). They never change form and must be added to the base of a verb or auxiliary, for example, "I <u>must go</u> home" or "I <u>must have gone</u> home." Each modal adds its own meaning to the verb, but those meanings can vary. Context is very important. For example, the meanings of "would" in the following two sentences differ:

I knew that the doctor <u>would help</u> you.
                    ↑ used as the past form of "will"

The doctor <u>would advise</u> her patients to take vitamin D for brain health.
                    ↑ implies a repeated action

Modals reflect a speaker's stance by showing politeness, uncertainty, intention, and so on. For example, a modal can soften requests, such as "Could you take out the garbage?" versus "Take out the garbage." They can signal formality as in "You may enter" versus "You can enter," or signal lack of certainty as in "She might have visited" versus "She visited." As mentioned above, the modal is always followed by the base form of the verb or auxiliary:

*The psycholinguist **might study** speech errors.*
*The psycholinguist **might have** studied speech errors.*
*The psycholinguist **might be** studying speech errors.*
*The psycholinguist **might have** been studying speech errors.*

Exercise 1.10 Getting a Grip on Verbs

In the following paragraph, underline every verb. Include all of the auxiliaries with the head verb.

One psycholinguistic experiment is the lexical decision task. In this task, participants must decide between words and nonwords on a screen. They push a "word button" for a real word and a "nonword button" for a nonword. For example, participants should push the "word button" for a string of letters like "brim," but not for "brif." Then the researcher measures the speed of word/nonword decisions. She also records the correctness of the decisions. This type of test can inform the experimenter about our mental dictionaries. Psycholinguists have been using such experiments to gather data about our brain functions.

DID YOU KNOW?

Only one modal can be used with a verb according to the prescriptive rules of English; however, some spoken Southern dialects take a more creative approach to the modal system by doubling them up. For example, one common double modal is "might could" as in "I might could go." The two modals used together seem to indicate something different from "I might go" or "I could go." Makes sense to me, but be careful about where and when you use this "creative" double modal because strict grammarians could get annoyed by its use. You should definitely avoid using it in professional or academic writing.

Adverbs

The **adverb** is often misunderstood. Some take the approach that if it doesn't look like a noun, adjective, or verb, then it must be an adverb, right? Well, often eliminating what a word can't be does help when choosing a specific word class. But in reality, adverbs have their own jobs in sentences and can be recognized doing those jobs. Traditional grammar describes an adverb as a modifier of adjectives, verbs, or other adverbs. Below, we will expand on that traditional definition by examining single-word adverbs in terms of how they function in a sentence and how we identify them. We will revisit adverbs in each of the following chapters when we examine prepositional phrases, infinitive phrases, and adverb clauses.

Adverbs are used to add information to a sentence—information about manner, time, place, purpose, frequency, and degree. As such, they answer questions related to how, when, where, why, how often, and to what extent. For example, in the following sentence, the adverb *rapidly* answers the question "**How** do our brains process information?":

> *Our brains process a great deal of information rapidly.*

Some adverbs are easily recognized because they are movable components in a sentence (note how *rapidly* can move to the slot before the verb *process*) and are marked by the "–ly" suffix. Other adverbs don't have these "clues." Rather, they are recognized by their functions as modifiers of verbs, adjectives, and adverbs and by the specific questions that they answer (e.g., "how?" in the above example).

Here we examine single-word adverbs and how to identify them. Unlike adjectives that have only one job (to provide more information about a noun or pronoun), adverbs can modify verbs, adjectives, and other adverbs. We begin by examining adverbs that modify verbs: adverbs of manner, time, place, and frequency. Then we examine adverbs of degree that modify adjectives and adverbs.

Adverbs Modifying Verbs

One characteristic of adverbs that modify verbs is that they are often movable. They also answer specific questions, such as how, when, where, and how often.

Adverbs of Manner

The most recognizable adverbs are the **adverbs of manner** because they answer the question "How?" They are generally movable and often end in "–ly." Our earlier example with *rapidly* illustrates this type of adverb. These "–ly" adverbs are derived from adjectives:

> Adjectives: *rapid, quick, clear, different*
> Adverbs: *rapidly, quickly, clearly, differently*

Here are some examples of these adverbs in context:

> *Brain scan technology is improving rapidly.*
> *When reading, we recognize common words quickly.*
> *She spoke clearly.*
> *Felipe speaks Spanish fluently.*

Note that we can easily move these adverbs: *Brain scan technology is rapidly improving.* Also, they are answering the adverb question "how?" *Improving* how? (*rapidly*) *Recognize* how? (*quickly*) *Spoke* how? (*clearly*) *Speaks* how? (*fluently*) These adverbs also have comparative and superlative forms, as in the following example:

> *When reading, we recognize common words more rapidly than uncommon words.*
> *Short, common words like pronouns are recognized the most rapidly.*

Adverbs of Time, Place, and Frequency

Adverbs of time, **place**, and **frequency** generally answer the questions when, where, and how often. They usually do not have the "–ly" suffix (though exceptions exist):

> *Today, we better understand the cause of dyslexia.*
> (*understand* when? *Today*)
>
> *After surgery, she went home.*
> (*went* where? *home*)
>
> *Dyslexia sometimes goes undiagnosed.*
> (*goes undiagnosed* how often? *sometimes*)

The above examples show adverbs modifying verbs, which are often movable; however, notice that in the second example, *home* functions as an adverb answering the question "Where did she go?" *Home* is not movable like the adverbs in the other two sentences. Also, isn't *home* a person, place, or thing? Isn't it a noun? Not so fast . . . Recall that we are looking at how a word functions, not what it looks like, and *home* is definitely functioning as an adverb in that sentence answering "She went where?" Movability is one characteristic of many of these adverbs, but not all (e.g., *home*); however, it remains a good test for identifying adverbs. Here are more examples of movable single-word adverbs:

> *We rarely remember a course lecture after a week.*
> *We remember a course lecture after a week rarely.*
>
> *Context usually influences word recognition.*
> *Usually, context influences word recognition.*
>
> *They analyzed the brain scans here.*
> *Here, they analyzed the brain scans.*
>
> *The brain surgeon examined the scans yesterday.*
> *Yesterday, the brain surgeon examined the scans.*

Adverbs Modifying Adjectives and Adverbs

Adverbs that modify adjectives (ADJ) and adverbs (ADV) are different from those discussed above that modify verbs because they cannot be moved from their positions. Look at the following examples and note how the adverbs *incredibly* and *very* cannot move away from the adjective (*complex*) and the adverb (*quickly*).

The brain is <u>incredibly</u> complex.
           ADV   ADJ

Her brain reacted <u>very</u> quickly to the stimulus.
                ADV ADV

These are called **adverbs of degree**, and they modify both adjectives and adverbs, as shown in the two examples above. They are often called **intensifiers** because they intensify the adjective or adverb. In the example sentence, *incredibly* is describing the degree to which something is *complex*, and *very* is intensifying quickly—*very quickly*. The slot preceding the adjective and adverb is a common location for adverbs of degree. Below are some other examples of adverbs modifying the following adjectives and adverbs.

Adverbs of degree modifying adjectives:

The brain is <u>quite</u> complex.
          ADV   ADJ

The brain is <u>unbelievably</u> complex.
          ADV   ADJ

Adverbs of degree modifying adverbs:

Her brain deteriorated <u>very</u> quickly.
                 ADV ADV

Damage to her left hemisphere affected her language <u>rather</u> severely.
                                           ADV   ADV

Other common adverbs of degree are almost, barely, highly, slightly, really, and so on. Sentences can contain multiple adjectives and adverbs. The next example illustrates this by using arrows below the sentence to show adjective-noun relationships and arrows above to show the adverb-adjective relationships:

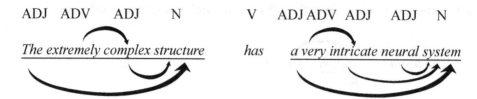

In sum, adverbs have their own specific jobs in a sentence. They give us more information by answering a set of questions, such as how, when, where, how often, and to what extent. They can modify verbs, adjectives, and other adverbs. Those that modify verbs are often movable and also often end in "–ly." Understanding their roles in a sentence will help keep you from confusing them with other word classes.

Exercise 1.11 Getting a Grip on Adverbs

In the sentences below, circle Y (yes) if the underlined word functions as an adverb; if not, circle N (no).

1. Y N   The corpus callosum is a <u>bundle</u> of nerve fibers that connect the brain's two hemispheres.
2. Y N   The corpus callosum allows <u>instant</u> communication between hemispheres.
3. Y N   Some patients with epilepsy have the corpus callosum cut to relieve <u>epileptic</u> seizures.
4. Y N   After "split brain" surgery, the two hemispheres cannot communicate <u>anymore</u>.
5. Y N   Patients who undergo this surgery can <u>often</u> adapt to the situation with few problems.
6. Y N   Researchers have conducted <u>fascinating</u> split brain studies on these patients.
7. Y N   However, this type of surgery has become <u>rather</u> rare.
8. Y N   <u>Recently</u>, fewer and fewer of these patients are available for split brain research.
9. Y N   What we have learned is that the brain is an <u>amazing</u> organ of extreme complexity.
10. Y N   Modern imaging is providing us with <u>extremely</u> important data about the mechanics of the brain.

Exercise 1.12 Getting a Grip on Adverbs Versus Adjectives

In the paragraph below, decide whether the underlined words function as adverbs (ADV) or adjectives (ADJ) and label them accordingly.

The word "bank" is very ambiguous. (How many things can the word "bank" represent?) Does it take much longer for our brains to process "bank" because of its multiple meanings? Studies show that the brain processes ambiguous and unambiguous words differently. The brain must work harder to process ambiguous words.

Prepositions

We use **prepositions** all of the time (I just used one!). They add essential elements to the sentence (another!). Prepositions are followed by a noun or pronoun and are part of a structure called a **prepositional phrase**. Most prepositions situate events, things, and people in time and space. Teachers often teach prepositions that show place by illustrating their usage with two objects, such as a box and a pen. The position of the pen in relation to the box is the preposition—*in* the box, *on* the box, *under* the box, *next to* the box, and so on. Below is a list of some of the most common prepositions. Please note that some are phrasal prepositions, meaning that they consist of more than one word but are treated as one unit.

Table 1.4
Common Prepositions

aboard	at	despite	next to	thanks to
about	because of	down	of	through
above	before	during	off	throughout
according to	behind	except	on	till
across	below	for	on account of	to
after	beneath	from	on behalf of	toward
against	beside	in	onto	under
ahead of	between	in back of	out	underneath
along	beyond	in case of	out of	until
along with	but (except)	in front of	outside	up
amid	but for	in spite of	over	up to
among	by	instead of	past	upon
around	by means of	into	per	with
as	concerning	like	regarding	within
aside from	contrary to	near	since	without

We will continue our discussion about prepositional phrases in Chapter 2. For now, let's focus on recognizing them within sentences.

Remember that a preposition exists within a prepositional phrase, which means that it must be followed by a noun or pronoun (as usual, there are exceptions to this). If there is no noun or pronoun, then it most likely is an adverb, as in the following example:

The surgeon walked out.

In this sentence, *out* cannot be a preposition because it is not part of a phrase. It is telling us where he walked, so it is a single-word adverb. However, it would be easy to give the sentence a prepositional phrase:

The surgeon walked out the door.

Now we have a preposition (*out*) plus a noun (*door*), which means we have met the requirements for a prepositional phrase. Here are some more examples of adverbs versus prepositions:

The researcher fell down. ←*down* = adverb
The researcher fell down the stairs. ←*down* = preposition; *stairs* = noun

They taped the electrodes on. ←*on* = adverb
They taped the electrodes on his head. ←*on* = preposition; *head* = noun

---

Exercise 1.13 Getting a Grip on Prepositions

In the sentences below, circle P if the underlined word is a preposition and A if it is an adverb.

1. P A   Our knowledge about brain functions is still limited.
2. P A   Early researchers examined the brains of dead people.
3. P A   They often went out and gathered brains from morgues.
4. P A   In the 1800s, a man had a 43-inch iron rod blown through his head, and he survived.
5. P A   The man, Phineas Gage, gave brain researchers a lot of information to work with.
6. P A   Researchers found that the front of his brain was damaged.
7. P A   Phineas's personality changed after his accident.
8. P A   He became aggressive, showing that damage to the frontal lobe can change personality.
9. P A   Early researchers determined women were less intelligent than men from brain size.
10. P A   Thus women were expected to stay in and not get an education.

Conjunctions

"Conjunction junction, what's your function?" Sound familiar? Many students today can still sing parts of songs from the *Schoolhouse Rock!* series, which tells you a lot about the role of music in learning. The songs are still available today on YouTube.

So what is the function of a **conjunction**? Its job is to conjoin. The traditional definition of a conjunction is that it connects words or groups of words. Below we will look at two types of conjunctions: **coordinating** and **correlative**. We will revisit conjunctions in Chapter 2 with conjunctive adverbs and in Chapter 5 with subordinating conjunctions.

Both correlative and coordinating conjunctions connect words and sentences. Let's start by looking at coordinating conjunctions and what units of language they commonly conjoin.

Coordinating Conjunctions

The **coordinating conjunctions** (for, and, nor, but, or, yet, so) are best remembered as FANBOYS:

F—for	**B**—but
A—and	**O**—or
N—nor	**Y**—yet
	S—so

In the following example, the conjunction "and" conjoins two nouns in the subject position:

Paul Broca and Carl Wernicke became famous for their brain studies conducted in the 1800s.

We can conjoin words and phrases, such as two nouns, two verbs, two prepositional phrases, two adjectives, and even two sentences. The rule is to conjoin like structures. Here are some examples:

Paul Broca examined the brains of (human cadavers) and (animals).
↑ two nouns ↑

Broca (measured) and (weighed) each brain.
↑ two verbs ↑

Broca thought women should stay (in the home) and (out of the way).
↑ two prepositional phrases ↑

According to Broca, women were (unintelligent) and (uneducable).
↑ two adjectives ↑

(Broca was considered a "freethinker" of his time), yet (his research supported the socially accepted concept of male superiority). ←two sentences

One mistake writers make (not just beginning writers) is that they use conjunctions to conjoin different structures:

Paul Broca weighed brains, measured skulls, and was making assumptions.

This is referred to as a nonparallel structure. Notice that three verbs are in a series conjoined by *and;* however, the last verb is not in the same form as the first two: *weighed, measured, was making.* You can fix this by changing the last verb so that it is parallel with the first two: *weighed, measured, made.* Checking for parallel structures is easy to do, and the payoff for doing it is that you have a much better text.

PUNCTUATION ALERT!

In the example above, the conjunction joins a series of three verb phrases, and each verb phrase is followed by a comma (except the last verb phrase). When a conjunction joins two sentences, the first is followed by a comma, which is the general rule in grammar handbooks, for example,

Broca was a French physician, and Wernicke was a German neurologist.

DID YOU KNOW?

One of the coordinating conjunctions is the third most commonly used word in the English language. Which one do you think it is?

Correlative Conjunctions

Correlative conjunctions are made up of two parts: both/and, not only/but also, either/or, neither/nor. Like coordinating conjunctions, these also conjoin grammatical structures, but they consist of two words and change the meaning or focus of the sentence. Compare the following:

In the 1800s, (Paul Broca) and (Carl Wernicke) made major discoveries concerning language locations in the brain.

Coordinating

> *In the 1800s, <u>both</u> (Paul Broca) <u>and</u> (Carl Wernicke) made major*
> *discoveries concerning language locations in the brain.*

In the first sentence above, the coordinating conjunction *and* conjoins two nouns in the subject slot. In the second sentence, the correlative conjunction *both/and* is used to conjoin the same two subject nouns. Note how this correlative conjunction changes the emphasis of the sentence. Below are more examples of correlative conjunctions joining nouns:

> *Today, Broca would be considered <u>both</u> a brilliant man <u>and</u> a misogynist.*
> *<u>Neither</u> Broca <u>nor</u> Wernicke truly understood how the brain works.*
> *Aristotle believed that the brain controlled <u>neither</u> sensations <u>nor</u> movement.*

Let's examine another sentence with a correlative conjunction:

> *Broca <u>not only</u> (studied brains) <u>but also</u> (conducted comparative studies of*
> *the brain based on race).*

The correlative conjunction *not only/but also* conjoins two verb phrases, *studied brains* and *conducted comparative studies of the brain based on race*. It's clear that correlative conjunctions can add life to sentences by emphasizing specific elements. However, they should be used in small doses.

Exercise 1.14 Getting a Grip on Coordinating and Correlative Conjunctions

In the paragraph below, underline the coordinating and correlative conjunctions. Mark them as CC (coordinating conjunctions) or COR (correlative conjunctions). Remember that correlative conjunctions have two parts, so draw a line to connect the parts, as seen in the example below:

<u>Both</u> Paul Broca <u>and</u> Carl Wernicke made major discoveries about the brain.

COR

The brain has a right hemisphere and a left hemisphere. Much of language is processed in the left hemisphere. Aphasia is the loss of language due to brain damage to the left hemisphere. Two types of aphasia are Broca's aphasia and Wernicke's aphasia. Broca's area is in front of the left ear and slightly above it. Patients with damage to Broca's area (Broca's aphasia) not only may have trouble producing grammatically correct sentences but also may have problems producing speech in general. Patients with Wernicke's aphasia have damage to an area farther back from Broca's area but slightly higher above the left ear. Patients with damage to Wernicke's area sound fluent yet oddly incoherent.

DID YOU KNOW?

Your brain and body are wired contralaterally. That means that the left hemisphere of your brain (put your left hand on the left side of your head—that is your left hemisphere) controls the right side of your body, and the right hemisphere controls the left side. If someone has a stroke that damages the brain's right hemisphere, he or she will most likely experience problems with the left arm, left leg, or left side of the face.

Interjections

Following the example of most grammar books, we give little space to **interjections**. However, interjections are still mentioned in some traditional grammar books, so we will take a quick look at them. Basically, an interjection is a word or short phrase that is added to a sentence as an exclamation, such as the following:

Holy smokes! I didn't know words were so powerful!
Man, oh man, she impressed me with her quick recovery from brain surgery.
Well, if you want my opinion . . .

Interjections are not part of the sentence structure, and that is why they are often left out of discussions of sentence grammar; however, they are important enough to have their own category. We all use them, although many would not be appropriate to use in a formal setting. But go ahead and add some of your own colorful interjections to complete the sentence below . . . silently, please.

[Appropriate interjection]! I didn't know a parking fine could cost so much!

Chapter Review

Now you have the opportunity to show your expertise in identifying word classes. These are critical building blocks needed for the next chapters. If you do not have a good grip on them, you will struggle with the remaining chapters. Be sure to go back and review the discussions of word classes in this chapter as needed.

Exercise 1.15 Getting a Grip—Review of Word Classes

Mark the function of each underlined word as noun (N), pronoun (PRO), adjective (ADJ), adverb (ADV), verb (V), preposition (P), interjection (I), or conjunction (C). Also mark correlative conjunction pairs as C.

1. ___ ___ The ethics of research is always a sensitive issue.

2. ___ ___ Researchers are interested in how children learn language.

3. ___ ___ What about children who never learn language?

4. ___ ___ Research suggests a critical period for learning language, and children never achieve full language abilities if exposed to language after that time.

5. ___ ___ Researchers have not agreed on the exact time of the critical period, but most believe that the critical period ends at puberty at the latest.

6. ___ ___ A feral child is one who has had little or no human contact; thus she has no human language.

7. ___ ___ Feral children provide evidence concerning the critical period.

8. ___ ___ Discovered in 1970, a girl named Genie is an American example of a child deprived of language.

9. ___ ___ She was not only locked in a room but also punished for making any noises.

10. ___ ___ Genie had been closed in a dark room since birth when she was discovered at the age of thirteen.

11. ___ ___ She was tied to a potty chair during the day and caged in a crib at night.

12. ___ ___ After her rescue, Genie lived with researchers who studied her to gain insight about language acquisition and socialization processes.

13. ___ ___ Genie learned vocabulary quickly, but she never grasped word order.

14. ___ ___ The researchers received grants to support their studies of Genie.

15. ___ ___ When the money ran out, Genie was placed in foster care. Wow, what a sad ending for Genie.

Exercise 1.16 Getting a Grip—Review of Word Classes

Label the function of every word in each sentence as noun (N), pronoun (PRO), adjective (ADJ), adverb (ADV), verb (V), preposition (P), conjunction (C), or interjection (I).

Example:

```
ADJ    N      V      N        P     ADJ  ADJ   N
```
Feral children provide evidence concerning the critical period.

1. The doctor tested the baby's language.
2. Some psycholinguists study the organization of the brain.
3. Many reading studies track eye movements.
4. Researchers examined Einstein's brain for "clues" to his intelligence.
5. Male subjects with an attractive female experimenter made more speech errors.
6. Genie learned vocabulary quickly, but she never grasped word order.
7. Broca was both a brilliant man and a misogynist.
8. Researchers have not agreed on the exact time of the critical period.
9. The left hemisphere of our brain controls the right side of our body.
10. Both Broca and Wernicke made major discoveries about the brain.

Exercise 1.17 Getting a Grip—Review of Word Classes

Read each sentence carefully and circle T (true) or F (false).

1. T F An adjective must modify an adverb.
2. T F Correlative conjunctions can be remembered through the acronym FANBOYS.
3. T F The most common slot for an adjective is immediately following the noun it modifies.
4. T F A preposition exists in a prepositional phrase.
5. T F There are three articles in English: a, an, and the.
6. T F The past participle of "run" is "run."
7. T F Adverbs can modify adjectives, verbs, adverbs, and nouns.
8. T F When a coordinating conjunction conjoins two sentences, a comma separates the two.
9. T F Every noun phrase must have a head noun, and every verb phrase must have a head verb.
10. T F The singular/plural test helps you to identify adverbs.

DID YOU KNOW?

You can learn more about the tragic story of Genie, the fourteen-year-old girl who was closed in a room and not allowed to speak. The PBS program *Nova* has a fifty-five-minute video (1997) available on YouTube at www.youtube.com/watch?v=hmdycJQi4QAr (search "Genie-Secret of the Wild Child"). You can also watch an excellent twelve-minute TLC documentary (2003) by searching "Genie Wiley," or go to www.youtube.com/watch?v=VjZolHCrC8E.

2
Extending The Basics

This chapter focuses on extending our knowledge of nouns, prepositions, verbs, and conjunctions. Chapter 1 provided the essential foundation upon which this chapter builds. In this chapter, important grammatical concepts to learn are **noun phrase**, **appositive**, **adjectival prepositional phrase**, **adverbial prepositional phrase**, **phrasal verb**, **active voice**, **passive voice**, and **conjunctive adverb**.

Language Focus: The Sounds of Language

Phonology and phonetics are fields of linguistics that investigate the sound systems of languages. Some of the questions that linguists ask include: How do English sound patterns and articulations differ across dialects? How do the sound patterns of our language affect our ability to sound fluent in a second language? What is the inventory of speech sounds across all languages? What factors influence the way we pronounce words?

Because the language focus of this chapter is on speech sounds, you will be introduced to the **International Phonetic Alphabet** (IPA), a set of symbols that represent the speech sounds of languages. The speech sounds are placed between slashes / / to distinguish them from letters of the alphabet. For example, the first sound in "cat" is represented by the IPA symbol /k/, and the last sound is represented as /t/ (rather than as the letters "c" and "t").

In this chapter, we extend our work on nouns by learning new tests that we can use for identifying nouns and learning a new noun structure, the appositive. Then we look at the adjectival and adverbial functions of prepositional phrases. Verbs are extended by examining active and passive voice. Finally, we look at another type of adverb called a conjunctive adverb; its job is to conjoin two sentences and to signal a particular relationship between the two. We will start this chapter by extending our knowledge of nouns.

Extending Nouns

In Chapter 1, we learned that nouns can be modified by a determiner such as "the" or a number (the phoneme, one phoneme), and they have both singular and plural forms (one phoneme, two phonemes). However, we found that not all nouns can be recognized by these two tests; for example, the noun "honesty" can't be counted (*the honesty, *one honesty, *two honesties—the asterisk is used to indicate un-grammatical usage). In this section on nouns, we will add two more tests to help identify nouns (even nouns like "honesty"). Then, we will examine another noun form called an appositive.

Let's begin with some new terminology that we will use in our discussions of nouns. The sentences below will help illustrate:

> *Bostonians have distinct accents.*
> *Many Bostonians have distinct accents.*
> *My relatives have a distinct Boston accent.*

The subjects of the sentences above are underlined. We learned in the last chapter that, in most cases, subjects are nouns or pronouns. In the first sentence, the subject is *Bostonians*; in the second, *Many Bostonians*; and in the third, *My relatives*. We will now use the term **noun phrase (NP)** to describe these subjects. Here, the term "phrase" encompasses both single words and groups of words that serve as a single functional unit—in this case, as nouns. So, we classify *Bostonians*, *Many Bostonians*, and *My relatives* as subject NPs. Even a pronoun in the subject position would be referred to as a subject NP; this is in keeping with current grammar terminology. At the same time, we want to be aware of traditional terminology, which uses the term "phrase" only for groups of words, like *Many Bostonians*, but not for single-word nouns like *Bostonians*.

In a group of words that function as a single NP, there must always be a head noun, a term first introduced in Chapter 1. In the second example above, the head noun is *Bostonians*, with *Many* functioning as an adjective.

> ADJ   Head Noun
> *Many Bostonians have distinct accents.*
>   NP

Additionally, as discussed in the previous chapter, we will use the term **verb phrase (VP)** to label everything that comes after the subject. Remember that the VP must include at least a head verb (also referred to as the "main verb"). In the above example, the VP is *have distinct accents*, and the head verb is *have*.

A sentence in English is composed of a subject noun phrase and a verb phrase. Here are examples with the subject NPs and the VPs labeled:

> *Bostonians have distinct accents.*
>   NP   VP

Many Bostonians have distinct accents.
    NP   VP

My relatives have a distinct Boston accent.
    NP   VP

They have a Boston accent.
  NP   VP

Not surprisingly, not all sentences adhere to the subject noun phrase–verb phrase pattern. For example, an adverb that is modifying the verb of the sentence can precede the subject NP:

Recently, the Brahmin dialect of Boston was studied by my students.
                NP   VP

Because many adverbs are movable within the sentence, this is not unusual. We can put the adverb back in the VP so that it reflects the subject noun phrase–verb phrase pattern:

The Brahmin dialect of Boston was studied recently by my students.
         NP   VP

The Pronoun Substitution Test

Subjects are NPs, so finding the slot before the verb guides us to the subject (identifying the subject and verb is an essential first step in analyzing a sentence). Other slots that NPs occupy depend on the verb in the sentence, which we will examine more closely in Chapter 3. The **pronoun substitution test (PST)** is one of the most useful tests for identifying NPs here and in the next chapters. If you can substitute a word or phrase with a pronoun, then you know that it is a noun phrase—that's the job of a pronoun, right? Let's look at some earlier examples:

Bostonians have distinct accents.
Many Bostonians have distinct accents.
My relatives have a distinct Boston accent.

Notice that *Bostonians*, *Many Bostonians*, and *My relatives* can be replaced by the pronoun *They*. This is evidence that they are NPs. Only NPs can be substituted with pronouns. Also note that the head noun and all of its adjectives must be substituted with the pronoun, not just the noun. For example, *They* must replace both the adjective (*Many*) and the head noun (*Bostonians*): *Many Bostonians*→ *They have distinct accents*. We can also find object NPs (objects follow the verb) in the three sentences using the PST. The object *distinct accents* can be substituted with the

pronoun "them," and *a distinct Boston accent* can be substituted with the pronoun "one" (other pronouns would work as well, e.g., "it"): *Bostonians have them*; *My relatives have one.*

Now examine the following sentence: "I went home." Is "home" an NP? It is a person, place, or thing, right? Try the PST: *"I went it." It doesn't work. Here, "home" functions as an adverb telling us <u>where</u> I went. How does "home" function in this next sentence? "<u>Home</u> is where the heart is." Apply the PST: "<u>It</u> is where the heart is." Yes, it is functioning as a noun. Remember, we are examining grammatical units in terms of their function within a specific context, not their form.

Let's look at an earlier sentence that we claimed did not have an object NP and check it with the PST:

> <u>*My friend*</u> *speaks rapidly.*
> She   it   ←NO

> <u>*My friend*</u> *speaks Arabic.*
> She   it   ←YES

In the first sentence, the adverb *rapidly* cannot be substituted with the pronoun *it* because *rapidly* answers <u>how</u> she speaks, and substituting *it* changes the meaning of the original sentence; therefore, it fails the PST. In the second sentence, *Arabic* can be replaced with a pronoun while keeping the original meaning of the sentence. Here is another example that uses the PST to find the NPs:

> <u>*Some children*</u> *find* <u>*the "th" sound*</u> *difficult to pronounce.*
> They/Some   it

There may be more than one pronoun that can substitute for the NP, as you can see in the example above. To identify NPs by replacing them with pronouns, you must know your pronouns. Students sometimes forget that indefinite pronouns can also be used to substitute for nouns (e.g., one, this, some, others, something). Go back and review them in Chapter 1, Table 1.2 if needed.

Exercise 2.1 Getting a Grip on Noun Phrases with the Pronoun Substitution Test

Underline the noun phrases in the parts of the sentences that are in parentheses (ignore the parts not in parentheses) and apply the pronoun substitution test. The number of noun phrases that you should identify is indicated at the end of the sentence. (Do not underline pronouns in this exercise.) There may be more than one pronoun that can substitute for a noun—just choose one.

Example:

At the back of your throat, (the hanging appendage is your uvula). (2)
it   it

1. In English, (some vowels are rounded, and other vowels are considered
   unrounded). (2) these   those
   They

2. (Nasal consonants are produced through the nose. Try to hold your
   nose) and make the sounds /m/ and /n/. (3) It   it

3. (Vowels become nasalized when they are next to nasal consonants.) (2)
   The   it

4. (You produce friction in your mouth to make sounds) such as /s/ as in
   "sit." (3)
              It

5. (A sound produced with the lips is called a "labial"), for example, the
   sound /b/ as in "boy." (3)
                    they

6. In English, (do all of the past-tense endings have the same
   pronunciation)? (2)

7. (Your tongue position influences your speech sounds.) (2)

8. (English language learners often first pronounce English words with an
   accent.) (3)

9. (Many languages have clicks in their sound systems.) These clicks
   function as consonants. (3)

10. (One click is similar to the sound that a rider makes to get a horse to
    move forward.) (4)

DID YOU KNOW?

The larynx (located behind your Adam's apple) contains vocal cords, which vibrate to produce sounds. Follow the link below to see vocal cords (also called vocal folds) vibrating in slow motion. I guarantee that you will be intrigued. Search for "vibrating vocal folds" at the University of California, Los Angeles, or go to www.phonetics.ucla.edu/vowels/chapter2/vibrating%20cords/vibrating.html.

Noun Phrase Appositives

We have looked at NPs in the subject and object positions, which we will examine in greater detail in Chapter 3. There is another type of NP that we haven't explored yet, and that is the **appositive**. An appositive is an NP that identifies, explains, or renames another noun. Sounds like the job of an adjective, right? The two may seem similar, but an appositive functions as a noun and refers to a noun that refers to it. What does that mean? For example, in the following sentence, *a native Bostonian* is an appositive NP that refers to the subject NP, *My mother*, which refers back to it. (*My mother* and *a native Bostonian* are the same person.)

My mother, a native Bostonian, doesn't pronounce the "r's" in some words.
　　　　↑ Appositive

Here are some more examples of appositive NPs:

Most Americans pronounce the "t" in "butter" as a flap, a quick tap to the
　　　　　　　　　　　　　　　　　　　　　　↑ Appositive

roof of the mouth.

Martha Stewart, a wealthy celebrity, pronounces "butter" with a carefully
　　　　　　　　↑ Appositive

articulated "t."

In the 1960s, William Labov, a famous sociolinguist, measured New
　　　　　　　　　　　↑ Appositive

Yorkers' use of "r" in words like "park" and "car," as in, "Pahk the cah"

instead of "Park the car."

In the first example above, the appositive refers to an object NP (*a flap*); in the second and third examples, the appositives refer to subject NPs (*Martha Stewart, William Labov*). Generally, they follow the NP that they are referring to, but they also can precede the NP, as in the following example:

A native Bostonian, my mother doesn't pronounce the "r's" in some words.
　　↑ Appositive

A wealthy celebrity, Martha Stewart pronounces "butter" with a carefully
   ↑ Appositive

articulated "t."

A famous sociolinguist, William Labov measured New Yorkers' attitudes.
   ↑ Appositive

PUNCTUATION ALERT!

If the appositive comes before the noun it refers to, as in the examples above, it is followed by a comma. In our other examples, the appositives come after the nouns they refer to, and so they are set off with commas (before and after the appositive). Appositives like these are not essential to the meaning of the nouns that they refer to (they do not restrict the meaning of their referent), and that is the reason they are set off with commas. If the appositive is essential for identifying the noun (it restricts the noun it is referring to), we do not set it off with commas. Take the following sentences as examples of essential appositives:

> *Your classmate Laura has an interesting accent.*
> *My friend Jose invited me to visit his home in Santiago.*
> *The African language Xhosa has many click sounds.*

The appositives *Laura, Jose,* and *Xhosa* are not set off with commas because the names restrict which *classmate, friend,* or *language* is being referred to (not just any classmate, but your classmate *Laura*; not just any friend, but my friend *Jose*; not just any African language, but the *Xhosa* language). We will get more practice with the punctuation of restrictive and nonrestrictive sentence elements in Chapters 4 and 5. Just remember, there is a system to punctuation, and it is best if you start to pay attention to it!

Exercise 2.2 Getting a Grip on Appositives

Underline the appositive noun phrase (NP) and draw an arrow to the NP that it explains or renames. In each example, there is only one appositive, even where there are two sentences.

Example:

Articulatory phonetics, the study of speech sounds, examines how speech sounds are produced.

1. The International Phonetic Alphabet (IPA), a set of symbols, represents the sounds of languages.

2. The IPA symbol for the first sound in the word "unhappy" is called a schwa.

3. A common sound in English, the schwa is produced in unstressed syllables. The IPA symbol is /ə/ and sounds like "uh" as in "duh."

4. The word "California" is pronounced with two schwas in English. Can you find them?

5. English spelling, an outdated system, is not a good phonetic representation. For example, how many ways can /k/ (as in "kite") be spelled (e.g., cat, aqua, ache)?

6. A great tool for learning a language, the IPA gives the learner the ability to transcribe words as they sound.

7. Do you think "ng," a common ending in English words such as "sang" and "thing," is pronounced as one or two sounds?

8. The IPA, the system mentioned above, represents "ng" as one sound/ one symbol. The IPA symbol is /ŋ/.

9. Men have larger voice boxes, larynxes, than women.

10. Phoneticians can compare the sound systems of many languages because they use the same phonetic symbols, the IPA, when analyzing the sound structures.

DID YOU KNOW?

What does English sound like to speakers of other languages? We are so used to the rhythms, sounds, and intonation patterns of English that it is difficult to imagine what it sounds like to others. Filmmakers Brian Fairbairn and Karl Eccleston produced a four-minute film using "fake" English. Experience "Skwerl" at www.youtube.com/watch?v=Vt4Dfa4fOEY.

Extending Prepositional Phrases

Prepositions do not work in isolation—they work in conjunction with an NP to form a **prepositional phrase (PP)**. In general, a PP needs a preposition (P) and an NP to be complete; for example, the PP "on the tongue" consists of the preposition "on" and the NP "the tongue," which is called the **object of preposition**. (Another slot for NPs, in addition to the subject and object slots. Only NPs can be objects of prepositions.) Of course, there are exceptions to the rule that all prepositions must be followed by an NP (the preposition may get "separated" from its NP in the sentence). However, for our purposes, we will examine prepositions that exist in prepositional phrases. We begin by examining prepositional phrases in general and then look at how they function as adjectives and adverbs in sentences. You may also want to go back to Table 1.4 in Chapter 1 and review the most common prepositions.

Below are some examples of PPs with the preposition marked as P and the noun phrase as NP. Remember that the NP in a PP functions as the object of preposition (OP) (OMG, another acronym!):

P   NP

Many speech sounds are made <u>with the tongue</u> touching different parts

PP

P   NP

<u>of the mouth.</u>

   PP

P   NP   P NP   P   NP

The first sound <u>in the word</u> "the" is produced <u>with the tip</u> <u>of the tongue</u>

PP   PP   PP

P   NP

<u>between the teeth.</u>

    PP

As you probably noticed, one prepositional phrase can immediately follow another, as in the second example above: (1) *<u>with the tip</u>* (2) *<u>of the tongue</u>* (3) *<u>between the teeth</u>*. Below is another example of a sentence with a series of PPs:

> *You push the back* (1) *<u>of your tongue</u>* (2) *<u>to the back</u>* (3) *<u>of your mouth</u> to produce the sound /k/.*

Beginning writers sometimes use too many prepositional phrases. Eliminating some of them may make the text more focused. For example, rather than writing "the tip of the tongue," the NP "the tongue tip" may be more efficient. Note the difference in the number of words—five versus three.

WARNING!

Another structure called an infinitive consists of the word "to" plus a verb, for example, "to produce." Infinitives may easily be misidentified as prepositional phrases. The confusion arises from the use of "to" in the infinitive, which has the same form as the preposition "to" (infinitives are examined in detail in Chapter 4). Here are some examples of prepositional phrases (P + NP) and infinitive phrases (to + V):

The researcher wanted to record the child's speech patterns.
↑ INF: *to + record (V)*

The researcher went to school for the meeting.
↑ PP: *preposition to + school (NP)*

The word was difficult to pronounce.
↑ INF: *to + pronounce (V)*

The student went to the lab to practice Romanian.
↑   ↑
PP: *to + the lab (NP); INF: to + practice (V)*

He wanted to practice, but he had to go to class.
↑   ↑   ↑
INF: *to + practice (V); INF: to + go (V); PP: to + class (NP)*

Exercise 2.3 Getting a Grip on Prepositional Phrases

In the following sentences, underline the prepositional phrases (PPs) and label the prepositions with P and the noun phrases with NP. The number at the end of the first five sentences indicates how many PPs you must find. Warning: There are infinitives in these sentences (to + V), so be sure not to mark them as PPs. Also, do not mark "for example" as a prepositional phrase in your answers.

Example:

    P NP   P   NP   P NP
The "th" in "thin" is written in the International Phonetic Alphabet (IPA) as /Θ/. (3)

1. The sound /Θ/ ("th") is an uncommon sound in other languages. (1)

2. In many parts of the country, "Mary," "merry," and "marry" are pronounced the same. (2)

3. People who live in isolated areas speak with accents that differ from other accents. (3)

4. For example, in Appalachian English, "fire" and "tire" rhyme with "car." (2)

5. In Appalachian English, the "r" sound is inserted into words like "wash" ("warsh"). (3)

6. Some languages have a consonant-vowel (CV) structure. For example, Japanese change the pronunciation of some English words to reflect the CV structure of Japanese: "bay su bo ru" (baseball).

7. Not all languages have the same contrasts between sounds. For example, in English, the sounds /p/ and /b/ are in contrast, that is, they change meaning (pat/bat).

8. In Arabic, /p/ and /b/ do not signal a change in word meaning, so they can sound the same to those speakers.

9. Speakers of Arabic may have trouble hearing the difference between the words "pat" and "bat."

10. My friend, who is an Arabic speaker, says "bebzi" for "Pepsi."

Above, we focused on simply identifying prepositional phrases. Now we are ready to examine how they function as adjectives and adverbs in sentences. To determine their function, we must look at what each PP is doing in the sentence. Always ask the following questions:

1. Is the PP preceded by a noun or pronoun? If the answer is no, you're FINISHED! It is an adverb. If yes, go to the next question.
2. Is the PP describing the preceding noun or pronoun by answering the question "which/which one?" If yes, it is an adjective; if no, it is an adverb.

Let's examine prepositional phrases in greater detail, starting with those that function as adjectives.

Adjectival Prepositional Phrases

Like all other adjectives, **adjectival prepositional phrases** have one job, and that is to modify a noun or pronoun. Examine the following sentence:

The tip of the tongue is used to produce speech sounds.

To decide whether the PP *of the tongue* is functioning as an adjective, follow the two steps listed above. First, look for an NP in front of the PP. The NP (*The tip*) precedes the PP, so now we must determine whether the PP (*of the tongue*) is describing *the tip*—which *tip*? Yes, it is the *tip of the tongue* (not the tip of your nose). We can now say that the PP *of the tongue* is indeed functioning as an adjective modifying the NP *The tip*.

Here are some more examples of PPs functioning as adjectives (underlined with arrows pointing to the nouns they modify):

Speakers of Arabic can have problems producing the /p/ sound.

The middle sound in "butter" is called a flap.

Many languages around the world use a "click" as part of their sound system.

Many people in the South pronounce "pin" and "pen" the same.

Another test that can be used to confirm that a PP functions as an adjective is the PST. Remember that a pronoun substitutes for a head noun and all of its adjectives (the entire NP). So, if a PP is an adjective, then the PP and the noun it is modifying should be able to be replaced with a pronoun. Let's revisit the first example above to see whether we can substitute *Speakers of Arabic* with a pronoun.

Speakers of Arabic can have problems producing the /p/ sound.

Apply the PST:

They can have problems producing the /p/ sound.

The PST proves that *Speakers* is the head noun and *of Arabic* is an adjective modifying it—*of Arabic* must be included in the NP or else you would get this:

*They of Arabic can have problems producing the /p/ sound.

Let's try another sentence to verify whether the PP is an adjective modifying its preceding noun using the PST:

The middle sound in "butter" is called a flap.
It is called a flap.

If you don't include *in "butter"* in the PST, you would get this:

*It in "butter" is called a flap.

The PST proves that *in "butter"* is an adjective PP modifying the noun *sound*.

Let's try another sentence but analyze it in two ways:

Larry studied Xhosa in Africa.

Apply the PST:

Larry studied Xhosa in Africa.
Larry studied it in Africa.

The PST shows that the pronoun substitutes for *Xhosa* only—*in Africa* is not part of the NP—and it answers the adverb question "where?" Another check is to see whether you can move the PP away from the noun it follows. An adjective cannot be moved away from its noun and maintain the original meaning of the sentence.

In Africa, Larry studied Xhosa.

We were able to move it, so it is most likely an adverbial prepositional phrase, which we will examine next.

In sum, to check that a PP functions as an adjective, be sure that there is a noun or pronoun in front of it, make sure that it is describing the noun or pronoun (answers "which?" or "which one?"), and then try the PST, which, if passed, reveals that the PP is an adjective attached to a noun. Practice using the PST in the following exercise.

Exercise 2.4 Getting a Grip on Adjectival Prepositional Phrases

Apply the pronoun substitution test to the prepositional phrases and their preceding nouns (both underlined) to determine if the prepositional phrases function as adjectives (and must be included in the pronoun substitution). Based on the results of the PST, circle Y (yes) if the prepositional phrase is modifying the preceding noun; N (no) if it is not.

Example:

Y (N) They recorded the endangered language after the interview.

Apply the PST:
They recorded it after the interview.

    1. Y N I studied click sounds in linguistics class.
    2. Y N My friend from South Texas pronounces "Dawn" and "Don" the same.
    3. Y N Writer Mark Twain provided examples of a rural Missouri dialect in his book *Huckleberry Finn*.

4.   Y   N   The migration patterns of settlers influenced local speech patterns.
5.   Y   N   Spanish has influenced the dialects of the Southwest.
6.   Y   N   The vowels of English are categorized as tense or lax.
7.   Y   N   In Chicago, the pronunciation of vowels can differ within a couple of miles.
8.   Y   N   Discriminatory practices have harmed people with accents.
9.   Y   N   Sometimes an accent is considered a speech impediment by others.
10. Y   N   Some students with accents are sent to "speech" classes.

Adverbial Prepositional Phrases

An **adverbial prepositional phrase**, like other adverbs, must modify a verb, adjective, or adverb. To identify the PP's function, look for a preceding noun. If there is no noun or pronoun for it to modify, then it functions as an adverb:

   She screamed *in my ear.*

The sentence above is easy because the PP *in my ear* does not have a noun directly in front of it to modify, so it can't be an adjective. In fact, it is an adverbial PP that modifies the verb *screamed—screamed* where? *in my ear*. But not all sentences are so easy. Look at the following sentence and decide whether the PP is functioning as an adjective or an adverb by asking the same two questions we used above:

   She shouted the word *in anger.*

1. Is there an NP in front of the PP *in anger*? Yes, *the word* is an NP.
2. Is the PP *in anger* describing which *word*? No, it is telling us <u>how</u> she shouted—*in anger.*

Remember that adverbs answer "how" questions (as well as why, where, when, how often, and to what extent). Here, the PP functions as an adverb modifying the verb *shouted*. Even though there is an NP in front of the PP, the PP is not describing that NP; thus, the PP functions as an adverb. You could also apply the PST as a check:

   She shouted the word in anger.

Apply the PST:

   She shouted <u>it</u> in anger.

Notice that the pronoun logically substitutes only for the NP *the word* and not *the word in anger*—they are not linked. This provides additional evidence that *in anger* functions as an adverb. Below are some examples of adverb PPs modifying verbs:

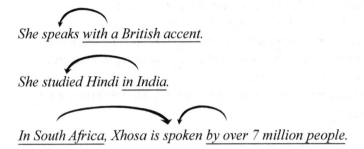

She speaks <u>with a British accent</u>.

She studied Hindi <u>in India</u>.

<u>In South Africa</u>, Xhosa is spoken <u>by over 7 million people</u>.

In addition to verbs, adverbial PPs can modify adjectives. Below are three PPs modifying predicate adjectives—*surprised*, *ready*, and *worried*:

He was surprised <u>at your accent</u>.

I was ready <u>for my Chinese test</u>.

Larry was worried <u>about the click sounds</u>.

PPs functioning as adverbs can also modify preceding adverbs. The examples below show PPs modifying the adverbs *closer* and *later*:

Her accent changed when she moved closer <u>to the city</u>.

Louis arrived much later <u>to his Urdu class</u>.

It is time to practice using the two steps to identify the functions of the PPs in the exercises below.

Exercise 2.5 Getting a Grip on Prepositional Phrases Used as Adjectives and Adverbs

Label the function of each underlined PP as an adjective (ADJ) or an adverb (ADV).

1. _____ The bump <u>behind your top teeth</u> is called the alveolar ridge.
2. _____ The sounds /t/, /d/, and /n/ are produced <u>with the tongue</u> hitting the alveolar ridge.

3. _____ The roof of your mouth is called the palate.
4. _____ An important organ for speech sounds is the larynx.
5. _____ The vocal cords vibrate in your larynx.
6. _____ Put your hand on your Adam's apple and produce the sounds /s/ ("hissssssss") and /z/ ("buzzzzzzzzzzzzzzzzzzz").
7. _____ Can you feel the vibration of your vocal cords?
8. _____ The difference between /s/ and /z/ is vibrating vocal cords.
9. _____ Can you pinch the nostrils of your nose and produce /m/? "mmmmmmmmmmmm"
10. _____ No, you can't. The sound /m/ is a nasal sound that exits from your nose.

Exercise 2.6 Getting a Grip on Prepositional Phrases Used as Adjectives and Adverbs

Find and underline the prepositional phrase(s) in each sentence. (There may be more than one.) Label each as an adjective (ADJ) or an adverb (ADV).

Example:

ADJ
You can feel the vibration of your larynx?

1. Our intonation can express feelings of happiness, sadness, etc.

2. Usually, we do not clearly enunciate each sound of a word.

3. Intonation is the pattern of tones.

4. Your tongue is a speech organ that produces a variety of sounds.

5. The IPA is used by linguists.

6. The English spelling system is not a good reflection of our sound system.

7. The "th" sound is produced with your tongue between your teeth.

8. The consonant sound /t/ is usually pronounced /d/ between vowels.

9. Word stress changes the meaning of "record."

10. Your lips and your tongue are important in the production of speech sounds.

Exercise 2.7 Getting a Grip on Prepositional Phrases Used as Adjectives and Adverbs

Go to the **Language Focus** box at the beginning of the chapter. Find all of the PPs and label them as adjectives or adverbs. You should find eight of them in the paragraph plus one in the heading.

Prepositional Phrases Versus Phrasal Verbs

The purpose of this section is to give you a quick overview of **phrasal verbs** because they can be confused with prepositional phrases. A phrasal verb consists of a verb plus a **particle.** Particles are words that look suspiciously like prepositions but are not. Let's examine a sentence with a phrasal verb:

> She *handed in* her phonetics homework.

The particle *in* completes the verb and is not part of a prepositional phrase. The verb and particle function as one unit, here meaning "submitted."

 She *handed in/submitted* her phonetics homework.

We have a number of verbs like this that contain particles. Some common phrasal verbs are "deal with," "give up," "lie down," "throw away," "blow up," and so on. The examples below are sentences with phrasal verbs, and they are compared to prepositional phrases preceded by similar verbs—notice the changes in meaning (and function) between the phrasal verbs and prepositional phrases. The phrasal verbs have their own idiomatic meaning that is difficult to deduce from the individual words:

Phrasal Verb: verb + particle:

She *turned in* the homework.	←Phrasal verb meaning: She *submitted* her homework.
She *turned down* the scholarship.	←Phrasal verb meaning: She *refused* the scholarship.
She *came back* at midnight.	←Phrasal verb meaning: She *returned* at midnight.
She *looked into* being a linguist.	←Phrasal verb meaning: She *investigated* being a linguist.

Single Verb + prepositional phrase:
> She *turned* in the wrong direction.
> She *turned* down the wrong street.
> She *looked* into the microscope.

As you can see from the above examples, the same word form may function as a preposition or a particle, for example, "in." You have to examine what it is doing in the sentence. The verb plus particle creates its own meaning that cannot always be understood by examining the individual words. The prepositional phrase consists of a preposition and a noun phrase, which may follow the verb but does not affect the meaning of the verb. There are a number of other nuances to phrasal verbs, but the focus of this section is simply to give you a heads-up that they exist and that they are different from prepositional phrases. You can practice identifying them in the exercise below.

Exercise 2.8 Getting a Grip on Prepositions and Particles

Examine the following sentences and determine whether the underlined word is a preposition in a prepositional phrase (PP) or a particle in a phrasal verb (PV).

1. _____ She received a grant from the National Science Foundation.

2. _____ The participant had a video camera inside her mouth to film her vocal cords.

3. _____ The participant didn't come back to the lab.

4. _____ The researcher turned down the money for her book.

5. _____ The student came across two relevant journal articles.

6. _____ The participants dropped off their voice recordings.

7. _____ Two of the participants got out quickly.

8. _____ The sounds came from the back of the throat.

9 _____ Nasal vowels are produced through the nose.

10. _____ She turned off the recorder.

DID YOU KNOW?

Many languages in Africa use click sounds as consonants. Imagine using a sound similar to what you would use to get a horse moving (something like "tchick") every time you wanted to pronounce a /k/ sound. Try it with the word "keep"—"tchick eep." Want to learn how to pronounce the three click sounds of Xhosa, a South African language? Go to www.youtube.com/watch?v=31zzMb3U0iY or search "Xhosa Lesson 2: How to Say "Click" Sounds."

Extending Verbs with Active and Passive Voice

In the last chapter, we examined verb forms, verb tenses, and auxiliary verbs. Here we will look at how subject-verb relationships (as well as the verb form) can change in **active** and **passive voice**. Voice influences the form that a verb takes. Because of this relationship, some grammar books use the terms "active verbs" and "passive verbs." Have you ever had an instructor say "avoid passives," but you had no idea what that meant? Here you will get the answers to all of your burning questions about passive voice.

Voice has to do with the structure of the sentence. Remember, a sentence has to have a subject noun phrase and a verb phrase to be complete:

> *John   produced a strange sound.*
>   NP   VP

In the above sentence, *John* is the subject NP, and *produced a strange sound* is the VP. Notice how *John* is the doer of the verb *produced*. This is an example of a sentence in active voice—the subject is doing the action. Sentences that use passive voice differ in that the subject of the sentence is not the doer; instead, the object from the active sentence is placed in the subject position. Below is the same sentence in its passive form:

> *A strange sound was produced by John.*

The doer of the action (*John*) has been placed at the end of the sentence in a "by" phrase (*John* has now become part of a prepositional phrase). *A strange sound* (the receiver of the action) has been moved into the subject slot. Let's explore further how voice influences sentence structure.

If we think of active voice as the "norm" (the subject doing the action), then passive voice is created by transforming the structure and verb of the active sentence. This is done in four steps that will be illustrated using the previous sentence (verb in parentheses):

> *John (produced) a strange sound.*

Step 1: Move the subject NP *John* to the end of the sentence:

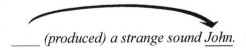

> _____ *(produced) a strange sound John.*

Step 2: Insert "by" in front of the moved subject:

_____ *(produced) a strange sound by John.*
             ∧

Step 3: Move the object NP _a strange sound_ to the subject position:

A strange sound (produced) _____ *by John.*

Now we have the sentence *A strange sound produced by John*; however, it needs one more step—we must transform the verb to reflect passive voice.

Step 4: Insert the appropriate form of the verb "be" in front of the head verb and change the head verb to its past participle (Ven) form. Verb transformation = be + Ven.

A strange sound (was produced) by John.
                be + Ven

The "be" verb's form depends on the tense of the original active verb—in this case, *produced* is past tense; therefore, the past tense of "be" (*was*) is used. The head verb's past participle form is *produced*. If you need a refresher on past participle forms, go back to Chapter 1, Table 1.3. It's important that you are clear about this verb terminology before moving on.

Let's look at some more active-voice sentences and their transformations to passive voice.

Your lips (produce) the /b/ sound.

Step 1: Move subject NP to the end of the sentence:

_____ *(produce) the /b/ sound your lips.*

Step 2: Insert "by" in front of the moved subject:

_____ *(produce) the /b/ sound by your lips.*
                              ∧

Step 3: Move object NP to subject position:

The /b/ sound (produce) _____ *by your lips.*

Step 4: Insert a form of the verb "be" (*produce* is present tense, so we must use *is*) and change the head verb *produce* into its Ven form, *produced*.

> *The /b/ sound (is produced) by your lips.*

Changing the verb can seem tricky when verbs have auxiliaries, but you just follow the same steps. Here are some examples of active-voice sentences that have been changed to passive voice. Look closely at the verb changes:

Active 1: *A speech therapist can help people with lisps.*
Passive 1: *People with lisps can be helped by a speech therapist.*

Active 2: *A speech therapist should help people with lisps.*
Passive 2: *People with lisps should be helped by a speech therapist.*

Active 3: *A speech therapist will help people with lisps.*
Passive 3: *People with lisps will be helped by a speech therapist.*

Active 4: *A speech therapist helped my friend.*
Passive 4: *My friend was helped by a speech therapist.*

Active 5: *A speech therapist is helping my friend.*
Passive 5: *My friend is being helped by a speech therapist.*

Active 6: *A speech therapist was helping my friend.*
Passive 6: *My friend was being helped by a speech therapist.*

Active 7: *A speech therapist has helped my friend.*
Passive 7: *My friend has been helped by a speech therapist.*

The verbs in the first three active sentences have modals (*can*, *should*, and *will*, respectively), so we need to retain the modals and then proceed with "be" + Ven form of *help* (*can be helped*). In Active 4, the past tense form *helped* is transformed into its passive form, *was helped*. In Active 5 and Active 6, the head verb is *helping*, used in present progressive form (*is helping*) and past progressive form (*was helping*). The "be" verb takes on the progressive forms (*is being* and *was being*), followed by the Ven form of *help*, which is *helped*. Active 7 shows the verb *help* being used in the present perfect form, the form now used by the "be" verb in the passive voice (*has been*) = *has been helped*.

Exercise 2.9 Getting a Grip on Active and Passive Voice

Complete the passive-voice sentences by filling in the blanks with the missing verb forms.

1. Active: Some people pronounce "pin" and "pen" the same.
   Passive: "Pin" and "pen" _are_ pronounced the same by some people.
2. Active: Some Northeasterners may not pronounce the "r" after vowels in words like "park."
   Passive: The "r" after vowels in words like "park" may not _be_ pronounced by some Northeasterners.
3. Active: Speakers of Indian English might produce the sounds "t" and "d" with the underside of the tongue rather than the tip of the tongue.
   Passive: The sounds "t" and "d" _____ be produced with the underside of the tongue rather than the tip of the tongue by speakers of Indian English.
4. Active: The bottom of the tongue hitting the ridge behind the teeth creates a retroflex sound.
   Passive: A retroflex sound is _____ by the bottom of the tongue hitting the ridge behind the teeth.
5. Active: Our first language can influence our pronunciation of a second language.
   Passive: Our pronunciation of a second language _____ _____ influenced by our first language.
6. Active: Americans are changing the pronunciation of vowels in some words.
   Passive: The pronunciation of vowels in some words is _____ changed by Americans.
7. Active: Australians and Americans speak different dialects of English.
   Passive: Different dialects of English _____ _____ by Australians and Americans.
8. Active: Americans might not completely understand Australian English.
   Passive: Australian English _____ not _____ completely _____ by Americans.
9. Active: For thousands of years, people have used clicks as speech sounds.
   Passive: For thousands of years, clicks as speech sounds have been _____ (by people).
10. Active: To produce a click sound, your tongue must suck air from the roof of your mouth.
    Passive: To produce a click sound, air from the roof of your mouth _____ _____ _____ by your tongue.

Not all passives have the "by doer" phrase at the end for a number of reasons; for example, we may not know who or what did something, the doer may be obvious and, therefore, does not need to be included (see number 9 in the exercise above), or the doer just may not be important. You often find passive voice used in scientific writing. For example, you will read "The mouse's brain was removed for analysis" rather than "The scientist removed the mouse's brain for analysis" (unless the scientist's name is relevant). Here are some more examples:

> *The research records were stolen.* (by whom?)
> *The research was conducted in Iceland.* (by someone whose name is
> known)
> *The speech sounds were recorded.* (by someone who isn't important for this
> discussion)
> *The cookies in the lab were eaten!* (I want someone to confess to the crime!)

Not all verbs allow for passive voice. For example, if there is no object NP to move to the subject position, then the sentence cannot be made passive:

> *She studied for the exam.*

This sentence is not a candidate for passive-voice transformation because of the lack of an object NP (it only has a prepositional phrase). If you moved the prepositional phrase to the front, you would have an ungrammatical sentence:

> Active: *She studied for the exam.*
> Passive: **For the exam was studied by her.*

 Also, some verbs such as "have" and the linking verb "be" cannot be used in passive voice. Here are examples of these verbs used in passive sentences (a question mark in front of a sentence indicates that its grammaticality is questionable):

> Active: *I am a student.*
> Passive: **A student is been by me.*

> Active: *John was a lab assistant.*
> Passive: **A lab assistant was been by John.*

> Active: *John has an accent.*
> Passive: *?An accent is had by John.*

> Active: *John had a headache.*
> Passive: *?A headache was had by John.*

Would you accept the last sentence as a grammatical sentence of English? It is very odd, although you do see this structure in the sentence: "A good time was had by all."

Why do instructors tell students to avoid the passive voice? First of all, passive sentences have more words than their active versions. If you look at the sentences in Active 7 and Passive 7 above, you can see that the active sentence has seven words, but the passive version has nine. Students may use this to their advantage when given specific lengths for their essays without considering the appropriate voice for their texts.

Grammarians argue that passive voice obscures meaning and slows down the text, which makes it less interesting. Active voice, with the subject doing the action, keeps the text more focused and forward moving. Of course, there are times when passive voice is more appropriate; for example, in scientific writing, the doer may not be known or may be unimportant to the topic under discussion (as mentioned above).

The general rule is to avoid passive voice whenever possible. Even in my own academic writing, I always do a final check for passive-voice sentences and change them if needed. Sometimes they cannot be avoided. (That was a passive sentence!) Sometimes, I cannot avoid them. (Better?)

Exercise 2.10 Getting a Grip on Active and Passive Voice

Mark each of the sentences below as active (A) or passive (P) voice.

1. __P__ The speech study was conducted by the graduate students.
2. __A__ The speech sounds from our first language can give us an accent in our second language.
3. __P__ In some dialects, "Dawn" may be pronounced as "Don."
4. __P__ A Coca-Cola may be called "pop" in parts of the United States.
5. __A__ In Vanuatu, the Lemerig language is dying.
6. __P__ Lemerig is spoken only by two adults.
7. __A__ Many languages are in danger of dying.
8. __P__ Language death means the loss of a wealth of cultural knowledge.
9. __A__ Many nonstandard dialects in the United States are stigmatized.
10. __A__ His West Virginian parents pronounce "storm" as "starm."

Extending Conjunctions with Conjunctive Adverbs

In the previous chapter, we examined coordinating conjunctions (FANBOYS) and two-part correlative conjunctions (e.g., not only/but also). In Chapter 5, we will look at subordinating conjunctions, another important group of conjunctions that conjoin grammatical structures. Here we take a quick look at **conjunctive adverbs**, a group of words that signal relationships among grammatical structures that they conjoin—in this case, between two sentences.

Conjunctive adverbs do some conjunction work and some adverb work. They conjoin sentences—in fact, some grammar books refer to them as "linking adverbials" rather than conjunctive adverbs because they link sentences. Like other adverbs, they show contrast, time, cause and effect, addition, concession, summary, and so on. Table 2.1 provides a list of some of the most common conjunctive adverbs.

Table 2.1
Common Conjunctive Adverbs

accordingly	however	meanwhile
also	in addition	moreover
as a result	in conclusion	nevertheless
consequently	in contrast	still
for example	in fact	that is
for instance	in other words	therefore
furthermore	instead	thus

We examine how these conjunctive adverbs conjoin sentences, what slots they fill in a sentence, and how they are punctuated. To help in our discussion, let's use the conjunctive adverb "however" as an example. We know that when it shows up in a sentence, there is going to be some sort of contrast:

The sound "th" as in "thank" may seem very easy to pronounce; however, for many non-English speakers, the sound is very challenging.

The structure above has two sentences (also referred to as "clauses," a topic explored in Chapter 5). The first one sets up the situation (*The sound "th" as in "thank" may seem very easy to pronounce*) that is contrasted in the second (*however, for many non-English speakers, the sound is very challenging*). The conjunctive adverbs "however," "on the other hand," "in contrast," and "nevertheless" set up this type of relationship. Because they are adverbs, they share the adverb quality of movability within their sentences:

> *The sound "th" as in "thank" may seem very easy to pronounce; for many non-English speakers, <u>however</u>, the sound is very challenging.*

Let's examine another commonly used conjunctive adverb, "therefore," which sets up a consequence:

> *French does not have the "th" sound; <u>therefore</u>, "th" may be difficult for French speakers to pronounce when first learning English.*

Therefore, like *however*, can also move around in a sentence:

> *French does not have the "th" sound; "th," <u>therefore</u>, may be difficult for French speakers to pronounce when first learning English.*

Note that the conjunctive adverb is always in the second sentence. When it is the first word of the sentence, it is followed by a comma, and when it is moved away from the front, it is punctuated with commas before and after.

The punctuation of these conjunctive adverbs is different from that of coordinating conjunctions. Coordinating conjunctions that conjoin two sentences are separated by a comma:

> *The "th" sound is easy for English speakers, <u>but</u> a French speaker may have trouble using it when first learning English.*

Unlike coordinating conjunctions, the conjunctive adverb requires either a semicolon or a period to separate the two sentences:

> *French does not have the "th" sound; <u>therefore</u>, "th" may be difficult for French speakers to produce when first learning English.*
> OR
> *French does not have the "th" sound. <u>Therefore</u>, "th" may be difficult for French speakers to produce when first learning English.*

Learning the simple punctuation rules for conjunctive adverbs and coordinating conjunctions can alleviate some of the most common punctuation errors found in student papers. The exercise below will give you practice punctuating conjunctive adverbs and reviewing the punctuation of coordinating conjunctions that conjoin sentences (not phrases).

Exercise 2.11 Getting a Grip on Conjunctive Adverbs and Coordinating Conjunctions

Punctuate the sentences by adding commas and semicolons where needed. Both conjunctive adverbs and coordinating conjunctions are used below to conjoin sentences.

1. I learned French in Africa as a result my French is different from the French spoken in France.
2. British English is different from American English we nevertheless can communicate.
3. The English spelling system can be difficult to learn children therefore spend a great deal of time learning how to spell.
4. We often drop sounds in a word and we sometimes add sounds as in real^{uh}tor.
5. "You and I" is often pronounced "You n I" but that does not cause a loss of understanding.
6. Some dialects of English have unique characteristics that mark them as different from Standard English consequently these characteristics are sometimes ridiculed by others.
7. Forty years ago, children learned to spell through memorization in contrast children more recently have been taught through phonics.
8. Some languages do not use an alphabet for writing instead they use symbols to represent meanings.
9. Our first language influences the pronunciation of our second language for example Spanish speakers may say "eschool" for the English word "school."
10. Many linguists are interested in articulatory phonetics therefore they may focus on how speech sounds are produced.

Chapter Review

Exercise 2.12 Getting a Grip—Review of Noun Phrases

Label the underlined NPs as a subject (S), appositive (A), object (O), or object of preposition (OP).

1. _____ Some foreign language sounds may be difficult to pronounce even after a lot of practice.

2. _____ /m/ and /n/, two nasal sounds, are produced in the nasal cavity.

3. _____ In your larynx, your vocal cords vibrate to produce sound.

4. _____ A head cold affects the sound of your voice.

5. _____ Gullah, a dialect with African roots, is spoken along the Southeastern U.S. coast.

6. _____ The first sound in "dog" is called a "stop" because air is stopped and then released.

7. _____ Spanish, a commonly spoken language, is generally written the way it is pronounced.

8. __S__ The English alphabet has twenty-six letters, but English has more than twenty-six sounds.

9. _____ Do you pronounce "Don" and "Dawn" with the same vowel sound?

10. _____ My friend from East Texas often feels self-conscious about her accent.

Exercise 2.13 Getting a Grip—Review of Prepositional Phrases

Below are some sentences that we have examined before; this time, find and underline all of the prepositional phrases (PPs). Label each one as an adjective (ADJ) or an adverb (ADV). Warning: There are some phrases that look like PPs, but they are not. They (infinitives) consist of "to" plus a verb. Remember that PPs have a preposition plus an NP. (Hint: There may be more than one PP in a sentence.)

Example:

                              ADV   ADJ
Some sounds are aspirated at the beginning of a word, meaning they get an

              ADJ
extra puff of air.

1. We may have difficulty pronouncing some foreign language sounds even after months of practice.

2. /m/ and /n/, two nasal sounds, are produced in the nasal cavity.

3. In your larynx, your vocal cords vibrate to produce sounds.

4. Gullah, a dialect with African roots, is spoken along the Southeastern U.S. coast.

5. My friend from East Texas often feels self-conscious about her accent.

6. The size of your larynx influences the sound of your voice.

7. Languages with few speakers will most likely disappear.

8. Lemerig is spoken only by two adults.

9. The speech sounds from our first language can influence our second language.

10. The speech study was conducted by the graduate students.

Exercise 2.14 Getting a Grip—Review of Active and Passive Voice

Examine the sentences in Exercise 2.12 and decide whether they are written in active (A) or passive (P) voice.

1. _A_   6. _____

2. _A_   7. _____

3. _A_   8. _____

4. _A_   9. _____

5. _P_   10. _____

Exercise 2.15 Getting a Grip—Review of Active and Passive Voice

Transform the following active-voice sentences into passive-voice sentences.

Example:
The students can recognize passive sentences.

Change active to passive:
Passive sentences can be recognized by the students.

1. The size of the vocal cords affects *can* speech sounds.

2. Some teachers demand the use of active voice in papers.

3. The tip of the tongue produces sounds like /t/ and /d/.

4. English borrows words from other languages.

5. According to some, English has killed other languages.

Exercise 2.16 Getting a Grip—Review of Active and Passive Voice

Transform the passive-voice sentences into active-voice sentences.

Example:
"Don" and "Dawn" are pronounced the same by some English speakers.

Change passive to active:
Some English speakers pronounce "Don" and "Dawn" the same.

1. Word meaning ~~can be~~ *is* changed by tone.
2. The sound of my voice was affected by a head cold.
3. Spanish as a first language is spoken by almost 400 million people.
4. Possibilities are created by language. *Language has many possibilities*
5. My personal history is reflected by my dialect.

Exercise 2.17 Getting a Grip—Review

Read each statement carefully and circle T (true) or F (false).

1. T F Following the terminology introduced in this chapter, a one-word noun is categorized as a noun phrase.
2. T F Prepositional phrases function as adjectives, verbs, and adverbs.
3. T F Conjunctive adverbs only conjoin sentences, unlike coordinating conjunctions.
4. T F Verbs in passive-voice sentences are recognized by a form of the verb "be" plus a present participle form (Ving) of the head verb.
5. T F All passive-voice sentences must have a clear "doer" in a "by" phrase at the end of the sentence.
6. T F A phrasal verb consists of a verb plus a particle.
7. T F The object of preposition must follow a preposition.
8. T F An active-voice sentence has fewer words than its passive version.
9. T F The conjunctive adverb in the second sentence sets up the relationship to the first sentence, for example, "therefore" indicates a cause and effect.
10. T F A sentence with a conjunctive adverb must be separated from the preceding sentence with a period or a semicolon.

3
Sentence Patterns

This chapter focuses on seven basic sentence patterns of English. These patterns demonstrate that verbs are powerful elements in the construction of sentences. In this chapter, important grammatical concepts to learn are **linking verb**, **action verb**, **intransitive verb**, **transitive verb**, **adverbial subject complement**, **predicate adjective**, **predicate nominative**, **subject complement**, **indirect object**, **direct object**, and **object complement**.

Language Focus: Sociolinguistics

Sociolinguistics is the study of language in its social context. It covers multiple areas of language research concerning language and identity. Sociolinguists investigate the following questions (among many others): Should English be the official language of the United States or not? Why? For what reasons do people shift from one language to another? Why do languages die? How is the language or dialect you speak a marker of your identity? Do men and women speak differently?

First we will look at the traditional classification of verbs: **linking verbs** and **action verbs**. Distinguishing between the two is essential to the discussion of sentence patterns that follows. The verb drives which patterns are allowed in the verb phrase (VP); for example, some verbs require at least one object noun phrase (NP, e.g., "She likes them"), whereas others cannot have any (e.g., "She laughed"). The terminology used in the VP depends on whether the verb is a linking verb or an action verb. If you cannot recognize the class of verb, you will not be able to analyze the VP correctly. This terminology is also relevant for the next two chapters. So if it seems like we are spending a great deal of time on these verbs, there is a good reason for it.

Verb Classes

As noted in Chapter 1, a sentence is divided into the subject noun phrase and the verb phrase. In this chapter, we will focus on the verb phrase, in particular, the terminology associated with the common sentence patterns of linking and action verbs.

The job of a linking verb is to link what follows it—an adverb, an adjective, or a noun—back to the subject. For example, in the sentence "John is bilingual," "bilingual" is an adjective describing the subject "John." So, if a linking verb's job is to link, it would follow that the job of an action verb is to show action, right? Yes, action verbs can show action, as in "John sings in Lithuanian." However, not all action verbs show action, for example, "John has an electronic translator." Not much action going on there!

In traditional grammar, action verbs are subcategorized as intransitive and transitive. However, contemporary grammar texts now use the terms "intransitive" and "transitive" only, and the traditional term "action verb" has been dropped. It is important that you are familiar with the term "action verb" because some traditional textbooks continue to use the linking-action verb classification.

Recognizing the class of verb is crucial in determining the structure of the verb phrase and the associated terminology. Some verbs take **complements**—grammatical structures that complete the verb phrase. Some of the complement terminology may sound familiar to you: **adverbial subject complement, predicate nominative, predicate adjective, direct object, indirect object,** and **object complement**.

We will start with linking verbs and then examine intransitive and transitive verbs. After we have a good grip on these verbs, we will dive into the seven sentence patterns. At the end of the chapter, Table 3.1 summarizes all of the terminology and provides examples of each sentence pattern.

Linking Verbs S-LV-PA

This is not the first time linking verbs have been mentioned in this book. (Linking verbs are also referred to as **copular verbs** in some texts.) In the section on adjectives in Chapter 1, we briefly discussed linking verbs as "be" verbs. We learned that adjectives regularly fill two slots—one slot occurring in front of the nouns they modify (e.g., strange sound), and the other slot being after linking verbs (LVs). Here is one of the linking verb examples from Chapter 1:

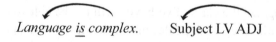

Language is complex.   Subject LV ADJ

In addition to adjectives, linking verbs can also link adverbs and noun phrases (NPs) back to the subject. The most common linking verb is "be" (is, are, was, were, has been, had been, will be, etc.). Below are sentences with "be" linking verbs. The first three examples have nouns following the linking verbs, the third has an adverb, and the last two have adjectives—all of them link back to the subject.

very test

Literacy is a social equalizer.

Bilingualism has been part of Southwestern U.S. culture for generations.

John is president of the Arabic club.

The vote on the language bill is tomorrow.

My mother is anxious to learn Chinese.

Our language is important to our identity.

Other verbs can do the same linking job as "be." These are verbs of sense, such as "seem," "feel," "sound," "grow," "taste," "become," "appear," and so forth. Below are examples of these verbs functioning as linking verbs:

English became an official language of Hong Kong in 1883.

Language seems complex.

My friend feels insecure about her dialect.

She appeared comfortable speaking Urdu.

These linking verbs link what comes after them back to the subject. Only linking verbs can do this.

We can use the **BE substitution test** to determine whether a "non-be" verb is functioning as a linking verb. The test is as follows: if you can substitute a "be" verb for the "suspected" linking verb and maintain the sentence's meaning, then it is a linking verb. Let's apply the BE substitution test to the verbs in these sentences:

English became an official language of Hong Kong. → *English is an official language of Hong Kong.*

Language seems complex. → *Language is complex.*

My friend feels insecure about her dialect. → *My friend is insecure about her dialect.*

She appeared comfortable speaking Urdu. → *She was comfortable speaking Urdu.*

It worked! The four sentences passed the BE substitution test, which proves that *became, seems, feels,* and *appeared* are linking verbs. You also should make sure that what follows the linking verb refers back to or describes the subject because that is the job of a linking verb. We will examine linking verbs in closer detail in the next section on sentence patterns.

WARNING!

In addition to functioning as linking verbs, "be" verbs can also be used as helping verbs. Examine the following sentences:

> The students *are studying* Hindi for their trip to India.
> My mother *is studying* Chinese.
> John *is reading* about gender and language.
> Our language *is evolving.*
> She *is promoting* bilingual education.

In the first two sentences, *studying* is the head verb, and *is* and *are* are used as helping verbs to form the present participle verb *are studying/is studying.* The same pattern is found in the next three sentences: *reading, evolving,* and *promoting* are head verbs and *is* functions as a helping verb. In all of the above examples, the "be" verb is not a linking verb; it simply helps the head verb show a continuous action. This is an important distinction that you must recognize because confusing "be" linking verbs with "be" helping verbs will cause problems in this chapter and in the upcoming chapters.

Exercise 3.1 Getting a Grip on "Be" Verbs

Let's check our knowledge of "be" verbs. Each sentence below has a "be" verb that functions as a linking verb. Using the cues in the sentences, fill in the blanks with the correct forms of "be." If there are two blanks, the verb form must have two parts.

1. Today, gender _____ an important area of sociolinguistic research.
2. For my current research, I _____ very interested in gender issues.
3. Thirty years ago, gender _____ a biological construct and not a social factor in research.
4. Over the last decade, knowledge about the social dimensions of gender _____ _____ a pivotal factor in producing rich sociolinguistic research.
5. In the future, gender _____ _____ an essential factor in language studies.

DID YOU KNOW?

"Be" is the most commonly used verb in English, and it is also the most irregular. The reason for its irregularity can be found in its history—"be" represents a merger of two Old English verbs with remnants of both in our modern language. You can see traces of the Old English forms of "be" in the Bible, as in "Our Father who *art* in heaven."

Exercise 3.2 Getting a Grip on Linking Verbs

Examine each underlined verb and decide whether it is a linking verb. Circle Y (yes) if it is a linking verb and N (no) if it is not. (Hint: Watch out for "be" used as a helping verb.)

1. Y   N   An official language bill is undergoing revisions in the Senate.
2. Y   N   The Chinese writing system is different from English orthography.
3. Y   N   I have a Chicago accent.
4. Y   N   Spanish is a common second language in the United States.
5. Y   N   French accents sound intriguing to many Americans. Why?

6. Y   N   My Chinese language skills <u>grew</u> weak from lack of practice.

7. Y   N   Many people in the United States <u>can</u> not <u>speak</u> the language of their grandparents.

8. Y   N   Many children <u>have been punished</u> for speaking Spanish in school.

9. Y   N   Language <u>has been</u> a controversial topic in the United States.

10. Y   N   Language <u>is</u> part of your identity.

Intransitive and Transitive Verbs   S-TV-DO

Intransitive and **transitive verbs** (traditionally known as **action verbs**) are very different from linking verbs. Only linking verbs can link the complement back to the subject. Intransitive and transitive verbs do not allow for this type of relationship between the complement and the subject. Intransitive verbs cannot be followed by a noun phrase object; transitive verbs require at least one NP object after the verb. Let's begin by examining intransitive verbs.

Intransitive Verbs - don't take objects   IV

An intransitive verb does not have an object NP after it (i.e., there is no complement). One good way to remember this is to think about the prefix "in" in the word "intransitive." The prefix means "not." Remember the prefix and associate it with the idea that a transitive verb does NOT have an NP after it. Here is a simple example of a sentence with an intransitive verb.

> *Languages <u>change</u>.*

An intransitive verb may be followed by an adverb or a prepositional phrase (PP)—but there can be no NP immediately after it. Below are examples of sentences with intransitive verbs that are followed by PPs and adverbs:

> *English vocabulary <u>evolved</u> from many languages.* ←followed by PP
> *As children, we <u>talk</u> like other family members.* ←followed by PP
> *You <u>speak</u> softly.* ←followed by adverb
> *Many Americans <u>talk</u> louder when speaking to foreigners.* ←followed by adverb

These verbs are intransitive because they do not have NPs directly following them. See if you can recognize intransitive verbs in the next exercise.

Exercise 3.3 Getting a Grip on Intransitive Verbs

Decide whether the underlined verb is intransitive (no NP immediately following it). Circle Y (yes) if it is intransitive and N (no) if it is not.

1. Y   N   Women generally <u>use</u> fewer swear words than men.
2. Y   N   Do you <u>agree</u> with the sentence above?
3. Y   N   Children <u>learn</u> gendered speech styles at a very young age.
4. Y   N   Little girls <u>use</u> more inclusive speech, for example, "Let's do this."
5. Y   N   Little boys often <u>speak</u> more directly, using commands like "Do this."

Transitive Verbs - take objects.   She likes cats. *[handwritten: never just she likes.]*

Three of the seven sentence patterns that we will examine next are based on transitive verbs (TVs), so recognizing them is critical. As mentioned above, a verb phrase with a transitive verb must have at least one object NP in it, for example,

$$
\begin{array}{cc}
\text{TV} & \text{NP} \\
\end{array}
$$

Hong Kong <u>has</u> <u>two official languages</u>.

VP

The verb *has* is followed by the NP *two official languages*, so it fills the requirement of a transitive verb. Below are other examples of sentences with transitive verbs:

$$
\begin{array}{cc}
\text{TV} & \text{NP} \\
\end{array}
$$

Some cartoons <u>promote</u> <u>language stereotypes</u>.

VP

$$
\begin{array}{cc}
\text{TV} & \text{NP} \\
\end{array}
$$

Researchers <u>have found</u> <u>negative attitudes</u> <u>toward certain dialects</u>.

VP

Transitive verbs can have more than one object NP; for example, in the following sentence, the transitive verb *teach* is followed by the NPs *children* and *language stereotypes*.

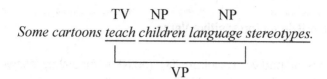

It is critical that you are able to distinguish transitive verbs from intransitive verbs before moving on to the different sentence patterns. After you test your knowledge below, decide whether it would be prudent to go back and review this section before proceeding to sentence patterns.

Exercise 3.4 Getting a Grip on Intransitive and Transitive Verbs

Label the underlined verbs as either intransitive (IV) or transitive (TV).

1. IV TV   Dialects <u>emerge</u> from immigration patterns.
2. IV TV   Everyone <u>has</u> an accent.
3. IV TV   My friend <u>switches</u> between Japanese and English in conversations.
4. IV TV   Writer Chinua Achebe <u>includes</u> Africanized English words in his novels.
5. IV TV   Some Japanese women <u>use</u> a language style different from men's.
6. IV TV   Along the U.S.–Mexico border, most people <u>understand</u> English and Spanish.
7. IV TV   Some children <u>have</u> not <u>learned</u> their parents' native language.
8. IV TV   Those children <u>lost</u> their opportunity to be bilingual.
9. IV TV   In many instances in our history, school systems <u>discouraged</u> bilingualism.
10. IV TV   I <u>use</u> my mother tongue when I am angry, not English.

Of course, nothing is ever straightforward in grammar, right? So here comes the heads-up—sometimes the same verb form can function as *both* a linking verb and an (in)transitive verb, depending on the context. (Rather than repeating intransitive and transitive, I will use the term "(in)transitive" to stand for both terms.) The verbs may appear to be the same, but they have different meanings:

> Julio <u>felt</u> confident about learning Arabic.
> Julio <u>felt</u> the braille.

Let's try the BE substitution test on the two sentences:

> *Julio <u>was</u> confident about learning Arabic.*
> *Julio <u>was</u> the braille.*

The BE substitution test shows that *felt* in the first sentence is a linking verb, but in the second sentence, *felt* is used as a transitive verb—we know this because the BE substitution test failed. Also, note that in the first example, the verb (*felt*) is linking *confident* to the subject; however, in the second example, *the braille* does not link back to the subject (*Julio = braille?*). This adds to the evidence that the verb *felt* in the second sentence is <u>not</u> a linking verb.

When a verb form is used as both a linking verb and an (in)transitive verb, the meaning of the verb is not the same in its two roles. Here are some other examples of verbs that can be used both ways. Notice how the nouns and adjectives following the linking verbs refer back to the subject, but those following the (in)transitive verbs do not.

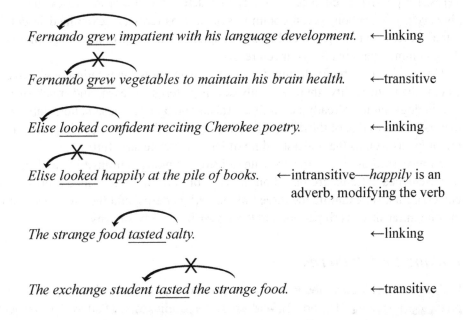

Fernando grew impatient with his language development.   ←linking

Fernando grew vegetables to maintain his brain health.   ←transitive

Elise looked confident reciting Cherokee poetry.   ←linking

Elise looked happily at the pile of books.   ←intransitive—*happily* is an adverb, modifying the verb

The strange food tasted salty.   ←linking

The exchange student tasted the strange food.   ←transitive

Exercise 3.5 Getting a Grip on Linking, Intransitive, and Transitive Verbs

Go to the **Language Focus** box at the beginning of the chapter. Copy the first two sentences from the box, underline the verbs, and mark them as linking (LV), intransitive (IV), or transitive (TV).

DID YOU KNOW?

"Vocal fry" is a relatively new term that describes a speech pattern used by young women, particularly students at universities. It is a lowering of the voice into a creaky sound—a vocal affectation used by popular stars (e.g., Katy Perry, the Kardashians, Gwen Stefani)—and is now being used by young women to feel as if they fit in. *CBS Sunday Morning* takes a humorous look at vocal fry. Search for "Faith Salie on Speaking with Vocal Fry" or go to www.cbsnews.com/video/watch/?id=50154925n.

Sentence Patterns

Verbs are powerful sentence elements that determine the structure of the verb phrase. In this section, seven common sentence patterns are examined in detail (other patterns exist). At the end of this chapter, Table 3.1 provides a summary of these common patterns for your reference.

This section may be frustrating for students who allow the terminology to overwhelm them. In reality, there are only seven patterns to learn, and much of the terminology should already be familiar. Taken one by one, these patterns are easy to grasp. Knowledge of these basic patterns supports the learning of important terminology as well as the understanding of basic sentence structures.

As discussed above, verbs are categorized as linking, intransitive, and transitive. Sentence patterns are based on the type of verb in the sentence (verbs have power!). First we examine the three linking verb patterns, and then we will examine one intransitive verb pattern and three transitive verb patterns.

Linking Verb Patterns

Linking verbs (LV) take the following types of complements: adverbs (Pattern 1), predicate adjectives (Pattern 2), and predicate nominatives (Pattern 3). **Subject complement** is the umbrella term for all adverbs, predicate adjectives, and predicate nominatives that refer back to or modify the subject. Because of this unique relationship between the subject and the complement, the term "subject complement" can only be used in linking verb patterns.

Some traditional grammar books do not include adverbs as subject complements. However, because of their unique relationship to the subject, they are included in our discussion of linking verbs.

Pattern 1, Subject-LV-Adverb

Linking verbs (in parentheses) can be followed by an **adverbial subject complement** (underlined)—adverbs of time or place that situate the subject:

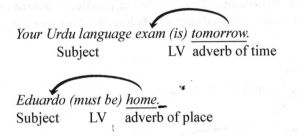

Your Urdu language exam (is) tomorrow.
    Subject   LV adverb of time

Eduardo (must be) home.
Subject   LV   adverb of place

Prepositional phrases can also fill this adverbial slot:

Our Urdu exam (was) on Monday.
    Subject   LV adverb of time

Yulianti (is) in Indonesia.
Subject LV adverb of place

Pattern 2, Subject-LV-PA

A linking verb can also be followed by an adjective. This subject complement is called a **predicate adjective (PA),** and its function is to describe the subject. Only adjectives that follow linking verbs and modify subjects are called predicate adjectives. Below are four examples of Pattern 2 sentences:

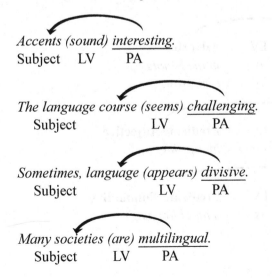

Accents (sound) interesting.
Subject   LV   PA

The language course (seems) challenging.
   Subject   LV   PA

Sometimes, language (appears) divisive.
   Subject   LV   PA

Many societies (are) multilingual.
Subject   LV   PA

As you can see, the predicate adjectives *interesting, challenging, divisive,* and *multilingual* describe subjects of the sentences, *accents, course, language,* and *societies.*

Pattern 3, Subject-LV-PN

Nouns can also be subject complements. This is called a **predicate nominative (PN)**, and it, too, must refer back to the subject NP. Below are three examples of Pattern 3:

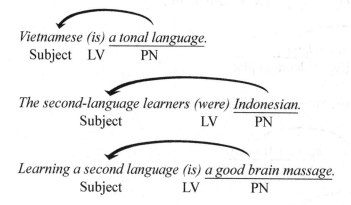

Vietnamese (is) a tonal language.
　Subject　LV　　PN

The second-language learners (were) Indonesian.
　　Subject　　　　　LV　　PN

Learning a second language (is) a good brain massage.
　　Subject　　　　　LV　　　PN

In the first example above, the predicate nominative *a tonal language* refers back to the subject NP *Vietnamese*; in the second example, the predicate nominative *Indonesian* refers back to the subject NP *The second-language learners*; and in the third example, the predicate nominative *a good brain massage* refers back to the subject NP *Learning a second language*.

In sum, the adverbial, predicate adjective, and predicate nominative subject complements refer to or describe their subjects. Below is a summary of the three linking verb patterns:

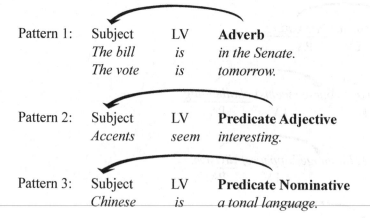

Pattern 1:　Subject　　LV　　**Adverb**
　　　　　　The bill　　*is*　　*in the Senate.*
　　　　　　The vote　　*is*　　*tomorrow.*

Pattern 2:　Subject　　LV　　**Predicate Adjective**
　　　　　　Accents　　*seem*　*interesting.*

Pattern 3:　Subject　　LV　　**Predicate Nominative**
　　　　　　Chinese　　*is*　　*a tonal language.*

Exercise 3.6 Getting a Grip on Sentence Patterns with Linking Verbs

In the sentences below, decide how the underlined subject complements function and identify each one as an adverb (ADV), a predicate adjective (PA), or a predicate nominative (PN).

1. ____ The second-language learners were <u>in the audience</u>.
2. ____ Spanish is <u>a common second language</u>.
3. ____ English is not <u>the official language of the U.S. government</u>.
4. ____ William Labov is <u>a famous sociolinguist</u>.
5. ____ Louisiana Cajun is <u>a mix of English, French, African, and Native American languages</u>.
6. ____ The needs of English language learners should be <u>a priority</u> in schools.
7. ____ Many people are <u>supporters of bilingual education</u>.
8 ____ Bilingual individuals are <u>fortunate</u> to have two languages available to them.
9. ____ Many languages of the world will be <u>extinct</u>.
10. ____ A language death is <u>a loss of important cultural knowledge</u>.

Exercise 3.7 Getting a Grip on Sentence Patterns with Linking Verbs

Write the six sentences from Exercise 3.2 that have linking verbs. Underline and label the adverbial (ADV), predicate adjective (PA), and predicate nominative (PN) subject complements.

Intransitive and Transitive Verb Patterns

There is one intransitive verb pattern (Pattern 4) and three patterns with transitive verbs (Patterns 5, 6, and 7). The terminology below differs from that used for linking verbs. The mixing of linking verb terminology with this terminology is one of the biggest problems that students have when first learning these patterns, so be alert!

Intransitive Verb Pattern

Pattern 4, Subject-IV

The intransitive verb pattern is the easiest to recognize because the verb is not followed by an NP. It may have other word classes following it, such as an adverb or a PP, but there is no NP object:

Everyone (speaks) with an accent.
I (speak) in my native tongue when angry.
Do Northerners (speak) rapidly?
My mother (speaks) loudly to my Japanese friends. She thinks it helps them
understand her!

In the first two examples above, the intransitive verb *speaks/speak* is followed by a PP (*with an accent, in my native tongue*). In the next two examples, *speak/speaks* is followed by an adverb (*rapidly/loudly*). Even though there are nouns in all of the PPs, they are tied up in their roles as objects of prepositions, so they cannot function as complements.

Transitive Verb Patterns

Pattern 5, Subject-TV-DO

Unlike an intransitive verb, a transitive verb must have at least a **direct object (DO)**. Our first TV pattern has just one NP, the DO, which receives the action of the verb:

> *Armando (speaks) three languages.*
> Subject   TV   DO

> *Your social network (influences) your speech.*
>   Subject   TV   DO

> *Caretakers (provide) linguistic input to the child.*
>   Subject   TV   DO

Notice that in the last example, there is a prepositional phrase following the direct object. The PP is not considered a complement in sentences with transitive verbs, so it is not labeled. Before we move on to the next two patterns, let's check our knowledge of Pattern 4 (intransitive verb) and Pattern 5 (transitive verb followed by a DO).

Exercise 3.8 Getting a Grip on Sentence Patterns 4 and 5

Underline the verb and then identify the pattern of each sentence: Pattern 4 (Subject-IV) or Pattern 5 (Subject-TV-DO).

1. DO   Children <u>learn</u> the dialect of their peers.
2. _____   Different regions of the United States have different words for soft drinks (e.g., soda, pop, Coke).

3. ____ I recognized her West Virginia accent.
4. ____ Students have varied cultural backgrounds.
5. ____ We all speak with an accent.
6. ____ Some children may not speak the classroom dialect.
7. ____ Teachers must demand respect for children's home languages and dialects.
8. ____ Some dialects have more prestige than others.
9. ____ According to many studies, women speak a more standard language variety than men.
10. ____ Language reflects cultural patterns.

Pattern 6, Subject-TV-IO-DO

Transitive verbs can be followed by two NPs, as we will see in Pattern 6 and Pattern 7. In Pattern 6, the complement consists of an **indirect object (IO)** and a direct object. As stated above, the DO receives the action. The IO identifies to or for whom (or what) the action is done.

> *Nunami (gave) me French lessons.*
> Subject TV IO   DO

> *Caretakers (teach) children politeness formulas such as "please" and "thank you."*
> Subject   TV   IO   DO

> *Her confident tone (sent) the audience a strong message.*
> Subject   TV   IO   DO

The two NP complements in Pattern 6 are always in the order of IO DO. The IO precedes the DO. One test for this pattern is the **IO movement test**: first, move the IO to the position after the DO, and then insert "to" or "for" in front of it. If the sentence retains its meaning, this is evidence for the IO DO pattern. (You'll understand the importance of this test when you get to Pattern 7.) Let's look at the IO movement test step by step in the three sentences:

> *Nunami (gave) me French lessons.*

Step 1: Move the IO to after the DO:

> *Nunami (gave)____ French lessons me.*

Step 2: Insert *to/for* in front of the moved IO:

> *Nunami (gave) French lessons to me.*

Caretakers (teach) <u>children</u> <u>politeness formulas</u>.

Step 1: Move the IO after the DO:

Caretakers (teach) ____ <u>politeness formulas</u> <u>children</u>.

Step 2: Insert *to/for* in front of the moved IO:

Caretakers (teach) <u>politeness formulas</u> to children.

Her confident tone (sent) <u>the audience</u> <u>a strong message</u>.

Step 1: Move the IO after the DO:

Her confident tone (sent) ____ <u>a strong message</u> <u>the audience</u>.

Step 2: Insert *to/for* in front of the moved IO:

Her confident tone (sent) <u>a strong message</u> to the audience.

In all three sentences, the first NP after the verb could be moved and the meaning is preserved. The IO movement test proves that all three sentences follow the Pattern 6 structure. Note that once the IO is moved and "to" or "for" is placed in front of it, it is no longer an IO. It becomes the object of a preposition in a prepositional phrase. Move it back into its original position, and the NP takes on its role as the IO again.

Now let's examine our last pattern, Pattern 7. Like Pattern 6, it can have two NPs following the transitive verb.

Pattern 7, Subject-TV-DO-OC

The **object complement (OC)** follows the direct object. The OC can be an NP or an adjective. When it is an NP, the sentence can look like Pattern 6, which also has two NPs after the transitive verb. The job of the OC is to refer back to the DO. In the sentence below, the OC (*their national language*) is referring back to the DO (*Swahili*).

Kenyans (made) <u>Swahili</u> <u>their national language</u>.
  Subject   TV   DO   OC

Below are more examples of this pattern:

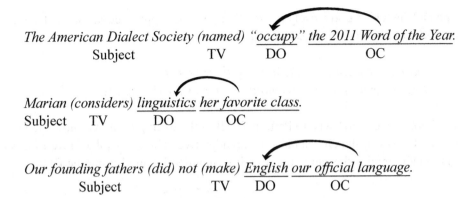

The American Dialect Society (named) "occupy" the 2011 Word of the Year.
    Subject   TV   DO   OC

Marian (considers) linguistics her favorite class.
Subject   TV   DO   OC

Our founding fathers (did) not (make) English our official language.
    Subject   TV   DO   OC

How do you know whether the two NPs after the transitive verb are Pattern 6 (IO DO) or Pattern 7 (DO OC)? Start with the IO movement test. If it works, then it is the IO DO pattern (Pattern 6). If it doesn't work, then check to see whether the second NP after the transitive verb refers back to the NP in front of it. If it does, then it is the DO OC pattern. Let's try the IO movement test using the second example above (which is kind of cheating because we already know that it is a DO OC pattern and not an IO DO pattern):

Original sentence:
    Marion (considers) linguistics her favorite class.
                       ?   ?
IO movement test applied:
    *Marion (considers) her favorite class to/for linguistics.

The IO movement test doesn't work (surprise!), indicating that it is <u>not</u> a Pattern 6 sentence (IO DO). Let's check to see whether the second NP is describing the first NP following the transitive verb (evidence for Pattern 7, DO OC).

    Marion (considers) linguistics her favorite class.

It works! *Her favorite class* refers back to or describes *linguistics*. We made the decision that the two NPs are DO OC by first checking to see whether the IO movement test worked (it failed) and then by examining the relationship between the two NPs. Notice the same relationship between the DO and the OC in the next two sentences:

    The students (made) bilingual education the focus of their report.

    Canada (considers) English and French essential languages for its citizens.

The DO and OC are so closely related that you could put an equal sign between the two NPs to illustrate that relationship:

bilingual education = the focus of their report
English and French = essential languages for its citizens

There is one more twist to Pattern 7. All of the examples above show the OC as an NP. However, the OC can also be an adjective. The OC's job of referring back to the DO remains the same, but now it is an adjective modifying the DO:

The governor's decision (made) the citizens angry.
   Subject   TV   DO   OC

Language policy discussions (can make) you frustrated.
   Subject   TV   DO   OC

Language policies (can leave) some people disenfranchised.
   Subject   TV   DO   OC

In the examples above, you can see that the adjectives *angry, frustrated,* and *disenfranchised* function as object complements describing the direct objects. Examine the four sentences below and see whether you can identify the <u>one</u> Pattern 7 sentence.

Men and women (may use) language differently.

Interesting research (examines) speech for gender differences.

Some research (investigates) interruptions in conversations.

The term "genderlect" (assumes) language differences by gender.

Victoria (calls) her dialect slang.

Only the last sentence provides us with an example of Pattern 7. The others are Pattern 5: Subject-TV-DO. Let's examine each more closely. In the first sentence, *language* is the DO; *differently* is an adverb modifying the verb *may use.* The second sentence has a DO followed by a prepositional phrase. The PP has an NP—the object of preposition, *gender differences;* however, this NP cannot be used as an OC because it is already occupied in its job as the OP. The third and fourth sentences are similar in that the DOs, *interruptions* and *language differences,* are followed by PPs, *in conversations* and *by gender*. The last sentence provides a good example of Pattern 7, with *slang* as the OC describing *her dialect*:

Victoria (calls) her dialect slang.
Subject   TV   DO   OC

DID YOU KNOW?

The American Dialect Society chooses a number of words each year that reflect new and popular usages—for example, most likely to succeed, least likely to succeed, and most useful, creative, unnecessary, outrageous, and euphemistic. Consider "grelfie," "teebowing," and "twerknado." "Hashtag" was the Word of the Year in 2012; the Word of the Year in 2013 was "because." See why "because" is the winner as well as the latest winners (and losers) at www.americandialect.org/woty or search for "American Dialect Society Words of the Year."

Exercise 3.9 Getting a Grip on Sentence Patterns 5, 6, and 7

First underline the verb and then identify the pattern of each sentence: Pattern 5 (Subject-TV-DO), Pattern 6 (Subject-TV-IO-DO), or Pattern 7 (Subject-TV-DO-OC).

1. __7__ We named "gleek" the Word of the Year. (A gleek is a fan of the television show *Glee*.)
2. __6__ Will Texas give the Spanish language official recognition?
3. __6__ Your accent gives you a regional identity.
4. __5__ Colonization spread the English language globally.
5. __7__ Many people consider their native language a part of their identity.
6. ____ She called the group's language "slang."
7. ____ We know the jargon of our profession.
8. ____ Young adults generally determine the success of new words.
9. ____ Local ecologies influence local languages.
10. ____ To solve crimes, forensic linguists analyze text and speech.

Exercise 3.10 Getting a Grip on Sentence Patterns with Transitive Verbs

Now test your ability to recognize all of the elements that can follow transitive verbs. Mark the underlined words as indirect object (IO), direct object (DO), or object complement (OC).

1. _____ Society plays a role in language attitudes.
2. _____ The Mandarin language has the largest number of speakers.
3. _____ Many Texans speak Spanish.
4. _____ The Endangered Language Fund supports the preservation of endangered languages.
5. _____ Many linguists give the Endangered Language Fund their support.
6. _____ Women use distinct female speech forms in some cultures.
7. _____ People argue language ideologies during election years.
8. _____ Schools should provide students second-language learning opportunities.
9. _____ They made bilingual education a priority.
10. _____ We consider sexist language inappropriate.

Table 3.1 provides a summary of the structures of the seven sentence patterns, the terminology associated with each, as well as two example sentences for each pattern.

not on text

Table 3.1
Linking , Intransitive, Transitive Verb Pattern Review

Linking Verb Patterns	Structure		
Pattern 1	Subject NP	LV	Adverb (Subject Complement)
Example:	Celeste	is	there.
Example:	Exams	are	tomorrow.
Pattern 2	Subject NP	LV	Predicate Adjective (Subject Complement)
Example:	Accents	seem	interesting.
Example:	Boston accents	are	different.
Pattern 3	Subject NP	LV	Predicate Nominative (Subject Complement)
Example:	Chinese	is	a tonal language.
Example:	Your dialect	is	an important part of your identity.

Intransitive and Transitive Patterns		Structure *Action verbs*		
Pattern 4	Subject NP	IV	(no NP)	
Example:	*Languages*	*evolve.*		
Example:	*Languages*	*evolve*	*over time.*	
Pattern 5	Subject NP	TV	Direct Object	
Example:	*Bilinguals*	*have*	*many cognitive advantages.*	
Example:	*My cousin*	*wrote*	*three letters.*	
Pattern 6	Subject NP	TV	Indirect Object	Direct Object
Example:	*Language*	*gives*	*people*	*power.*
Example:	*My mother*	*taught*	*me*	*French.*
Pattern 7	Subject NP	TV	Direct Object	Object Complement
Example:	*Iowans*	*voted*	*English*	*their official language.*
Example:	*Many people*	*consider*	*their language*	*beautiful.*

Finally, the next five exercises test you on all seven sentence patterns and their associated terminology. Remember to identify the verb first to determine whether it is a linking verb or not. Then you can move on to examine the structures following the verb. Good luck!

S → NP

Clause
—————
S   V

Chapter Review

Exercise 3.11 Getting a Grip—Review of Terminology

Write the following terms under the verb class to which they belong: adverbial complement, direct object, indirect object, object complement, predicate adjective, predicate nominative, subject complement.

LINKING VERB	TRANSITIVE VERBS
adv.	

Exercise 3.12 Getting a Grip—Review of Verbs and Sentence Patterns

Circle T if the statement is true and F if it is false.

1. T (F)   Linking verbs can sometimes take direct objects.
2. T (F)   An object complement can refer back to the subject.
3. T (F)   A direct object is always a noun phrase or an adjective.
4. T (F)   An object complement can sometimes precede the direct object that it modifies.
5. T (F)   A transitive verb always has a predicate nominative after it.
6. T F   The BE substitution test is helpful for finding direct objects.
7. T F   The "be" verb is always a linking verb.
8. T F   Some verb forms like "feel" can function as linking or action verbs (different meanings).
9. T F   An object complement can be a noun, adjective, or adverb.
10. T F   The IO precedes the DO.

Exercise 3.13 Getting a Grip—Review of Terminology

Label the underlined words as predicate adjective (PA), predicate nominative (PN), adverbial subject complement (AC), indirect object (IO), direct object (DO), or object complement (OC). If you label the word as PA, PN, AC, or OC, draw an arrow to the word that it is modifying or referring to.

Example:

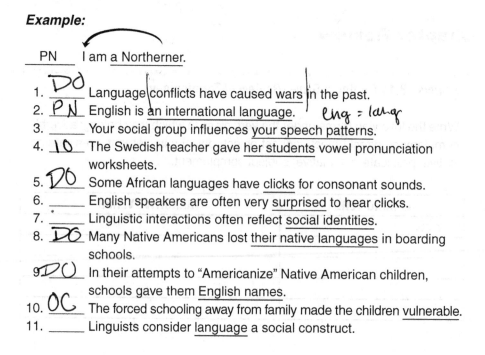

___PN___   I am a Northerner.

1. __DO__ Language conflicts have caused <u>wars</u> in the past.
2. __PN__ English is an international <u>language</u>.   eng = lang
3. _____ Your social group influences <u>your speech patterns</u>.
4. __IO__ The Swedish teacher gave <u>her students</u> vowel pronunciation worksheets.
5. __DO__ Some African languages have <u>clicks</u> for consonant sounds.
6. _____ English speakers are often very <u>surprised</u> to hear clicks.
7. _____ Linguistic interactions often reflect <u>social identities</u>.
8. __DO__ Many Native Americans lost <u>their native languages</u> in boarding schools.
9. __DO__ In their attempts to "Americanize" Native American children, schools gave them <u>English names</u>.
10. __OC__ The forced schooling away from family made the children <u>vulnerable</u>.
11. _____ Linguists consider <u>language</u> a social construct.

12. _____ Pragmatic studies are <u>valuable</u> to linguists.
13. _____ Language myths can create <u>language prejudices</u>.
14. _____ Some people consider certain dialects <u>incorrect</u>.
15. _____ Linguists provide <u>us</u> details about the structure of conversations.

Exercise 3.14 Getting a Grip—Review of Terminology and Sentence Patterns

Fill in the missing terminology indicated by blank lines in the chart below by using the following abbreviations: ADV (adverbial), PN (predicate nominative), PA (predicate adjective), IO (indirect object), DO (direct object), and OC (object complement). Some of the blanks have already been filled in—use them as clues.

Finally, write an example sentence for each pattern. Use family members or pets for your subjects. For example, all of your sentences with linking verbs could have a pet as the subject: Fido is outside (ADV). Fido is a mutt (PN). Fido is cute (PA). Then you would have a different subject for all of your (in)transitive verb patterns. This will help keep the patterns relevant and separate.

Linking Verb Patterns:

    Pattern 1 → Subject LV _____
        Example: _____

    Pattern 2 → Subject LV __PA__
        Example: _____

    Pattern 3 → Subject LV _____
        Example: _____

Intransitive/Transitive Verb Patterns:

    Pattern 4 → Subject IV _____
        Example: _____

    Pattern 5 → Subject TV_____
        Example: _____

    Pattern 6 → Subject TV _____ DO
        Example: _____

    Pattern 7 → Subject TV DO _____
        Example: _____

Exercise 3.15 Getting a Grip—Review of Terminology and Sentence Patterns

Now write the same seven sentences without looking back at what you wrote above. If you can't do it, study your sentences and write them again. Do this until you have successfully written them all down without "peeking." Be sure that you are able to label all of the verbs and complements.

Pattern 1: _____

_____

Pattern 2: _____

_____

Pattern 3: _____

_____

Pattern 4 :_____

_____

Pattern 5: _____

_____

Pattern 6: _____

_____

Pattern 7: _____

_____

4
Verbals: Gerunds, Participles, and Infinitives

This chapter focuses on verbals—words that look suspiciously like verbs but function as other word classes. Important grammatical concepts to learn in this chapter are **gerund, gerund phrase, participle, participle phrase, infinitive**, and **infinitive phrase**.

Language Focus: Language Acquisition

Linguists investigating first-language acquisition in children and second-language acquisition in children and adults pose a variety of challenging research questions. Second-language acquisition studies often focus on older language learners; however, interesting research is being conducted on young children's learning of two languages. Additionally, studies of language acquisition in primates have become quite controversial.

Some of the questions that language researchers explore include: How important is social interaction in language acquisition? In what order do language learners acquire the different structures of language? How does second-language learning differ from first-language acquisition? How do attitudes and motivation impact learning a second language? Can primates or other animals learn to use human language?

Verbals may look like verbs (e.g., going, gone, to go), but they do not function as verbs. Instead, they function as nouns, adjectives, or adverbs. I like to think of them as having been verbs in their past lives, but now they have been reincarnated into other word classes. Table 4.1 provides an overview of the three verbals that we will focus on in this chapter. Remember, these verbals are not verbs. Repeat after me—verbals are not verbs, verbals are not verbs . . .

verbals .. gerbals → nouns

Table 4.1

Verbals/Verbal Phrases

Type	Form	Function	Examples
Gerund	Ving	Noun	*Learning* can be rewarding.
			Learning a second language can be rewarding.
			I like *learning languages.*
Participle	Ving/Ven	Adjective	*Studying for hours*, I finally grasped the concept.
			Studying Spanish, I felt a connection to the culture.
			Spanish is an *established* language in the United States.
			Established by the Spanish conquistadores, Spanish has flourished in the United States.
Infinitive	to + V	Noun	*To learn another language* is a noble quest.
		Adjective	Today, a good language *to learn* is Chinese.
		Adverb	I was excited *to learn Chinese.*

Gerunds

A **gerund** functions only as a noun; therefore, the term "gerund noun" is redundant—we don't need the "noun" part of it. As you can see in Table 4.1, a gerund takes the form of a present participle (Ving), for example, "learning," "walking," and "talking."

Identifying Gerunds

In previous chapters, we examined the many slots that can be filled by nouns—subject, appositive, direct object, indirect object, object complement, object of preposition, and predicate nominative. Gerunds fill these same slots.

As we have already dedicated a good amount of space in this book to learning about nouns, our understanding of gerunds should be an easy task. They are simply Ving forms used as nouns:

> *Practicing is vital to your success in learning a second language.*
>
> *The best route to successful language acquisition is practicing.*

In the first sentence above, the gerund *practicing* is used as a subject; in the second sentence, it is used as a predicate nominative. Gerunds can also be part of **gerund phrases**. Below are two examples of gerunds in gerund phrases. In these sentences, the gerund *practicing* is in parentheses and the entire gerund phrase is underlined:

(Practicing) as often as possible is vital to your success in learning a second language.

The best route to successful language acquisition is (practicing) as often as possible.

Here, we have expanded our one-word gerunds to gerund phrases. One way to think about a gerund versus a gerund phrase is to go back to the reincarnation metaphor. "Practice" was a verb in its past life as part of a verb phrase, for example, "I practice as often as possible." When the verb "practice" became reincarnated as a gerund (noun), it brought along its "baggage" from the verb phrase (objects, prepositional phrases, adverbs, etc.). In the above examples, the adverb phrase *as often as possible* got pulled into the gerund phrase along with the original verb "practice," which is now the head noun of the gerund phrase *practicing as often as possible*.

Gerunds fill noun phrase (NP) slots; however, they are not commonly used as object complements. Below are examples of gerunds used in noun slots.

Subject:	*Crying is a way for babies to communicate.*
Indirect Object:	*Francisco gave studying a try.*
Direct Object:	*The student tried strategizing.*
Predicate Nominative:	*My favorite language learning strategy is reading.*
Object Complement:	*Do you consider memorization of vocabulary learning?*
Object of Preposition:	*My strategy for learning is to read literature.*
Appositive:	*My favorite language learning tool, reading, makes a difference.*

As discussed above, a gerund phrase contains remnants of the gerund's past life as a verb. The entire gerund phrase functions as an NP, just like a single-word gerund does, and it occupies the same sentence slots. Below are examples similar to those above but with the gerunds (in parentheses) located in gerund phrases (underlined).

Subject:	*(Crying) loudly is a way for babies to communicate.*
Indirect Object:	*Francisco gave (studying) the Hausa language a try.*
Direct Object:	*The student tried (strategizing) his approach.*
Predicate Nominative:	*My favorite language learning tool is (reading) Japanese literature.*

Object Complement:	*Do you consider memorization of vocabulary language (learning)?*
Object of Preposition:	*My strategy for (learning) Japanese is to read Japanese literature.*
Appositive:	*My favorite language learning tool, (reading) literature, makes a difference.*

Tests for Gerunds

Because gerunds were verbs in their past lives, they do not have plural forms (e.g., *one practicing, *two practicings—the asterisk indicates an ungrammatical structure) and thus they fail the singular/plural test that we identified in Chapter 1. However, there are three tests that we can use to identify gerunds. The most useful test is one that we learned in Chapter 2—the **pronoun substitution test**. The others are the **possessive subject test** and the **verb conjugation test**. We will discuss each of these below.

⚰ Pronoun Substitution Test

Substituting the pronoun "it" (other pronouns work as well, e.g., "this") will help you identify gerunds. Below are examples of sentences used earlier, now with the pronoun substitution test applied to the gerunds:

Subject:	*Crying is a way for babies to communicate.* 　*It*
Indirect Object:	*Francisco gave studying a try.* 　　　　　　*it*
Direct Object:	*The student tried strategizing.* 　　　　　　*it*
Predicate Nominative:	*My favorite language learning tool is reading.* 　　　　　　　　　　　　　　*it*
Object Complement:	*Do you consider memorization of vocabulary learning?* 　*it*
Object of Preposition:	*My strategy for learning is reading Japanese* 　　　　　　*it* *literature.*
Appositive:	*My favorite language learning tool, reading, makes* 　　　　　　　　　　　　　　　　*it* *a difference.*

In Chapter 2, we learned that the pronoun substitutes for the head noun and all of its modifiers, for example, "My first language is Yoruba." → "It is Yoruba." Substituting the pronoun helps find the borders of the NP. You can see how it will identify your error if you identify the NP incorrectly, for example, *"My it is Yoruba." This indicates that "My" was part of the NP. Below are some examples to show you how the pronoun substitution test works well to identify the beginning and ending of the gerund phrase:

Subject: *(Crying) loudly is a way for babies to communicate.*
                                        It

Indirect Object: *Francisco gave (studying) the Hausa language a try.*
                                                it

Direct Object: *The student tried (strategizing) his approach.*
                                                    it

Predicate Nominative: *My favorite language learning tool is (reading)*
                                                         it
                                       Japanese literature.

Object Complement: *Do you consider memorization of vocabulary*
                                       language (learning)?
                                           it

Object of Preposition: *My strategy for (learning) Japanese is reading*
                                                  it
                                       Japanese literature.

Appositive: *My favorite language learning tool, (reading)*
                                                   it
                                       literature, makes a difference.

Exercise 4.1 Getting a Grip on Gerunds with the Pronoun Substitution Test

Find the gerunds and gerund phrases by applying the pronoun substitution test. Underline the gerund phrases and put the gerunds in parentheses. (Hint: There may be more than one gerund in a sentence.)

Example:

(Babbling) during infancy is a type of sound play by babies.
             It

1. Learning a first language seems to be an easy task.
2. According to some linguists, language learning is a uniquely human endeavor.
3. They believe that humans have a unique brain for learning a language.
4. Acquiring a first language means acquiring social rules.
5. Learning "please" starts from an early age.
6. In talking to babies, caretakers often use "baby talk."
7. Baby talk is the use of high-pitched, slow speech and specialized vocabulary for communicating with babies.
8. Gurgling and burping are seen as communicative events by parents.
9. The first stage of a child's language is called babbling.
10. After babbling, the child produces one-word sentences.

Possessive Subject Test

Another important test that helps identify gerunds is the **possessive subject test.** Because these gerunds had past lives as verbs, remnants of their past subjects may be found in the gerund phrases. These old subjects take the form of possessive nouns or pronouns preceding the gerunds:

> *A personal strategy for learning Japanese is my reading Japanese literature.*

In fact, we should be able to add a possessive noun or pronoun in front of the gerund phrase and still have a grammatical sentence—although sometimes the sentence may sound better without it (if the [past] subject of the gerund is the same as the subject or object of the sentence, the possessive may be unneeded or awkward). Below are examples of gerunds with possessive nouns or pronouns:

> *Babies' crying loudly is a way for them to communicate.*
>
> *Francisco gave his learning the Hausa language a try.*
>
> *The students loved their learning of a third language.*
>
> *One strategy for my learning Japanese is reading Japanese literature.*
>
> *A favorite language learning tool, my reading Japanese literature, makes a difference.*

The possessive subject test works well to identify gerunds because you can't add possessives to other Ving forms. For example, in the following two sentences, the verbs are in the present progressive form (be + Ving). Because these Ving forms are verbs and not gerunds, the possessive subject test will not work in the sentences.

The boy is learning French.

The boy is **his learning French.*

Waldo is studying for his Arabic exam.

Waldo is **his studying for his Arabic exam.*

Exercise 4.2 Getting a Grip on Identifying Gerunds with the Possessive Subject Test

Apply the possessive subject test by adding a possessive noun or pronoun before each "suspected" gerund. If the sentence is still grammatical, then you know the word or phrase is a gerund. (Hint: There may be more than one gerund in a sentence, and two sentences do not have gerunds.)

Example:

Burping is seen as a communicative event by parents.
A child's burping is seen as a communicative event by parents.

1. The parents were asking about using baby talk with their four-year-old.
2. The baby's Language learning is linked to the baby's cognitive development.
3. Little Jenny's way to communicate is by her crying loudly.
4. We enjoyed her studying the stages of first-language acquisition.
5. Producing words in a sequence is a big step.
6. The one-year-old was speaking at an advanced level.
7. Children are always learning from the language around them.
8. Children go through stages of language learning.
9. Pronouncing the "th" sound is difficult for children.
10. Children start learning speech through babbling.

★ *Verb Conjugation Test*

One challenge is to distinguish between the Ving form used as a gerund predicate nominative and the Ving form used as a verb. In the **verb conjugation test**, you consider that the Ving form is (or may be) the head verb and try to change its tense. If the tense can be changed successfully, then you know it is a verb. You cannot change the tense of a gerund. Here is an example of a gerund in the predicate nominative slot that was used earlier:

My favorite language learning tool is (reading) Japanese literature.

We already know that *reading* is a gerund, but it looks suspiciously like the head verb in *is reading*. Remember that a verb can have a helping verb "be" in the present progressive form (Ving). To test whether *reading* is a gerund or a verb, you apply the verb conjugation test by changing (or trying to change) *read* to the past and the future tense:

Present progressive: *My favorite language learning tool is reading Japanese literature.*

Past: *My favorite language learning tool read Japanese literature.*

Future: *My favorite language learning tool will read Japanese literature.*

It fails the verb conjugation test because you cannot conjugate a gerund. Notice that a *tool* cannot read *Japanese literature*. The verb consists of *is*, and the phrase *reading Japanese literature* is a gerund. Let's check the verb *is* for its ability to be conjugated:

Present: *My favorite language learning tool is reading Japanese literature.*

Past: *My favorite language learning tool was reading Japanese literature.*

Future: *My favorite language learning tool will be reading Japanese literature.*

Think of a sentence with a predicate nominative as an equation that shows the linked relationship between the subject and the gerund predicate nominative:

My favorite language learning tool = reading Japanese literature.
  Subject   Predicate Nominative

Let's look at one more sentence: "The boy is learning French." If "learning" is the head verb of the sentence, you should be able to apply the verb conjugation test (change the tense of "learn"), and the sentence will still be grammatical. If it fails the test, then "learning" is most likely a gerund:

Present progressive: *The boy is learning French.*

Past tense:	*The boy learned French.*
Future tense:	*The boy will learn French.*

ed

will

We see that *learn* can be conjugated, which provides evidence that *learning* is a verb and not a gerund. The next exercise gives you practice applying the verb conjugation test to help identify gerunds. (Gerunds fail the test.)

Exercise 4.3 Getting a Grip on Identifying Gerunds with the Verb Conjugation Test

Examine the following sentences and apply the verb conjugation test (VCT) to determine if the underlined form is the head verb of the verb phrase (passes VCT) or if it is a gerund functioning as a predicate nominative (fails VCT). Indicate whether the underlined word is a verb (V) or gerund (G).

Example:

V	Babies are <u>showing</u> word development when using incorrect word forms.
Past tense:	Babies showed word development when using incorrect word forms.
Future tense:	Babies will show word development when using incorrect word forms.

1. V ___ Researchers are <u>discovering</u> the principles of language acquisition.
2. G ___ A child's goal is <u>communicating</u> with caretakers.
3. V G One objective is <u>procuring</u> food from a caretaker.
4. ___ The child's cry is <u>indicating</u> a specific need.
5. V ___ A child in the two-word stage is <u>using</u> two words as a complete sentence.
6. V ___ An early stage of language production is <u>babbling</u>.
7. V ___ Children are <u>learning</u> words rapidly when they are three to four years old.
8. √ ___ The child is <u>throwing</u> a tantrum to communicate.
9. √ ___ Scientists have been <u>linking</u> language development to emotional, physical, and cognitive development.
10. G ___ A concern of parents is <u>being</u> able to understand the needs of their child.

This next exercise puts your knowledge of gerunds to the test. Remember, gerunds are nouns; therefore, they can be found in noun slots in a sentence. Gerunds will also pass the pronoun substitution test and the possessive subject test, but they will fail the verb conjugation test.

Exercise 4.4 Getting a Grip on Gerunds

Underline the gerunds and gerund phrases. If the gerund is in a gerund phrase, put the gerund in parentheses. Mark how each functions in the sentence: subject (S), predicate nominative (PN), indirect object (IO), direct object (DO), object complement (OC), object of preposition (OP), or appositive (A). (Hint: There may be more than one in a sentence.)

Example:

In the past, some educators believed bilingualism had a negative effect on children's (learning).
OP

1. Children overgeneralize rules during their language learning.
2. For example, a child may overgeneralize by calling all four-legged animals "doggie."
3. Putting "–ed" on all verbs is another way children overgeneralize, for example, "hitted."
4. These overgeneralizations show a child's learning of rules.
5. Understanding language precedes producing language.
6. Deleting sounds is very common in a child's speech, for example, "Barbara" becomes "Baba."
7. Baby talk, also called "motherese," includes using a higher voice pitch.
8. Using exaggerated speech tones is also a feature of motherese.
9. Before talking to a child, adults often first say the child's name to get his or her attention.
10. Parents imitating the child's baby talk is common.
11. Parents avoid using difficult words with their babies.
12. People enjoy interacting with babies.
13. Babies learn the intonation patterns of their language very early, even before talking.
14. A baby's language learning coincides with motor skills development.
15. Her goal, learning two languages simultaneously, was more difficult than she expected.

DID YOU KNOW?

Some researchers claim that primates can learn language. Because they do not have human vocal tracts, primates—bonobos in particular—are being taught language through lexigrams (symbols) at the Iowa Primate Learning Sanctuary. To communicate, bonobos point at specific symbols. Researchers there claim that some primates can learn to understand spoken language if they are given enough time. As you can imagine, this claim is very controversial. See Dr. Susan Savage-Rumbaugh's TED talk, in which she shares videos of her bonobos engaged in human-like tasks. Search for "Susan Savage-Rumbaugh: The Gentle Genius of Bonobos," or go to www.ted.com/talks/susan_savage_rumbaugh_on_apes_that_write.html.

Participles

A **participle** is an adjective, so we will not use the term "participle adjective"—it is redundant. Below, we will examine participles and participle phrases, their placement in sentences, their punctuation, and their possible confusion with gerunds.

At the beginning of the chapter, Table 4.1 showed that participles have two forms: present participle (Ving)—"learning," "walking," "talking"—and past participle (Ven)—"learned," "walked," "talked." Below are more examples of Ving and Ven forms:

Present Participle Form (Ving)	Past Participle Form (Ven)
eating	eaten
interesting	interested
studying	studied
finding	found

In previous chapters, we learned that adjectives must always modify a noun or pronoun; they can change, expand, qualify, add to, or enrich the concepts of the nouns or pronouns they modify. That's what participles do. It helps to think of them as having been reincarnated from their past lives as verbs, like gerunds; however, participles function as adjectives (whereas gerunds function as nouns).

As mentioned above, participles can have two forms, Ving and Ven. Below are examples of both forms with the participles underlined and arrows pointing to the nouns that they modify.

Ving Participles:

I think Chinese is an interesting language.

The Chinese language is interesting.

The motivating factor was that she planned to live in a Chinese-speaking country.

Many of our founding fathers spoke two or three languages.

Ven Participles:

She gave me a worried look during our Hindi exam.

She was worried.

The motivated student talked freely to others to practice the language.

Participles also can bring their baggage from their past lives as verbs to the **participle phrase**:

(Learning) three languages simultaneously, Geraldo impressed me with his abilities.

(Trying) to learn a second language in a classroom, Juan felt frustrated.

Participles can be particularly difficult for students of English as a second language. The choice of a present participle (Ving) or past participle (Ven) form changes the meaning of a sentence. For example, a language learner may claim to be "boring" rather than "bored." For native speakers, the difference is obvious. Simply put, these adjectives come from two different forms of the verb based on voice—active or passive. With Ving, you are the doer—you bore someone, thus you are a boring person. With Ven, you are the receiver—you were bored by something or someone, so you are a bored person.

There are two challenges when identifying participles and participle phrases. The first is their placement in relation to the nouns they modify. They often have more freedom than descriptive adjectives. The second challenge is that participles share the same present participle form with gerunds. We begin by examining participle placement and punctuation. Then we will learn how to tell them apart from gerunds.

Identifying Participles

As adjectives, participles and participle phrases can precede or follow the nouns that they modify; however, single-word participles almost exclusively precede the noun that they modify, with the exception of those following linking verbs. Below are examples of sentences with single-word participles:

Single-word participle after linking verb:

The language class was challenging.

Single-word participles before the nouns they modify:

Teaching a bonobo to learn language is an intriguing idea, and a very controversial one.

Memorized vocabulary quickly becomes forgotten vocabulary.

Although a participle phrase can come before or after the noun it modifies, it must be clear from the context which noun the participle is modifying. Which noun is the participle phrase modifying in the following sentence?

Pablo felt comfortable speaking Thai to his teacher, (encouraged) by his increasing fluency.

There are two nouns that the participle phrase could modify (*Pablo, teacher*). To avoid confusion, the participle phrase should be near the noun it is modifying. Because the phrase *encouraged by his increasing fluency* follows the noun *teacher*, the reader may assume that the *teacher* is encouraged. However, if the author means for the phrase to modify *Pablo*, then the phrase is incorrectly placed and should be moved near *Pablo*:

> *(Encouraged) by his increasing fluency, Pablo felt comfortable speaking Thai to his teacher.*
>
> *Pablo, (encouraged) by his increasing fluency, felt comfortable speaking Thai to his teacher.*

If there is only one possible noun, then there is more flexibility in the placement of the phrase—clarity is the goal:

> *Pablo felt comfortable speaking Thai, (encouraged) by his increasing fluency.*
>
> *(Encouraged) by his increasing fluency, Pablo felt comfortable speaking Thai.*
>
> *Pablo, (encouraged) by his increasing fluency, felt comfortable speaking Thai.*

No matter where it is placed in a sentence, the participle must have a noun or pronoun to modify. In fact, the noun or pronoun that it modifies was the participle's subject from its past life when it was a verb. For example, the sentence above could have come from two separate sentences: "Pablo was encouraged by his increasing fluency" and "Pablo felt comfortable speaking Thai." When these two sentences were combined to form one sentence, *encouraged* got demoted from a passive verb form ("was encouraged") to an adjective. Do you see how the participle, now an adjective, is still tied to its past subject? Here's another example that helps show where the participles come from:

> *Geraldo is learning three languages simultaneously.*
> *Geraldo impressed me with his abilities.*

Combine the two sentences, and you get the following sentence:

> *Learning three languages simultaneously, Geraldo impressed me with his abilities.*

Learning three languages simultaneously is modifying the noun *Geraldo*. You can see how the noun that the participle modifies is the subject from its past life as a verb. This type of sentence combination exercise is often used in middle school and high school to help students develop more "sophisticated" sentence structures.

If the participle does not logically modify a noun or pronoun, it is called a **dangling participle**. I admit that I have dangled modifiers in the past, so I always check my sentences carefully for this error. Let's look at an example of a dangling modifier:

> *Speaking Spanish since the age of four, the book* El Camino de Mi Vida *was easy to read.*

The participle phrase begins the sentence, but what noun is it modifying? *The book?* No. *The book* does not speak Spanish—the participle phrase does not logically modify any noun in the sentence, and the result is a dangling modifier. How can we rewrite this sentence to make it correct? I suggest the following:

> *Speaking Spanish since the age of four, I found the book* El Camino de Mi Vida *easy to read.*

Now the participle phrase has a pronoun (*I*) to modify. Here are some more examples of sentences with dangling modifiers:

> *Being sixty-five years old, learning a second language was more difficult than expected.*
>
> *Living in China for ten years, my Chinese was becoming more fluent.*
>
> *Arriving at a higher level of language fluency, more communication was occurring.*

How would you fix these sentences? Give the participle phrases nouns or pronouns to modify:

> *Being sixty-five years old, I found learning a second language was more difficult than expected.*
>
> *Living in China for ten years, I started to speak Chinese more fluently.*
>
> *Arriving at a higher level of language fluency, he found that more communication was occurring.*

DID YOU KNOW?

Koko, a female gorilla who lives in a special preserve on the island of Maui, has learned to sign more than 1,000 words. A website devoted to Koko that gives up-to-date news about her can be found at www.koko.org. An interesting YouTube video showing how Koko reacted to the news of the death of her cat All Ball can be seen at www.youtube.com/watch?v=AJglyBAqBBU, or search for "Koko the Gorilla Cries over the Loss of a Kitten."

Exercise 4.5 Getting a Grip on Participles

Underline the participles and participle phrases and draw arrows to the nouns or pronouns that they modify. There is only one participle or participle phrase in each sentence. One sentence contains a dangling participle; rewrite the sentence and give it a noun to modify.

Example:

Parents, responding to baby's sounds with smiles and responses, teach conversation skills.

1. Learning two languages from birth, the child had many cognitive advantages.
2. Spanish, spoken as a first or second language by many Americans, is not allowed in some schools.
3. An older person learning a second language has unique challenges.
4. Those who speak two and three languages are often very motivated learners.
5. Exposed to a second language at an early age, fluency was not a problem.
6. Learning sign language from his parents, the baby signed "hungry."
7. The students learned French quickly, immersing themselves in the language for six months.
8. Students studying a foreign language may have few chances to practice outside the classroom.
9. Motivation is an important factor for someone trying to learn a second language.

re-write

10. There is interesting research on the differences between first- and second-language acquisition.
11. Speaking three languages, the applicant was considered a strong candidate for the job.
12. Genie, being isolated for many years, had cognitive and physical problems.
13. Locked in a room for almost fourteen years, Genie was unable to learn language after her discovery.
14. Taught three languages from birth, the linguist's child became his father's research subject.
15. Diaries kept by linguists were often used for studies on child language acquisition.

Punctuation of Participles

Like any introductory phrase, a participle phrase is set off with commas at the beginning of a sentence:

> *Pointing to symbols, the bonobo Kanzi communicated that he wanted to go outside.*

> *Using Dr. Savage-Rumbaugh's lighter, Kanzi started the campfire.*

In Chapter 2, we discussed that if an appositive (NP) is essential to identifying the noun it is referring to, no commas are used. Let's revisit the appositive rule and apply it to participles. Here are examples of appositives (underlined) with and without commas:

> *Dr. Sontasa, my university professor, started the experiment.*

> *My university professor Dr. Sontasa started the experiment.*

In the first example, *my university professor* is not essential to identifying Dr. Sontasa (her name identifies her), so the appositive is set off with commas. If it is taken out, we don't lose any essential information. In the second example, *Dr. Sontasa* is essential information needed to identify exactly which university professor started the experiment, so no commas are used. These are examples of appositives (nouns) that we discussed in Chapter 2. Now let's extend the same concepts of "essential" and "nonessential" to participles.

> *The bonobo shrieked at a boy standing close to the cage.*

If we remove the participle, we still have a grammatical sentence, but we don't know which boy was shrieked at. The participle provides essential information about the noun, so it is not set off with commas. Here are some other examples of essential participle phrases (no commas):

A chimpanzee taught sign language from birth passed the skill to her infant.

In the 1980s, a gorilla caring for a kitten while in captivity signed words such as "bad," "sad," and "frown" when the kitten was killed by a car.

Language research is being conducted on bonobos living at the Great Ape Trust research facility.

Again, note that the participle phrases can be deleted and the sentences remain grammatically correct; however, essential information about the nouns being referred to is lost. For example, not just any chimpanzee passed a signing skill to her infant—it was the *chimpanzee taught sign language from birth* that did; similarly, not just any gorilla signed about the loss of her kitten, it was the gorilla *caring for a kitten,* and so on. If the participle phrase begins the sentence, it is always followed by a comma, even when it is essential for identifying the noun:

Caring for a kitten while in captivity, the gorilla signed words such as "bad," "sad," and "frown" when the kitten was killed by a car.

Here are some examples of participle phrases that are not essential to the meaning of the noun, and so they are set off with commas:

Koko, signing about her dead kitten, felt very sad according to her caretakers.

Dr. Savage-Rumbaugh, researching language acquisition in bonobos, has stirred up controversy.

Koko, upset by the loss of her kitten, signed "sad."

In each sentence above, the participle phrase is not essential for identifying the noun—it does not restrict it. It adds extra, nonessential information about the noun. Comma usage provides the reader with information. Can you sense the differences in meaning in the next two sentences by reading them out loud and pausing at the commas?

The actors using both Hindi and English made the movie more realistic.

The actors, using both Hindi and English, made the movie more realistic.

In the first sentence, only the actors who used Hindi and English made the movie realistic (no commas, essential information for identifying which actors). In the second sentence, the fact that they are using both Hindi and English may be important information, but it is not essential information needed to identify which actors we are talking about (commas, nonessential). Did you notice these differences when reading the sentences out loud? This same rule was applied to appositives (discussed in Chapter 2) and will be applied in the next chapter on clauses.

Exercise 4.6 Getting a Grip on Participle Phrase Punctuation

In each sentence, find and underline participles and participle phrases; draw arrows to the nouns that they modify. Place commas where needed. (Hint: There may be more than one participle in a sentence.)

Example:

Hindi, a language spoken in India and elsewhere, has almost 400 million native speakers.

1. Learning Hindi online, I had to look for opportunities to practice speaking it.
2. On the Internet, you can connect with other motivated people learning Hindi.
3. A language spoken by millions of people, Hindi is one of the official languages of India.
4. *Slumdog Millionaire* filmed in India, had a bilingual cast.
5. To learn Hindi, I love watching any movie made in Bollywood.
6. Learning a lot of new vocabulary I watched Spanish soap operas for an hour each day.
7. The first language learned by a child is her link to her culture.
8. Hawaiian spoken by few people after colonization is becoming more widespread due to government language programs.
9. To achieve fluency, a person studying a second language must be very motivated.
10. Taking a Spanish language course taught in a Spanish-speaking country is a better option.

Exercise 4.7 Getting a Grip on Participles

Go to the **Language Focus** box at the beginning of this chapter. Find three participles or participle phrases in the first paragraph. Write the sentences and underline the participles and participle phrases.

Differences Between Gerunds and Participles

Gerunds and participles share a Ving (present participle) form. So, how can you tell the difference between the gerund Ving form and the participle Ving form? It is all about function. Because gerunds are nouns, they will function as subjects, objects, and so on. Previously, we saw that the pronoun substitution test helps identify gerunds and gerund phrases. Nouns cannot be deleted without making the sentence ungrammatical (except for appositives, which can be deleted). As adjectives, participles and participle phrases often can be deleted and the sentence will remain grammatical (with the exception of participles that follow linking verbs—for example, "She is very amusing"). We can apply the **deletion test** and the pronoun substitution test to help identify gerunds and participles.

Sentence:
> Learning a second language requires a commitment.

Pronoun substitution test:
> It requires a commitment.

Deletion test:
> *___ requires a commitment.

The two tests identify *Learning a second language* as a noun (passes the substitution test, fails the deletion test); therefore, it is a gerund. Let's try applying the two tests to another sentence:

Sentence:
> Learning the language, I felt good about my upcoming trip.

Pronoun substitution test:
> *It, I felt good about my upcoming trip.

Deletion test:
> ___, I felt good about my upcoming trip.

Notice that the phrase fails the pronoun substitution test (it's not a noun), but passes the deletion test, verifying that it is a participle phrase. Remember, many participles can be deleted, but not all (e.g., predicate adjectives).

Exercise 4.8 Getting a Grip on Distinguishing Between Participles and Gerunds

Apply the pronoun substitution test (PST) and the deletion test (DEL) to the Ving phrases below to determine whether they are gerunds or participles. After applying the tests, mark each as a gerund (G) or participle (P) phrase.

Example:

   G   Genie was punished for <u>making sounds</u>.
  PST: Genie was punished for <u>it</u>.
  DEL: *Genie was punished for.

1. **G** <u>Being isolated for almost fourteen years</u> caused Genie to lose her ability to learn language.

2. **P** <u>Being isolated for almost fourteen years</u>, Genie was of interest to linguists and psychologists.

3. **~~G~~ P** My mother, <u>speaking loudly</u>, asked my Japanese friend a question.

4. **G** My mother's style of "foreigner talk" is <u>speaking more loudly</u>.

5. **G** <u>Learning a second language</u> requires a number of strategies.

6. **P** A good language learner has good <u>learning</u> strategies.

7. **G** <u>Practicing the language</u> can help learning.

8. **P** <u>Using the audio-lingual method</u>, my teacher made us listen to language recordings.

9. **G** <u>Language learning</u> is more than memorizing vocabulary.

10. **P** Young children <u>acquiring language concepts</u> may call all animals "doggie."

Exercise 4.9 Getting a Grip on Participles

Underline the participles and participle phrases in the sentences below and draw arrows to the nouns they modify. Beware of Ving forms functioning as verbs and gerunds. (Hint: There is only one participle in each sentence.)

Example:

At one time in Texas's history, teachers discouraged

Spanish-speaking parents from teaching their children Spanish.

1. In the United States, a growing number of people speak Spanish.
2. School systems used to tell Spanish-speaking parents that Spanish would have a negative impact on their children.
3. Losing their ability to speak Spanish, many second-generation Latinos struggle to communicate with relatives.
4. Older high school students trying to learn their heritage language may find it difficult.
5. Linguists researching second-language acquisition know the challenges for adult language learners.
6. Some universities with large numbers of Latino students provide heritage language classes, focusing on the students' unique experiences with Spanish.
7. Most university students sitting in foreign language classrooms will never achieve fluency in the second language.
8. Those immersed in a foreign culture often learn the second language more quickly.
9. Immersion in a foreign culture does not ensure success. People interacting and conversing with others in that country achieve higher levels of success.
10. In many countries, an adult speaking more than two languages is not unusual—it is the norm.

Infinitives

Infinitives are the last verbal that we will explore in this chapter. Infinitives are easy to recognize because they take the infinitive form of a verb (to + V), for example, "to speak," "to learn," "to be," "to study." Recognizing an infinitive is easy; the challenge is in determining how the infinitive functions in the sentence—as a noun, adjective, or adverb. Infinitives can function as all three word classes, so it is essential to look at what the infinitive is doing in the sentence.

Identifying Infinitives

Let's start with a general overview of infinitives and infinitive phrases to learn how to identify them before we move on to look at their functions as nouns, adjectives, and adverbs. Below are two sentences that have infinitives in subject NP slots—note that their form makes them easy to recognize, and their position in subject slots makes them easy to identify as nouns:

> *To learn* is my goal in this class.
>
> *To practice* is important.

Infinitives can also be part of **infinitive phrases**, meaning that they, too, can have baggage from their past lives as verbs. The infinitives *to learn* and *to practice* are expanded to include their "baggage" in the following sentences:

> *(To learn) a second language* requires a great deal of dedication.
>
> *(To practice) every day* is important for language acquisition.

Like gerunds, infinitives can have subjects from their past lives attached to them; their reincarnated subjects can be found as "for + NP" (reminder: a gerund's past subject is reincarnated as a possessive pronoun or noun in the gerund phrase, for example, "his learning a second language . . ."). The for + NP phrase helps us locate the infinitive in the sentence:

> *For you (to learn) a second language* requires a great deal of dedication.
>
> *For me (to practice) every day* is important.

The for + NP is not needed if the information is redundant. For example, in the infinitive phrase functioning as an adverb below, *For them* and *students* are the same, and so *For them* is unnecessary:

> *For them (to observe) bonobos,* the students had to visit the Language Research Center.

Instead, the following would be sufficient:

> *(To observe) bonobos,* the students had to visit the Language Research Center.

Here are more examples of infinitives with the for + NP signal. All three are examples of adjective infinitives:

> I will get permission *for Franco (to participate) in the research.*

The research for them (to conduct) requires special permission from the facility.

The best research for students (to conduct) requires observing children.

As mentioned above, infinitives can function as nouns, adjectives, or adverbs, which we will examine individually. Many of the tests that we used previously to identify nouns, adjectives, and adverbs also apply to infinitives. First, let's look at infinitives and infinitive phrases used as nouns.

Infinitives as Nouns

Common slots for infinitive nouns are subject, direct object, and predicate nominative. An infinitive can also fill an appositive slot, but it can never be the object of a preposition.

We can use the pronoun substitution test to identify infinitives and infinitive phrases functioning as NPs (again, it doesn't work very well with appositives). Remember that the test will help you find the borders of the infinitive phrase. Below are examples of infinitives and infinitive phrases functioning as nouns. The infinitives are in parentheses and the entire infinitive phrase is underlined.

Subject: *(To study) is my goal this semester.*
                          It

Subject: *(To study) Korean is my goal this semester.*
                          It

Subject Complement: *My goal this semester is (to study).*
                          it

Subject Complement: *My goal this semester is (to study) Korean.*
                          it

Direct Object: *The scientists decided (to investigate).*
                          it

Direct Object: *The scientists decided (to investigate) the*
                          it
                          bilingual brain.

Appositive: *Their project (to investigate) the bilingual brain*
                          it
                          was funded by their university.

Exercise 4.10 Getting a Grip on Infinitives as Nouns

Practice finding the infinitive phrases functioning as nouns by applying the pronoun substitution test. Underline the entire infinitive phrase and put parentheses around the infinitive. Above the infinitive, identify which noun slot it is occupying—subject (S), direct object (DO), or predicate nominative (PN). Don't forget that infinitives can begin with for + NP (its past subject). Be very careful to find the borders of the phrase—the pronoun substitution test will help with that. (Hint: There is only one infinitive in each sentence, and one sentence does not have an infinitive.)

Example:

DO

I have decided (to learn) a fourth language.

it

1. According to most research, children need (to learn) a second language earlier, not later.

it

2. (To learn) a second language after the age of ten often means a lot more work for the learner.

3. In many American schools, children are not taught (to speak) a second language until high school.

it

4. Many students are sent to language labs (for developing) their listening skills.

5. The purpose of the study is for us (to investigate) complex language processes.

it

6. To incorporate new knowledge about language acquisition is the goal of the new curriculum.

7. How many Americans want to learn another language?

8. Try to understand and control your fear of sounding "funny."

9. Your goal should be to lower your inhibitions in the language classroom.

10 For an adult to learn a second language requires a great deal of motivation.

Infinitives as Adjectives

Need I repeat what the function of an adjective is? I thought not! Infinitive adjectives function like other adjectives; they still answer the question "which?" Infinitive adjectives follow the nouns that they modify. Consider the examples below:

The bonobo (to observe) closely was Kanzi.

The bonobo for the researchers (to observe) closely was Kanzi.

In both of the above sentences, the infinitive modifies the subject noun *bonobo*, thus they function as adjectives. They tell us which bonobo—The bonobo to read about? No. The bonobo to make faces at? No. We are talking about *The bonobo to observe closely*. Also note that in the second sentence, the infinitive includes the infinitive's past subject in a for + NP phrase. The following four sentences show adjective infinitives modifying objects:

The Great Ape Trust facility achieved its goal (to raise) money for bonobo research.

Bonobos, a type of chimpanzee, have the ability (to make) tools.

The bonobo Kanzi had a desire (to communicate).

Dr. Savage-Rumbaugh believes in the facility's mission (to expose) bonobos to language and other cultural knowledge.

All of the above infinitives answer the question "which?": Which *goal*? Which *ability*? Which *desire*? Which *mission*?

The next exercise allows us to practice recognizing infinitives functioning as adjectives. There are going to be some "distractors" in the sentences, for example, prepositional phrases. At first glance, a prepositional phrase might seem to have a similar form as an infinitive, for example, "She went to class." However, a prepositional phrase requires a preposition and an NP. An infinitive requires "to" plus a verb.

Exercise 4.11 Getting a Grip on Infinitives as Adjectives

Underline only the infinitives and infinitive phrases that function as adjectives. Draw arrows to the nouns that they modify. (Hint: There will be infinitives used as nouns to divert your attention from adjectives, and it is possible that a sentence may have two adjective infinitives. Be alert!)

Example:

She knew the question to ask about research funding.

1. Her desire to learn about bonobos was almost as great as her desire to learn from the bonobos.
2. Kanzi, an intelligent bonobo, has been a good primate for researchers to study.
3. The quest to understand more about bonobos, a genetically similar species to humans, drives the research.
4. Kanzi learned to start a campfire, to peel an apple with a knife, and to ask for something to eat.
5. Kanzi can indicate his desire to eat a banana using a computer.
6. Specific tasks to highlight Kanzi's language ability were on display for the audience.
7. The researchers had evidence to prove Kanzi's ability to understand language.
8. The tasks for Kanzi to perform included pouring drinks and fetching items.
9. Many scientists are skeptical about Kanzi's ability to learn language.
10. Research to study language acquisition by nonhumans continues at the Great Ape Trust.

Infinitives as Adverbs

Adverb infinitives and infinitive phrases commonly modify verbs and predicate adjectives. In earlier chapters, we saw that adverbs modifying verbs are usually (but not always) movable; for example, "She researched the ape thoroughly" or "She thoroughly researched the ape." The same is true for infinitive adverbs—they can be moved around in the sentence when they modify verbs. Additionally, these infinitives answer the question "why?" Let's examine these infinitives and infinitive phrases used as adverbs modifying verbs, and then we will look at those that modify predicate adjectives.

Adverb Infinitives Modifying Verbs

Infinitives as adverbs modifying verbs answer the question "why?" and they can be moved in the sentence. When used as introductory phrases, you must set them off with a comma. Here are some examples:

The students sat behind a screen in the language lab to observe.

To observe, the students sat behind a screen in the language lab.

The researchers tested the language learners to understand their anxiety levels.

To understand the language learners' anxiety levels, the researchers tested them.

In each of the sentences above, the infinitive answers the question "why?" For instance, "Why did the students sit behind a screen in the language lab?" Additionally, each infinitive is movable—both are tests that almost always work to identify infinitive adverbs that modify verbs.

Adverb Infinitives Modifying Adjectives

A very common position for these adverb infinitives is immediately following the predicate adjectives that they are modifying. They are not movable like infinitives modifying verbs.

The child was happy (to cooperate).

The child was happy (to cooperate) with the researchers.

Many linguists were ready (to question) the evidence of bonobos learning language.

Some were ready (to accuse) the research of being unscientific.

It is sometimes difficult for some linguists (to accept) the findings of the studies.

In the last sentence, the infinitive's baggage includes its past subject in the for + NP (*for some linguists*) phrase at the beginning.

Exercise 4.12 Getting a Grip on Infinitives as Adverbs

Find and underline the infinitives and infinitive phrases that function as adverbs in the following sentences and draw arrows to the verbs or predicate adjectives that they modify. Be careful not to underline infinitives used as adjectives or nouns. There is only one infinitive functioning as an adverb in each sentence. (Hint: They are modifying the verb if they answer the question "why?")

Examples:

Her baby is fun to talk to.

The girl went quickly to settle the baby.

1. Bonobos are able to learn symbols for communication purposes.
2. Children learn a complicated system of symbols to communicate. Is it the same?
3. Baby talk is easier for the child to understand.
4. Are some languages more difficult to learn?
5. Many researchers compare different languages to identify the universal features of languages.
6. Interjections (e.g., "Wow!") are found in all languages to cover basic needs of expression.
7. Vowels are particularly important to have in a language.
8. It would be impossible to speak a language without vowels!
9. To speak any new language fluently, you must learn sounds not found in your first language.
10. Do you need social interaction to learn a second language?

Finally, let me address a "no-no" in prescriptive grammar—splitting an infinitive. What does that mean? It means that an adverb comes between "to" and the verb, for example, "She wanted to quickly return home." Note that the adverb "quickly" interrupts the infinitive "to return." This rule comes from a period in the seventeenth century when "scholars" decided to apply rules of Latin to English—two completely different languages. (They had too much time on their hands.) The short of it is that in formal writing, you want to definitely avoid what I just did—I split an infinitive.

Exercise 4.13 Getting a Grip on Infinitives as Nouns, Adjectives, and Adverbs

Underline the infinitives and infinitive phrases and mark each as a noun (N), adjective (ADJ), or adverb (ADV). Remember that the infinitive phrase may include the for + NP phrase at the beginning. (Hint: There may be more than one infinitive in a sentence.)

Example:

N
Genie did not learn to speak before puberty, so she had passed the critical language period.

1. One reason to learn a foreign language is the desire to experience another culture.
2. To learn a second language is a complex task.
3. Our ability to learn a first language disappears by puberty, according to much research.
4. After that critical period, a first language is most likely impossible to learn.
5. To speak a foreign language fluently shows a great deal of dedication to the task.
6. Language learners need interaction to develop language skills.
7. Oftentimes, language anxiety is difficult for second-language learners to overcome.
8. Not all second-language speakers want to sound like native speakers.
9. Young children with foreign accents often lose their accents quickly to fit in.
10. Young children have the ability to sound like native speakers, but this is rare in older language learners.
11. They went to Germany to study German for a semester as part of their degree requirement.
12. At many universities, a student must study abroad for a semester to receive an MBA in international business.
13. To study abroad, a student must be flexible and not get upset over miscommunication issues.
14. In Africa, I learned specific ritual greetings to use with the village elders.
15. Speak slowly to me to help me better understand.

Chapter Review

Exercise 4.14 Getting a Grip—Review of Verbals

Mark the underlined verbals as gerunds (G); participles (P); or infinitives as nouns (I-N), adjectives (I-ADJ), or adverbs (I-ADV).

1. _____ Languages with different writing systems may be more difficult to learn.

2. _____ A language learner may have the desire to assimilate into the new culture, which can affect the rate of language acquisition.

3. _____ For second-language learners, meaningful interaction is essential for learning the language.

4. _____ "Communicative Language Teaching" is an approach that uses activities focusing on effective communication rather than activities focusing on grammar.

5. _____ Learning to speak a second language fluently in a short period of time can be challenging.

6. _____ Language learners must learn to negotiate language, which includes asking questions and rephrasing sentences when communication breaks down.

7. _____ In second-language classrooms, the teacher must provide lots of opportunities for learners to practice their communication skills.

8. _____ A second language learned in adulthood rarely sounds native-like.

9. _____ People speaking English as a second language outnumber native speakers of English.

10. _____ Many people learn English to communicate in the global marketplace; sounding like a native speaker is not their goal.

11. _____ The grammar-translation method is an approach that focuses on translating texts.

12. _____ Some people have a special ability for learning languages.

13. _____ Many people learn English to communicate in the global marketplace; sounding like a native speaker is not a goal.

14. _____ Social and psychological factors can affect our ability to learn a second language.

15. _____ My goal to learn Spanish has become my obsession.

Exercise 4.15 Getting a Grip—Review of Verbals

In the following paragraph, underline all of the verbals and verbal phrases. Mark them as gerunds (G); participles (P); or infinitives as noun (I-N), adjective (I-ADJ), or adverb (I-ADV). (Hint: There are six verbals.)

Many people are learning English, but their goals are to communicate in a global world. A person in Indonesia may need to learn English for global commerce. Does he or she want to sound like someone from the United States? Most English spoken internationally is by non-native English speakers communicating with other non-native speakers; so why do many international language schools hire only native English speakers to teach English? Do you think that only native English speakers should teach English to second-language learners?

Exercise 4.16 Getting a Grip—Review of Verbals

Go to the **Language Focus** box at the beginning of this chapter. Find and underline all of the verbals and verbal phrases and mark them as gerunds (G), participles (P), or infinitives (I). (Hint: You should find seven.)

Exercise 4.17 Getting a Grip—Review of Verbals

First mark each statement as true (T) or false (F), and then correct the false statements to make them true.

1. _____ Gerunds function as nouns or adjectives.

2. _____ Participles may have a Ving or Ven form.

3. _____ Gerunds may modify the head verb of the sentence.

4. _____ Infinitives may use the form to + V or Ving.

5. _____ When a participle phrase begins a sentence, it is followed by a comma.

6. _____ Infinitives function as nouns, adjectives, adverbs, and verbs.

7. _____ The pronoun substitution test helps identify gerunds.

8. _____ Gerunds can take possessive forms, for example, "John's snoring kept me awake."

9. _____ Infinitives functioning as adverbs can modify adjectives and nouns.

10. _____ Infinitives functioning as adjectives are movable in the sentence.

11. _____ An infinitive's subject from its "past life" as a verb may be included in a for + NP phrase at the beginning of the infinitive phrase.

12. _____ A participle phrase often has more flexibility in terms of its location in a sentence than a descriptive adjective.

13. _____ Ven participles (past participles) derive from passive verbs.

14. _____ The verb conjugation test can be used to identify infinitives.

15. _____ A participle or participle phrase that restricts the meaning of the noun it is modifying is always set off with commas.

Phrase → no verb

clause → VS and verbs

"which" → ADJ

ADJ —
↳
- modify nouns
- noun usually preceeds ADJ
- ~~deletable~~
candelete

ADV —
↳ can
- delete
↳ don't modify nouns (modify everything else)
  ↳ ADV, ADJ, verbs
↳ movable (wherever they want)

NC —
↳ cannot be
deleted

↳ fit in noun slots
Substitution with
"it"
"them" if talking about people

5
Adjective, Adverb, and Noun Clauses

This chapter focuses on adjective, adverb, and noun clauses. Important grammatical concepts to learn in this chapter are **adjective clause, adverb clause, noun clause, independent/main clause, dependent/subordinate clause, relative pronoun, relative adverb,** and **subordinate conjunction.**

Language Focus: The History of English

Much of the history of the English language is a story of territorial invasions, bloody rebellions, and wars. The English language spoken today developed from the many invaders who took turns ruling the British Isles. Each invading group brought along its own culture and language, contributing to what is now called Modern English. Remnants of the Latin, German, French, and Scandinavian languages that were spoken by such conquerors hundreds of years ago are still part of the English language we speak today.

Among the questions that linguistic historians ask are: What historical events helped form the English language? How can dead languages such as Ancient Greek be reconstructed? How can we determine the pronunciation of old languages? What impact has English had on other languages as a result of colonization and globalization?

In this chapter, we analyze adjective, adverb, and noun clauses. You will find a number of exercises to serve as checkpoints for you to test your understanding of these grammatical concepts. Each section builds on the previous one, so be sure to go back and review if you find that you are having difficulty with any of the exercises.

Before we start our discussion of clauses, it is essential that you understand the difference between a phrase and a clause. **Clauses** are different from phrases in that they are grammatical units that contain both subjects and verbs, while phrases do not have subjects and verbs.

Clauses are divided into two types: independent and dependent. "Languages evolve" is a clause that can stand by itself as a grammatical sentence, so it is called an **independent clause** (also referred to as a **main clause**). Below are examples of sentences that contain two independent clauses, which are conjoined with "or" and "and." Conjoining two independent clauses with conjunctions is very common. The clauses can be separated and can function independently.

> *Languages can evolve, or languages can die.*
>
> *A language evolves over time, and this ensures its survival.*

Not all clauses can function independently, for example, "When languages evolve." Notice that the sentence is not grammatical (not a complete thought), even though it has a subject (languages) and a verb (evolve). This is called a **dependent clause** (also referred to as a **subordinate clause**). Here, to be consistent, the terms "independent clause" and "dependent clause" are used in our discussion. The adjective, adverb, and noun clauses that we examine in this chapter are all dependent clauses, meaning that they cannot function alone; they must be attached to other clauses to be grammatical.

> *When a language evolves, it reflects the needs of its speakers.*
>   ↑   ↑
>   dependent clause   independent clause

As you can see, the sentence above contains one dependent clause and one independent clause, each with its own subject and verb. Notice how the clause *it reflects the needs of its speakers* can function as a complete sentence, whereas *When a language evolves* (an adverb clause) cannot. Adjective and adverb clauses are dependent clauses and must be attached to independent clauses. (Noun clauses follow a slightly different rule that we will examine after adjectives and adverbs.)

Sentences can have more than two clauses. The following sentence has three different clauses—one independent and two dependent (the clauses are in parentheses, with the subjects and verbs underlined). The first clause is a dependent adverb clause, the middle clause is the independent clause, and the third clause is an adjective clause.

> *(When a language evolves), (it reflects the culture of its speakers), (whose environment is evolving).*

A common error is to confuse phrases such as those covered in Chapter 4—gerunds, participles, and infinitives—with clauses. Remember that a phrase does not have a subject and a verb, whereas a clause must have a subject and a verb, even if it is not a complete thought and cannot stand alone as a sentence. The exercise below will give you essential practice recognizing the differences between phrases and clauses. If you do not get them all correct, go back, review, and redo the exercise.

Exercise 5.1 Getting a Grip on Phrases and Clauses

Mark each underlined section as a phrase (P) or clause (C).

1. _P_ During the first century, the Celts living in the British Isles were invaded by Romans.

2. _P_ With the fall of the Roman Empire, Germanic tribes displaced the Romans.

3. _C_ The Germanic tribes moved into the British Isles, forcing the Celts outward toward present-day Scotland, Ireland, and Wales.

4. _C_ The Celtic language disappeared with the Celts when they fled from the Germanic invaders.

5. _P_ The three Germanic tribes—the Angles, Saxons, and Jutes— spoke languages understood by each tribe.

6. ____ Old English developed from the languages that the Angles, Saxons, and Jutes spoke.

7. _P_ Along with the Germanic languages, Latin influenced Old English.

8. _C_ In Old English, every noun had a different ending, depending on whether it was the subject, object, object of a preposition, and so on.

9. _P_ There was no standardization of spelling during the Old English period and very little literacy.

10. _C_ Old English is so different that it would have to be taught today as a foreign language.

DID YOU KNOW?

The Open University produced "The History of English in 10 Minutes" in a cartoon format. You know it's going to be entertaining when the first line is "The English language begins with the phrase 'Up yours, Caesar . . .'" (with the appropriate hand gestures). The video summarizes a long history in ten short segments at www.youtube.com/watch?v=H3r9bOkYW9s.

Now that you've had a little practice distinguishing between phrases and clauses, we will move on to explore the three types of dependent clauses: adjective, adverb, and noun.

Adjective Clauses

An **adjective clause** is a dependent clause that modifies a noun or a pronoun, which is often located in the independent clause (they can also modify nouns and pronouns in phrases and other dependent clauses). The adjective clause cannot function alone because it is a dependent clause. In terms of placement, an adjective clause follows the noun phrase (NP) that it modifies.

In this section, we will first become acquainted with relative pronouns that begin adjective clauses. Then we will look at the punctuation of adjective clauses and some "quirks" associated with them.

Relative Pronouns

Adjective clauses usually begin with a **relative pronoun**: who, whom, whose, that, or which. The **antecedent** of the relative pronoun is the noun that it modifies. Here are some examples of adjective clauses (underlined, with the relative pronoun in parentheses). Arrows point to the noun in the independent clause that the adjective clause modifies (which is the antecedent of the relative pronoun):

Indo-European, (which) is an ancient family of languages, evolved from European and Asian languages.

In the first century, the British Isles were invaded by Romans, (who) brought their Latin language with them.

The West Germanic tribes (who) came to the British Isles in the fifth century

spoke dialects (that) became "Old English."

The Angles, Saxons, and Jutes, (who) made up the West Germanic tribes, left their mark on modern-day English.

Today, we would not be able to understand Old English, (which) is also called Anglo-Saxon.

An adjective clause is also referred to as a **relative clause** in some texts because it begins with a relative pronoun. You choose the relative pronoun based on whether the pronoun refers to a human or nonhuman and whether it functions as a subject, object, or possessive within the adjective clause. "Who" and "whom" are used for humans (and often our pets), "which" for nonhumans, and "whose" for the possessive form. "That" is used for people or things.

To help understand relative pronouns and their roles in adjective clauses, let's look at some examples of two sentences being combined to form one complex sentence (one independent and one dependent clause). We begin with the relative pronouns "which" and "that" before we move on to adjective clauses that begin with the relative pronouns "who," "whom," and "whose."

Adjective Clauses with Relative Pronouns "Which" and "That"

Combining two or more sentences to form one complex sentence is an activity commonly used in middle schools and secondary schools to advance students' writing skills. We will look at examples below to explore how adjective clauses are derived from full sentences.

Relative Pronoun "Which"

Let's start with the two sentences below. We will subordinate the second sentence (i.e., make it an adjective clause) by using the relative pronoun "which" and put it into the first sentence (the independent clause) after the noun it modifies:

> *Old English emerged from various Germanic dialects.*

> *Old English is also called Anglo-Saxon.*

First, note that *Old English* is the repeated NP and the subject of both sentences. A relative pronoun's function is to replace the repeated NP in the new adjective clause. *Old English* is nonhuman, so here we use the relative pronoun "which." The transformation is completed in two steps.

> *Old English emerged from various Germanic dialects.*

> *Old English is also called Anglo-Saxon.*

Step 1: To transform the second sentence into an adjective clause, change the repeated NP to a relative pronoun:

> *which is also called Anglo-Saxon*

Step 2: Insert this adjective clause after the NP being modified:

> *Old English, which is also called Anglo-Saxon, emerged from various Germanic dialects.*

In the above and following examples, the adjective clause should be inserted into the independent clause <u>after</u> the noun that it modifies—the antecedent of the relative pronoun. (Adjective clauses can also modify nouns outside of the independent clause; however, in these examples, the adjective clauses are modifying nouns in independent clauses.) Seems easy enough, right?

Below is another example of two sentences combined into one. Note that the repeated NP in the second sentence (*Old English*) is not the subject of the sentence as it is in the example above—in this case, it is an object. Now we do the transformation in three steps:

> <u>Old English</u> is also called Anglo-Saxon.
>
> *The dialects of the Angles, Saxons, and Jutes helped form <u>Old English</u>.*

Step 1: To transform the second sentence into an adjective clause, change the repeated NP to a relative pronoun:

> *The dialects of the Angles, Saxons, and Jutes helped form <u>which</u>*

You have probably noticed that we cannot place the new adjective clause into the sentence as is, or else you will get this ungrammatical result:

> **Old English, <u>the dialects of the Angles, Saxons, and Jutes helped form which</u> is also called Anglo-Saxon.*

Step 2: The relative pronoun "which" must begin the adjective clause, so we move *which* to the front of the adjective clause:

> <u>*which* the dialects of the Angles, Saxons, and Jutes helped form</u> _____

Step 3: Now we can insert the adjective clause into the independent clause after the NP it modifies, *Old English*:

> *Old English, <u>which the dialects of the Angles, Saxons, and Jutes helped form</u>, is also called Anglo-Saxon.*

Let's practice with one more sentence combination task. Again, the second sentence needs to be changed to an adjective clause and inserted into the first:

Old English had different letters.

Modern English no longer uses different letters.

Step 1: To transform the second sentence into an adjective clause, change the repeated NP to a relative pronoun:

Modern English no longer uses which

Step 2: Move the relative pronoun to the front of the clause:

which Modern English no longer uses _____

Step 3: Insert this adjective clause after the NP being modified:

Old English had different letters, which Modern English no longer uses.

Relative Pronoun "That"

The relative pronoun "that" can be used to refer to people or things; however, it should be used only in essential clauses (adjective clauses without commas—a subject we will cover in the section on punctuation). The relative pronoun "that" would not work in the sentence above because the adjective clause is not essential information identifying the noun *Old English*. In fact, the sentence may seem odd to a native speaker of English (the question mark indicates that the grammar is questionable):

?Old English, that the dialects of the Angles, Saxons, and Jutes helped form, is also called Anglo-Saxon.

We could change the sentence to make the relative pronoun "that" work:

The dialects that the Angles, Saxons, and Jutes brought to England helped form Old English.

We use the relative pronoun "that" above because the adjective clause is essential in identifying which *dialects*—those *that the Angles, Saxons, and Jutes brought to England*—so no commas are used to set it off.

It has become more common to hear "which" used in this type of adjective clause, although some prescriptive grammar books discourage its use in essential adjective clauses. Substitute "which" for "that" in the sentence above and decide whether it sounds right to you. Most of us would agree that it sounds fine, which means that we most likely use this form in our spoken English; however, in formal papers, you would use the relative pronoun "that."

Here are three more sentences with adjective clauses introduced by the relative pronoun "that."

The man that wrote about Anglo-Saxon settlements was a monk.

The man that Bede admired most was another author.

Those that Bede admired most were other authors.

The adjective clauses are essential in identifying which *man* and the pronoun *those*, so no commas are used. Because *man* and *those* refer to people, the relative pronoun "who" could also be used in the first sentence and "whom" in the second and third. We will examine the relative pronouns "who," "whom," and "whose" next. But first let's practice identifying adjective clauses that use the relative pronouns "which" and "that."

Exercise 5.2 Getting a Grip on Relative Pronouns "Which" and "That"

Find the adjective clauses with the relative pronouns "which" and "that" and underline them. One sentence does not have an adjective clause. (Hint: Be sure that the clause you underline modifies a noun or pronoun.)

1. The "Great Vowel Shift," which affected the pronunciation of vowels in English, occurred systematically over hundreds of years.
2. The first Bible that was written in English caused great controversy because of the use of the "heathen" language.
3. The King James version of the Bible, completed in 1611, shows that language changes.
4. Languages that change have a better chance of survival.
5. Changes may occur in words that are difficult to pronounce. (We simplify them.)
6. There is a great deal of research that documents language change.
7. Because languages change, it is difficult to reconstruct those that are thousands of years old.
8. Many historical documents that were written in Old English were destroyed during battles.
9. English developed from the many languages and cultural heritages that came with the invaders.
10. Some sounds that have been lost are still visible in the spelling of certain words (e.g., "gh" in "night").

Adjective Clauses with Relative Pronouns "Who," "Whom," and "Whose"

The relative pronouns "who" and "whose" are commonly used in spoken and written English, whereas "whom" is rarely used in conversation—in fact, it can sound downright pompous in a casual conversation and may get a strange response (or worse). Thus many of us have lost our intuition regarding the use of "whom."

In academic writing and formal situations, however, "whom" is still used. Listen to some formal political speeches—you will hear "whom" inserted in all the right places (thanks to speechwriters). Let's first look at the use of "who" in adjective clauses and then move on to "whom" and "whose."

Relative Pronoun "Who"

To explore the use of the relative pronoun "who," we will continue to combine sentences. In the two sentences below, we will transform the second sentence into an adjective clause and place it inside the first, which will be our independent clause. Because *Bede the Venerable* is a person (and the subject of the second sentence), the appropriate relative pronoun to replace him with is "who." Why? Because the relative pronoun replaces the subject of the second sentence, and "who" is always the subject form:

> *Bede the Venerable wrote a critical book about the Anglo-Saxon settlements around 700 C.E.*
>
> *Bede the Venerable was a monk.*

Step 1: To transform the second sentence into an adjective clause, change the repeated NP to a relative pronoun:

> *who was a monk*

Step 2: Insert this adjective clause after the NP being modified:

> *Bede the Venerable, who was a monk, wrote a critical book about the Anglo-Saxon settlements around 700 C.E.*

Let's combine another two sentences, changing the second sentence into an adjective clause:

> *During the first century, Romans attacked the Celts.*
>
> *The Celts were living in the British Isles.*

Step 1: To transform the second sentence into an adjective clause, change the repeated NP to a relative pronoun:

who were living in the British Isles

Step 2: Insert this adjective clause after the NP being modified:

During the first century, Romans attacked the Celts, who were living in the British Isles.

Note that the newly formed adjective clause is modifying the direct object of the independent clause, *Romans attacked the Celts*. The relative pronoun *who* is used because it is the subject of the adjective clause that modifies *Celts*.

Relative Pronoun "Whom"

Are you ready for "whom"? The rule is simple: "who" is used in the subject slot (as we saw above), while **"whom" fills the object slot**. In a formal letter, you would not write "To Who It May Concern," right? We use "whom" in the salutation because it is the object of preposition "To."

For practice using "whom," let's look at two more sentences and change the second sentence into an adjective clause. Notice that *Bede the Venerable* in the second sentence below is in the object slot (*The church* is the subject, and *declared* is the verb). The "who" form cannot substitute for an object in formal English, so we must use the object form, "whom":

Bede the Venerable wrote a critical book about the Anglo-Saxon settlements.

The church declared Bede the Venerable a saint.

Step 1: To transform the second sentence into an adjective clause, change the repeated NP to a relative pronoun:

The church declared whom a saint

Now if we insert the new clause into the first sentence, the result is an ungrammatical sentence:

*Bede the Venerable, the church declared whom a saint, wrote a critical book about the Anglo-Saxon settlements.

In the previous section, "which" replaced an object and was moved to the front of the adjective clause. The same must be done here with "whom." Let's do all three steps, starting from the beginning:

Bede the Venerable wrote a critical book about the Anglo-Saxon settlements.

The church declared Bede the Venerable a saint.

Step 1: To transform the second sentence into an adjective clause, change the repeated NP to a relative pronoun:

The church declared whom a saint.

Step 2: Move the relative pronoun to the front of the clause:

whom the church declared ____ a saint

Step 3: Insert this adjective clause after the NP being modified:

Bede the Venerable, whom the church declared a saint, wrote a critical book about the Anglo-Saxon settlements.

"Whom" is also used in the object of preposition slot, as you can see in the following example in which *Bede* is the object of the preposition *to* in the second sentence:

Bede the Venerable wrote a critical book about the Anglo-Saxon settlements.

The church gave sainthood to Bede the Venerable.

Step 1: To transform the second sentence into an adjective clause, change the repeated NP to a relative pronoun:

The church gave sainthood to whom

Step 2: Move the relative pronoun to the front of the clause:

whom the church gave sainthood to ____

Step 3: Insert this adjective clause after the NP being modified:

Bede the Venerable, whom the church gave sainthood to, wrote a critical book about the Anglo-Saxon settlements.

In formal English (and we are obviously being formal because we are using "whom"), the preposition is often moved to the front of the clause with the relative pronoun:

> Bede the Venerable, <u>to whom the church gave sainthood</u> ___ , *wrote a critical book about the Anglo-Saxon settlements.*

Below are two more examples of adjective clauses with the relative pronoun "whom." Again, note that "whom" is located at the beginning of the adjective clause, but it is not the subject of the clause.

> King Alfred, <u>under whom the English language thrived</u>, *commissioned many Latin texts to be translated into English.*

> Bede wrote about Caedmon, <u>whom he praises for his Christian poetry written in Old English.</u>

To summarize the use of "who" and "whom" in adjective clauses, use "who" when a relative pronoun is in the subject slot of the adjective clause and "whom" in the object slot. Remember, whether you use "who" or "whom" is all about what is happening <u>within</u> the adjective clause itself; it has nothing to do with the noun the adjective clause is modifying in the independent clause.

Relative Pronoun "Whose"

The relative pronoun "whose" is the possessive form of "who" and is used regularly without problems by native speakers. What two sentences do you think the following sentence came from?

> Bede the Venerable, <u>whose account of early Britain provided important historical facts</u>, *was a monk.*

The two sentences would look like this before the second sentence was transformed into an adjective clause:

> <u>Bede the Venerable was a monk.</u>

> <u>Bede the Venerable's</u> *account of early Britain provided important historical facts*

Let's look at the steps again.

> <u>Bede the Venerable was a monk.</u>

Bede the Venerable's account of early Britain provided important historical facts.

Step 1: To transform the second sentence into an adjective clause, change the repeated NP to a relative pronoun:

whose account of early Britain provided important historical facts

Step 2: Insert this adjective clause after the NP being modified:

Bede the Venerable, whose account of early Britain provided important historical facts, was a monk.

The next exercise gives you practice choosing among the relative pronouns "who," "whom," and "whose." That exercise is followed by one requiring you to combine two sentences to form one sentence containing one independent and one adjective clause.

Exercise 5.3 Getting a Grip on Relative Pronouns "Who," "Whom," and "Whose"

Insert the correct relative pronoun in the blanks below, choosing from "who," "whom," or "whose."

1. The Germanic tribes were first asked to come to Britain to defend it from the Picts and Scots _____ were trying to take control of Britain in the fifth century.

2. The Germanic tribes, _____ the monk Gildes described as slaughtering tyrants, decided to stay in Britain.

3. The names of British towns provide information about the people_____ settled the areas.

4. Some British towns _____ names come from pagan words were most likely established earlier than towns with Latin names.

5. Cynewulf, _____ was a poet in Britain, wrote religious poems around 800 c.e. in the local dialect, not Latin.

6. The reintroduction of Latin by monks, _____ work was to bring Christianity to Britain, added new words to Old English vocabulary.

7. In the eighth century, the British Isles were attacked by Vikings, _____ brought their Scandinavian language to Britain.

8. Danish and Norwegian invaders, from _____ many British villagers fled, took over a great deal of land in Britain and settled there during the ninth century.

9. Modern English retains many words from those invaders, _____ spoke Danish and Norse.

10. According to some Norwegian researchers _____ ideas are quite controversial, Modern English actually developed from Old Norse, not Old English.

Exercise 5.4 Getting a Grip on Adjective Clauses Using "Which," "That," "Who," "Whom," and "Whose"

Combine the two sentences. Transform sentence (b) into an adjective clause. Replace the repeated noun in sentence (b) with a relative pronoun and insert it into sentence (a) after the NP it modifies.

Example:

(a) Early English was sometimes written with the runic alphabet.
(b) The runic alphabet consisted of twenty-four angular letters.
     Combined: Early English was sometimes written with the runic alphabet, which consisted of twenty-four angular letters.

1. (a) The Romans brought their language to the British Isles during the first century.
   (b) Their language was Latin.
        Combined:_____

2. (a) The Romans also brought the Latin script.
   (b) The Latin script was based on letters for consonants and vowels.
        Combined:_____

3. (a) The Romans left Britain to take care of conflicts back home around 400 C.E.
   (b) The Romans' rule lasted for more than 300 years.
        Combined:_____

4. (a) Today, we would have trouble understanding Old English.
   (b) Old English was formed from different West Germanic dialects.
        Combined:_____

5. (a) Old English resembles German more than it does modern-day English.
   (b) Old English used prefixes and suffixes to extend its vocabulary.
        Combined:_____

6. (a) One of the best-known literary works written in Old English is *Beowulf*.
   (b) *Beowulf* depicted the social conditions of the people at that time.
       Combined:_____
7. (a) The French occupied England for 300 years after the Norman Conquest of 1066.
   (b) The peasants disliked the French.
       Combined:_____
8. (a) French words were added to English during the French occupation of Britain.
   (b) French words covered matters of government and law.
       Combined:_____
9. (a) William Caxton made note of the irregularities of English spelling.
   (b) William Caxton brought the printing press to England in the mid-fifteenth century.
       Combined:_____
10. (a) Shakespeare lived during an exciting period of time.
    (b) The exciting period of time witnessed great changes to English.
        Combined:_____

Punctuation of Adjective Clauses

In almost all of the previous adjective clause examples, the clauses were set off with commas except those beginning with the relative pronoun "that." In Chapters 2 and 4, we investigated the use of commas to set off essential phrases in appositives and participles. The rule for clauses is the same: if the clause is essential to the meaning of the NP it is modifying, no commas are used; if the clause is not essential for identifying the NP it modifies, then it is set off with commas. The information may be important but is not essential for identifying or restricting the noun. For example, in a sentence from a previous exercise, the adjective clause modifies a person, *Cynewulf*.

> *Cynewulf, who was a poet in Britain, wrote religious poems around 800 C.E. in the local dialect, not Latin.*

Because *Cynewulf* is a proper noun, he is identified by his name; the adjective clause (*who was a poet in Britain*) is not essential information needed to identify him, so it is placed in commas. In the sentence below, *monks* is modified by the adjective clause *whose work was to bring Christianity to Britain*:

> *The reintroduction of Latin by monks, whose work was to bring Christianity to Britain, added new words to Old English vocabulary.*

By using commas, the writer is indicating that this is not essential information for identifying any particular monks—they all brought Christianity to Britain. If you wanted to make clear the difference between monks, you would not use commas. Look at the following sentence as an example:

Monks who lived in the north were driven out by the Danes.

The adjective clause *who lived in the north* is not set off by commas, marking it as essential information for identifying which monks were driven out by the Danes. This type of clause is also called **restrictive** in some books because it restricts the meaning of the noun. See how the meaning changes with the removal of the essential adjective clause:

Monks were driven out by the Danes.

It has changed the meaning of the sentence: it now indicates that all monks were driven out by the Danes. You can see why the adjective clause *who lived in the north* is essential to describing which monks were driven out by the Danes; therefore, it is not set off with commas. Here is another example of a sentence with essential adjective clauses:

Words that came from Scandinavian languages exist in English today, in particular words that have the sounds "sk."

In the example above, there are two essential adjective clauses. Both describe which *words* and add essential information—take them out to see exactly how important they are to identifying the NPs *words*:

Words exist in English today, in particular words.

Your choice of relative pronoun and commas can provide the reader with a great deal of information. Read the next pair of sentences, pausing at the commas, and then compare their meanings:

Monks who brought Latin to Britain dispersed the language through their religious teachings.

Monks, who brought Latin to Britain, dispersed the language through their religious teachings.

Can you tell the difference in meanings, even though these sentences have the same words? In the first sentence, *monks* is restricted to the monks *who brought Latin to Britain* (meaning that there may have been other monks who did not bring Latin). The second sentence has the same adjective clause, but because it is placed within commas, the author is indicating that the clause *who brought Latin to Britain* is not essential for identifying which *monks*—the adjective clause is extra information (possibly all monks dispersed Latin). Both sentences are correct, but they convey different meanings.

Let's try one more—a personal example:

My brother who lives in Atlanta is a teacher.

Notice that there are no commas around the adjective clause *who lives in Atlanta.* What does that tell you about my family? Do I have one brother or more than one? If you answered "more than one," you're right. No commas were used because *who lives in Atlanta* is essential information in identifying which brother is a teacher. It means that I have at least two brothers. Who knew that commas could provide so much information?

Exercise 5.5 Getting a Grip on Adjective Clauses and Their Punctuation

Find and underline the adjective clauses. There may be more than one in a sentence. Punctuate the adjective clauses with commas where needed.

1. Latin which was the language of Christianity never replaced English in Britain.
2. Old English which is very different from Modern English had complex word endings.
3. An Old English noun that functioned as a subject had a different ending from a noun that was used as a direct object.
4. "Fæder ure Þu Þe eart on heofonum" is Old English text that means "our father who is in heaven."
5. During the Norman occupation, Norman French which became the prestigious language in Britain was used for law and literature, and English remained the language that the common folk spoke.
6. Middle English which people spoke from around 1100 to 1470 C.E. is more understandable to us than Old English, but it still can be a challenge, for example, "Oure fadir that art in heuenes."
7. Spelling varied greatly in Middle English which also had dialectical variations.
8. In Middle English which was spoken for around three centuries many adjectives modifying plural nouns were also made plural with an "e," for example, "goode children."
9. An example of a Middle English pronoun that differs from Modern English is "you" which had a singular form and a plural form.
10. The *Canterbury Tales* were written by Geoffrey Chaucer whose work provided a descriptive account of fourteenth-century English society.

DID YOU KNOW?

The famous *Canterbury Tales* by Geoffrey Chaucer are written in Middle English, a language that is very difficult for us to understand. An interesting rap (yes, rap) version of the *Tales* with Modern English translations is available on YouTube at www.youtube.com/watch?v=4E-0PaK4Rtl, or search for "The Canterbury Tales Rap (General Prologue)-In Middle English."

Adjective Clause Quirks

There are a couple other quirks of adjective clauses that we need to discuss. First, some relative pronouns can be deleted from the adjective clause; second, some adjective clauses can be introduced by words that are not relative pronouns.

Relative Pronoun Deletion

If the relative pronoun introduces an essential adjective clause and replaces an object (remember, we moved the object to the front of the adjective clause), it can often be deleted. Let's look at a sentence from the previous exercise:

> *During the Norman occupation, Norman French, <u>which became the prestigious language</u>, was used for law and literature, and English remained the language <u>that the common folk spoke</u>.*

The two adjective clauses are underlined. The first is nonessential and is set off with commas. The relative pronoun *which* is the subject of the adjective clause, and *became* is its verb. We cannot delete this relative pronoun for two reasons. First, it is located in a nonessential adjective clause (marked by the use of commas), meaning that it doesn't restrict the meaning of the NP it is modifying (*Norman French*). Relative pronouns in nonessential adjective clauses cannot be deleted. Second, the relative pronoun is the subject of the adjective clause, and subject relative pronouns cannot be deleted (a clause must have a subject).

The next adjective clause is an essential clause that restricts *language*. In the adjective clause, the relative pronoun *that* replaced the repeated object NP (*the language*) and was moved to the front of the adjective clause. Because *that* is not the subject of the adjective clause (*common folk* is the subject, and *spoke* is the verb), and it is located in an essential adjective clause, it can be deleted:

> *During the Norman occupation, Norman French, <u>which became the prestigious language</u>, was used for law and literature, and English remained the language <s>that</s> the common folk spoke.*

Below are two more examples of deletable relative pronouns in essential adjective clauses:

> *The language ~~that~~ <u>people spoke in the eighth century</u> would be unintelligible to us.*

> *The wealthy people ~~whom~~ <u>the Normans killed</u> refused to be subjugated to the new king.*

In the first sentence above, the relative pronoun *that* is located in an essential adjective clause restricting which *language*, and it is not the subject of that clause (*people* is the subject, and *spoke* is the verb), so we can delete it. In the second sentence, the relative pronoun *whom* is the object of the adjective clause (remember that it was moved to the front of the clause), and it can be deleted.

In nonessential adjective clauses, however, the relative pronoun serving as the object <u>cannot</u> be deleted. The sentence below contains a nonessential adjective clause that modifies *Norman French*:

> *Norman French, <u>which the wealthy people spoke</u>, was the prestigious language after the Norman invasion.*

Note that *wealthy people* is the subject of the adjective clause, and *spoke* is the verb. The relative pronoun *which* is the object that was moved to the front of the clause. If the relative pronoun is deleted, you will get an ungrammatical sentence:

> **Norman French, ~~which~~ <u>the wealthy people spoke</u>, was the prestigious language after the Norman invasion.*

Below are two more examples of nonrestrictive adjective clauses with object relative pronouns that <u>cannot</u> be deleted:

> *The new French king of Britain, William of Normandy, <u>whom the peasants despised</u>, banished English from his courts.*

> *Rather than speaking French, the British peasants spoke English, <u>which the French rulers did not recognize in their courts</u>.*

Deleting the relative pronouns results in ungrammatical sentences:

> **The new French king of Britain, William of Normandy, <u>the peasants despised</u>, banished English from his courts.*

> **Rather than speaking French, the British peasants spoke English, <u>the French rulers did not recognize in their courts</u>.*

In general, we have good intuition on which relative pronouns can be deleted in a sentence. Because a relative pronoun clearly marks the beginning of an adjective clause, its deletion may make the adjective clause more difficult to identify:

> The language <u>people spoke in the first century</u> would be unintelligible to us.

If it helps, you can always put the relative pronoun back in the adjective clause:

> The language <u>that people spoke in the first century</u> would be unintelligible to us.

Adjective Clauses with Relative Adverbs

There are a few words that can substitute for relative pronouns in adjective clauses. They are the **relative adverbs** "where," "when," and "why." Below are some examples of these relative adverbs introducing adjective clauses:

> Westminster is the city <u>where the first printing press was set up in Britain.</u>
>
> The printing press was the reason <u>why English became more standardized.</u>
>
> The period of Norman rule was the time <u>when French vocabulary entered English.</u>

These clauses function as adjectives modifying nouns in the independent clauses. They still answer the question "which?" Which *city*? Which *reason*? Which *time*? We will see "where," "when," and "why" used later in both adverb and noun clauses, but they will function quite differently. This is just a heads-up for you to be aware of these possible "conflicts of interest."

Exercise 5.6 Getting a Grip on Adjective Clauses

Underline all of the adjective clauses in the sentences below. Remember that the relative pronoun may have been deleted. There is only one adjective clause per sentence.

1. The history of English is roughly divided into four time periods, which are Old English, Middle English, Early Modern English, and Modern English.
2. The division of English into Old, Middle, Early Modern, and Modern is mostly based on historical events that influenced the language.
3. The year 1066 is important in British history because it marks the conquest of England by the Normans, who came from what is now northern France.

4. The Norman Conquest of 1066, which marked the beginning of the Middle English period, started a decline in the use of English.

5. French, the language the invaders brought to Britain, was used by the elite class and kings.

6. Two hundred years after the Norman Conquest, English, which had been in decline, started to be used in literature and become more standardized.

7. Starting in 1272, King Edward I waged war against Wales and Scotland, two areas of Britain where the Celtic language was still spoken.

8. Middle English, which was not standardized, consisted of different dialects from the various regions of the country.

9. There are a number of differences between Old English and Middle English, the language Chaucer spoke.

10. English, which was being transformed, accepted, and rejected, finally became the language of the court and education in the second half of the fourteenth century.

Adverb Clauses ← movable

An **adverb clause** is a dependent clause that functions the same way that many single-word adverbs function. Adverb clauses answer the adverb questions of "when," "why," "how," and "to what extent," and they modify verbs, adjectives, and adverbs. As a dependent clause, an adverb clause must be inserted in a sentence with an independent clause.

Below, we will examine adverb clauses based on the word class that they are modifying—verbs, adjectives, or adverbs. But first, you must become acquainted with the words that introduce adverb clauses, called subordinating conjunctions.

Subordinating Conjunctions

Adverb clauses begin with **subordinating conjunctions**, which show time, condition, cause and effect, contrast, manner, or degree. Here are some of the most common subordinating conjunctions:

Time:	*before, after, even after, as soon as, until, while, when, whenever*
Condition:	*if, even if, unless, whether or not, provided that*
Cause and Effect:	*because, since, so that*
Contrast:	*though, although, even though, while, whereas*
Manner:	*as, as if, as though*
Degree:	*as . . . as, than, more than, less than, that*

Adverb clauses are introduced by subordinating conjunctions, which can indicate different relations between the two clauses (contrast, degree, etc.). These subordinating conjunctions are always found at the beginning of the adverb clause:

              adverb clause   independent clause
                ↓   ↓

__After__ the Romans conquered Britain in the first century, they were soon driven out by the Anglo-Saxon tribes.

      independent clause   adverb clause
              ↓   ↓

The Vikings were fiercer __than__ some of the earlier invaders had been.

Being able to recognize these subordinating conjunctions will aid in your recognition of adverb clauses. Below, we begin with adverb clauses that modify verbs in independent clauses. Pay attention to how these clauses are punctuated. Then we will investigate adverb clauses that modify predicate adjectives and adverbs in independent clauses.

Adverb Clauses Modifying Verbs

Adverb clauses that modify verbs begin with subordinate conjunctions that indicate time, condition, cause and effect, contrast, or manner. Below are examples with the adverb clauses underlined:

Time: *The Anglo-Saxons burned down Roman cities <u>while they were driving the Romans out of Britain.</u>*

Condition: *Our language would be quite different today <u>if the Romans had held control over Britain.</u>*

Cause and Effect: *The English language has a rich vocabulary <u>because the invaders' languages left their marks on English.</u>*

Contrast: *Most of the people of Britain continued to speak English, <u>even though the Norman Conquest of 1066 brought the French language.</u>*

Manner: *The French occupiers acted <u>as if the English language was unworthy of their attention.</u>*

One characteristic of adverb clauses that modify verbs is that they are almost always movable. Using the example sentences from above, let's move the adverb clauses to the front of the sentences. An exception to this rule is the adverb clause introduced by the subordinate conjunctions of manner (as if, as though, as).

Time: *While they were driving the Romans out of Britain, the Anglo-Saxons burned down Roman cities.*

Condition: *If the Romans had held control over Britain, our language would be quite different today.*

Cause and Effect: *Because the invaders' languages left their marks on English, the English language has a rich vocabulary.*

Contrast: *Even though the Norman Conquest of 1066 brought the French language, most of the people of Britain continued to speak English.*

PUNCTUATION ALERT!

Adverb clauses that modify verbs have a very simple punctuation rule. Look at the two sets of examples above and see whether you can describe the pattern. You should have noticed that if the adverb clause begins the sentence, it is followed by a comma. If it follows the independent clause, there is no comma. Of course, you know that there is always an exception, so here it is: an adverb clause introduced by a subordinate conjunction of contrast (e.g., though, although, even though) is separated from the independent clause with a comma in both positions. I will use one of the above examples to illustrate this exception to the rule:

Contrast: *Most of the people of Britain continued to speak English, even though the Norman Conquest of 1066 brought the French language.*

             Even though the Norman Conquest of 1066 brought the French language, most of the people of Britain continued to speak English.

For many students, learning this rule has lowered comma errors by at least 50 percent. I must also note that in other disciplines (e.g., history), the rules might be slightly different.

The good news is that commas are not used in adverb clauses modifying predicate adjectives or adverbs, as you will see next. But first, here is a short exercise that gives you practice identifying adverb clauses and punctuating them.

Exercise 5.7 Getting a Grip on Adverb Clauses that Modify Verbs

Underline the one adverb clause in each sentence and add a comma if needed. (Hint: Two sentences do not have adverb clauses.)

1. The Norman invaders killed members of the British aristocracy if they did not relinquish their lands.
2. After the Norman Conquest, some common folk spoke a mixed French-English language.
3. Although bilingualism (English/French) became more common among the ruling class, most of the peasants spoke only English during the eleventh century.
4. Middle English borrowed from French vocabulary because French was the language of the ruling elite in the eleventh century.
5. During the twelfth century, Middle English started to evolve and become distinct from Old English.
6. After people had been forced to speak French in government affairs for three centuries English finally marked its comeback in the fourteenth century through its use in literature, for example, the *Canterbury Tales*.
7. Even though English was the language of the common people a person could be killed for translating the Bible into English in the fourteenth century.
8. In 1380, as English began to be resurrected the people finally got a Bible in a language that they could read.
9. Because there was no printing press in England in the fourteenth century copies of the Bible were handwritten.
10. In the fifteenth century, as Britain developed economically schools and colleges were built.

Adverb Clauses Modifying Adjectives and Adverbs

Adverb clauses that modify adjectives and adverbs begin with the subordinate conjunctions "that" and "than." "That" is used to express the consequence of a degree expression (e.g., "I am happy that you called"). The other type is also an adverb clause of degree, but it is used with comparative forms of adjectives and adverbs (e.g., "Old English was more complex than English is today").

Adverb Clauses Introduced by "That"

An adverb clause with the subordinator "that" modifies a predicate adjective or an adverb that is usually located in the independent clause (but can modify adjectives and adverbs in dependent clauses as well). These adverb clauses sit in the slots following the predicate adjectives or the adverbs that they modify. Below are four examples of adverb clauses modifying the predicate adjectives in independent clauses and two examples of adverb clauses modifying adverbs in independent clauses:

Adverb clauses modifying predicate adjectives:

> *Many English speakers today are surprised that Old English would be unintelligible to them.*

> *We should be happy that Modern English does not have all of the prefixes and suffixes of Old English.*

> *The pope was extremely angry that John Wycliffe had translated the Bible into English in 1380.*

> *The church was sure that John Wycliffe was a heretic.*

Adverb clauses modifying adverbs:

> *Language was changing so rapidly that Shakespeare noticed and used this knowledge to his advantage.*

> *The first French rulers of England despised English so much that they ordered their troops not to learn it.*

These adverb clauses are relatively easy to identify because they predictably follow the predicate adjectives and adverbs that they modify. However, be careful not to confuse this type of adverb clause with adjective clauses using the relative pronoun "that." Let's revisit a sentence from the section on adjective clauses.

Adjective Clause:

> *The English that was spoken in the eighteenth century would be understandable to us.*

In the adjective clause above, *that* is the subject of the verb *was spoken*, and the clause modifies the noun *English*. However, in an adverb clause, "that" is just a flag word signaling the beginning of the adverb clause (it plays no role in the sentence), and, of course, an adverb clause would not be modifying a noun.

Now that you've learned the role of "that" in adverb clauses, feel free to delete it. "That" is the only subordinating conjunction in adverb clauses that can be deleted, making it quite special in the adverb clause world. The next examples illustrate this deletion:

> *Many English speakers today are surprised ~~that~~ Old English is unintelligible to them.*

> *We should be happy ~~that~~ Modern English does not have all of the inflections of Old English.*

> *The pope was extremely angry ~~that~~ John Wycliffe had translated the Bible into English in 1380.*

> *The church was sure ~~that~~ John Wycliffe was a heretic.*

When "that" is deleted, it may be more difficult to recognize the adverb clause. Its "essence" is still there, so you can put it back in if that helps you. We had the same challenge when relative pronouns in adjective clauses were deleted. The trick is to put it back into the clause. Below is an example of an adverb clause with "that" deleted and an adjective clause with "that" deleted—can you find the two different dependent clauses?

> *The translations the church banned were those of the Bible written in English.*

> *The church was furious John Wycliffe had translated the Bible into the heathen language.*

The adjective clause is modifying the NP *The translations* in the first sentence, and the adverb clause is modifying the predicate adjective *furious* in the second:

Adjective clause:

> *The translations ~~that~~ the church banned were those of the Bible written in English.*

Adverb clause:

> *The church was furious ~~that~~ John Wycliffe translated the Bible into the heathen language.*

Being able to distinguish between the two types of clauses is essential to your success in this chapter, so an exercise is included below to give you more practice identifying them.

Exercise 5.8 Getting a Grip on Adverb Clauses and Adjective Clauses with "That"

Practice distinguishing between adverb clauses and adjective clauses introduced by "that." Underline the clauses beginning with "that" and identify each as an adjective clause (ADJ) or an adverb clause (ADV).

1. ADJ (ADV) The pope was clear that English versions of the Bible would not be tolerated.

2. ADJ ADV The English versions of the Bible that were available in the fourteenth century were handwritten.

3. ADJ ADV During Shakespeare's time, there was great religious turmoil that pitted Catholics against Protestants (and others).

4. ADJ ADV In some of Shakespeare's plays, it is clear that he was in love.

5. ADJ ADV "Compare her face with some that I shall show, And I will make thee think thy swan a crow" is a quote from what play by Shakespeare?

6. ADJ ADV Plays that were written more than 400 years ago by Shakespeare are still relevant today.

7. ADJ ADV Shakespeare is still so popular that any American university student could probably name one of his plays.

8. ADJ ADV An interesting linguistic exercise that students can do is to translate Shakespeare into Modern English.

9. ADJ ADV English was considered so "vulgar" that most scholars of the sixteenth and seventeenth centuries refused to study it.

10. ADJ ADV A nineteenth-century exam that was taken to get into Harvard required the student to translate English into Latin and to write an essay in Greek.

Adverb Clauses Introduced by "Than"

Adverb clauses of degree modify predicate adjectives and adverbs in their comparative forms. They are introduced with the subordinating conjunction "than," which is the signal word for this type of adverb clause; it can never be deleted.

By the fourteenth century, literature written in English had become

more common than it had been in the previous centuries.

The Hundred Years' War with France (1337–1453) helped end French

usage in England faster than any other historical event had.

In the first example, the adverb clause modifies the comparative predicate adjective *common*. In the second example above, the adverb clause modifies the comparative adverb *faster*. Below are some more examples of comparative adverb clauses:

Adverb Clause Modifying Predicate Adjective:

The printing press was more influential than any other invention had been in promoting literacy.

Adverb Clauses Modifying Adverbs:

We can decipher ancient writings more accurately now than we were able to decipher them in the past.

The British government shipped criminals to Australia more

frequently than they sent other immigrant groups to Australia in

the late 1700s.

Did you notice that these adverb clauses of comparison aren't punctuated with commas?

Below you will have the opportunity to practice identifying adverb clauses that are introduced by the subordinating conjunctions "that" and "than." After you complete the exercise (and review your errors), go to the next exercise, which allows you to review all three types of adverb clauses.

Exercise 5.9 Getting a Grip on Adverb Clauses with "That" and "Than"

Find and underline the adverb clauses beginning with "that" and "than." Remember that the subordinate conjunction "that" may have been deleted. There is only one adverb clause in each sentence. (Hint: One sentence does not have an adverb clause.)

1. In the mid-1300s, English started to be used in the courts more often than French was used.

2. The plague of 1350 killed millions of people; as a result, social changes for the surviving peasants came more quickly than they had before.

3. The Black Death that ravaged Britain was so horrendous that thousands of city dwellers died.

4. The Catholic Church was so devastated by the plague that many unqualified men were allowed to enter the clergy.

5. Lollards, who advocated church reform in the 1300s, wanted more Bibles translated into English, but they were considered so subversive that they had to go into hiding.

6. The church authorities were sure that an English Bible would undermine their control of the people.

7. King Henry VIII started the Church of England, and his heirs to the throne moved England toward a religion that was in conflict with Catholicism and Latin.

8. The Hundred Years' War with France made Brits more nationalistic than they had been in the previous years.

9. The British were unhappy that French had been forced upon them for so many years.

10. By the mid-1300s, English as a literary medium became more accepted than it had been in the previous century.

Exercise 5.10 Getting a Grip on All Types of Adverb Clauses

Find and underline the adverb clauses that modify verbs, adjectives, and adverbs. There is only one in each sentence.

1. In the Early Middle English period, the plural noun marker "–s" became the standard, although the older form "–en" was often used for plural nouns in southern England.

2. Today, there are still vestiges of the "–en" plural marker in English, as you can see in the word "oxen."

3. During the Middle English period, Britain had many different dialects because the areas had different settlement patterns and foreign occupation histories.

4. As England kept trade ties with other countries such as Germany and Holland, Middle English became influenced by languages other than Latin and French.

5. Late Middle English spelling became more regularized than Early Middle English spelling had been.

6. Geoffrey Chaucer wrote the most famous literature of the Middle English period while he worked in service to the king.

7. At one time, the owning of a Bible written in English was considered so heretical that the person could be executed.

8. In the fifteenth century, the church became more accepting of English Bibles than it had been in the previous century.

9. King Henry V promoted the use of English and helped foment pride in the language and all things English while he reigned in Britain from 1413 to 1422.

10. After English had competed with French and Latin for centuries, it finally became adopted by the courts in the mid-fifteenth century.

Noun Clauses

In this section, we complete our discussion of clauses by examining those that function as nouns. **Noun clauses**, like adjective and adverb clauses, are dependent clauses and cannot stand alone as grammatical sentences. Unlike adjective and adverb clauses, noun clauses do not modify anything. Instead they fill noun slots in sentences. Let's first examine these slots and then look at the two types of subordinate conjunctions that introduce noun clauses, the "that type" and the "wh– type."

Noun Clause Slots

Noun clauses can be found in any slot that can be filled by a noun phrase (NP). We will continue to use the pronoun substitution test to identify these nouns. Below are some examples of noun clauses functioning as a subject, direct object, and object of preposition (OP), respectively. Go ahead and substitute the pronoun "it" or "this" for the noun clause:

Subject: *That English vocabulary developed from many languages* is well documented.

Object: Linguists have documented *how English vocabulary developed from many languages.*

OP: Linguists are knowledgeable about *how ancient languages are related.*

Noun clauses can also function as appositives (APPs) and predicate nomina-tives (PNs), as the two sentences below illustrate. As mentioned in earlier chapters, the pronoun substitution test doesn't work for appositives, and it is a little awkward with predicate nominatives:

APP

The fact that English has been influenced by multiple languages is well documented.

*The fact it is well documented.

PN

One question is whether or not English would be understandable to us in another 500 years.

One question is this.

Like adjective and adverb clauses, noun clauses are dependent clauses and do not form grammatical sentences on their own; however, unlike adjective and ad-verb clauses, which can often be deleted, noun clauses play essential roles within the sentence (e.g., subject, object), to which other sentence elements must be added. For example, if the noun clause is the direct object, then a subject (S) and verb (V) must be added to make a grammatical sentence:

S   V   DO
Everyone knows that the bubonic plague (Black Death) killed millions in Europe.

Everyone knows functions as the subject and verb of the direct object noun clause.
    In the example below, the noun clause is in the subject slot; minimally, a verb is required. Here, the linking verb is followed by a predicate adjective (PA):

S   V   PA
That the bubonic plague killed millions in Europe is well documented.

It is important to remember that all dependent clauses have their own subject-verb structures <u>within</u> them. Above, the noun clause structure is subject-verb-object-prepositional phrase (*bubonic plague killed millions in Europe*), and the entire clause is placed in the subject slot. Below the pronoun substitution test is applied to the two sentences to prove their noun functions:

> *Everyone knows <u>it</u>.*
> *<u>It</u> is well documented.*

Although we are familiar with the slots that nouns occupy in a sentence, we may not be so familiar with the types of subordinate conjunctions used to introduce noun clauses. They are generally divided into two types: those that play no role in the clause—that, whether, whether or not, if—often called "that type," and those that do have a function in the clause—who(ever), whom(ever), what(ever), how(ever), which(ever), where(ever), whose(ever), and why—called the "wh– type" because most begin with "wh." We will start with the noun clause introduced by "that type" subordinate conjunctions and address issues that can arise from the use of "that"; then we will look at "wh– type" noun clauses.

"That Type" Noun Clause

In **"that type" noun clauses**, the subordinate conjunction is a flag word that signals the noun clause. It plays no role inside the noun clause. "That" is the most common signal in this type of clause, although "whether," "whether or not," and "if" are also flag words for "that type" noun clauses. Below are noun clauses introduced by "that":

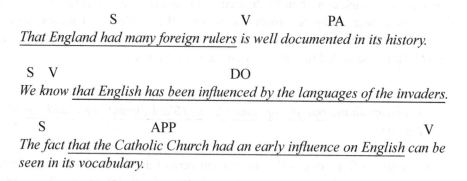

The one quirk regarding the use of *that* is that it can be deleted in the noun clause, except when the noun clause is in the subject slot:

> *_____ *England had many foreign rulers is well documented in its history.*

When used in other noun slots, such as in direct object and appositive noun clauses (see below), the flag word "that" can often be deleted while the sentence remains grammatical:

We know ~~that~~ English has been influenced by the languages of the invaders.

The fact ~~that~~ the Catholic Church had an early influence on English can be seen in its vocabulary.

The trick is to be able to recognize the noun clause without the flag word "that." You can put it back in to help find the beginning of the clause. The other subordinate conjunctions in this group (whether, whether or not, and if) cannot be deleted. Below are examples of these subordinate conjunctions flagging the noun clauses:

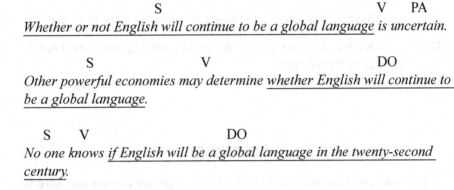

Notice the slots that these noun clauses occupy. In the first example above, the noun clause is in the subject slot; in the second and third examples, the noun clauses are in the direct object slots. The next exercise will give you practice identifying "that type" noun clauses.

Exercise 5.11 Getting a Grip on Identifying "That Type" Noun Clauses

Underline the entire noun clause and mark the noun slot that it fills in the sentence: subject (S), direct object (DO), appositive (AP), or predicate nominative (PN). (Hint: "that" is sometimes deleted from the noun clause, and there is one sentence with no noun clause.)

1. ____ Between Middle English and Early Modern English, vowels that Geoffrey Chaucer had used began to be pronounced differently.

2. ____ Whether or not people were aware of this vowel shift at the time is uncertain.

3. _____ An example of another change during this time is the "k," as in "knight," stopped being pronounced.

4. _____ That London was an important culture center in the fifteenth century has been well documented.

5. _____ Historians know that the patterns of migration into London helped form the London dialect.

6. _____ The belief that living languages don't change is wrong.

7. _____ Shakespeare believed that the changes in language should be taken advantage of.

8. _____ That no English dictionary existed during Shakespeare's time makes his writing even more historically important.

9. _____ Do you know whether Shakespeare could read Old English?

10. _____ I wonder whether or not we almost ended up speaking French rather than English.

WARNING!

Previously, we saw "that" used to introduce adjective clauses and adverb clauses. Remember that in adjective clauses, the relative pronoun plays a role in the clause itself (subject or object). The use of "that" in adverb and noun clauses is clearly different from its use in adjective clauses. In both adverb and noun clauses, "that" is simply a signal word that plays no role in the dependent clause. Let's look at some earlier examples of all three dependent clauses using "that."

Adjective Clause: *The man that Bede admired was a monk.*

Adverb Clause: *Many English speakers today are surprised that Early English would be unintelligible to them.*

Noun Clause: *We know that English has been influenced by the languages of the invaders.*

These three sentences illustrate how adjective and adverb clauses are modifiers, whereas the noun clause modifies nothing; it plays a major role in the syntax of the sentence (above as direct object).

The pronoun substitution test remains the best test to determine whether a "that" clause is a noun clause. Practice recognizing the different uses of "that" in the following exercise.

Exercise 5.12 Getting a Grip on Adjective, Adverb, and Noun Clauses Beginning with "That"

Determine whether the underlined clause beginning with "that" is an adjective clause (ADJ), an adverb clause (ADV), or a noun clause (N).

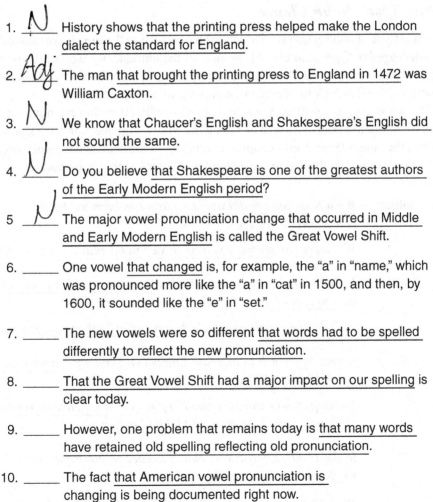

1. __N__ History shows that the printing press helped make the London dialect the standard for England.

2. __Adj__ The man that brought the printing press to England in 1472 was William Caxton.

3. __N__ We know that Chaucer's English and Shakespeare's English did not sound the same.

4. __N__ Do you believe that Shakespeare is one of the greatest authors of the Early Modern English period?

5. __N__ The major vowel pronunciation change that occurred in Middle and Early Modern English is called the Great Vowel Shift.

6. _____ One vowel that changed is, for example, the "a" in "name," which was pronounced more like the "a" in "cat" in 1500, and then, by 1600, it sounded like the "e" in "set."

7. _____ The new vowels were so different that words had to be spelled differently to reflect the new pronunciation.

8. _____ That the Great Vowel Shift had a major impact on our spelling is clear today.

9. _____ However, one problem that remains today is that many words have retained old spelling reflecting old pronunciation.

10. _____ The fact that American vowel pronunciation is changing is being documented right now.

DID YOU KNOW?

William Shakespeare's English sounded different from today's English. An interesting short video from the Open University gives examples of Shakespeare's work in both today's (British) English and Early Modern English (as Shakespeare spoke). It also explains how researchers figured out the pronunciation of the language as it was spoken 400 years ago. Go to www.youtube.com/watch?v=gPlpphT7n9s, or search for "Shakespeare: Original Pronunciation."

"Wh– Type" Noun Clause

The other type of noun clause is referred to as the **"wh– type" noun clause** (also called an **interrogative type** noun clause), as most of the introductory words are question words beginning with "wh–." Some of the most common are: who(ever), whom(ever), what(ever), how(ever), which(ever), where(ever), whose(ever), and why.

The interrogative words play a role (subject or object) within the noun clause. This is important because we will be facing the who/whom decision once again. Of course, the noun clause itself occupies a noun slot in the sentence (subject, object, etc.), as illustrated in the following examples of interrogative noun clauses:

Subject: *What Shakespeare did with his plays has been fodder for researchers since then.*

Whomever Shakespeare chose to star in his play became famous.

Object: *In 1600, Shakespeare didn't realize how famous his works would be 400 years later.*

In 1600, the people watched whatever play Shakespeare produced.

PN: *Borrowing words to increase English vocabulary is what was needed in the 1600s.*

Looking at how words rhymed in poetry is what gave researchers clues to the pronunciation of Middle English.

OP: *In the 1600s, English vocabulary needed to grow quickly in whatever way was possible at the time.*

Shakespeare had strong impact on whoever hoped to follow in his footsteps.

The use of "who" or "whom" in the noun clause depends on whether the "wh–" word fills the subject slot in the noun clause (who) or the object slot (whom):

Shakespeare had strong impact on whoever hoped to follow in his footsteps.

Whoever likes Shakespeare may also like the work of Ben Jonson, his contemporary.

Whomever the king admired became the court's poet laureate.

Remember, our choice of who or whom depends on the word's role in the noun clause (don't forget that this is true for who and whom in adjective clauses as well). You don't need to look at what slot the noun clause is filling in the sentence—focus on the structure of the noun clause itself. Because it is a clause, it has to have a subject and a verb.

In the first example above, even though the noun clause is the object of preposition *on*, *whoever* was chosen because it is the subject of the verb *hoped* in the noun clause (*whoever hoped to follow in his footsteps*). The entire noun clause is the object of the preposition *on*, not just the word immediately following it. In the second sentence, *whoever* was chosen because it is the subject of the verb *likes* in the noun clause (*Whoever likes Shakespeare*). In the third example, *whomever* is the direct object of the verb *admired* within the noun clause (*Whomever the king admired*). (Let's repeat: "who" is the subject form and "whom" is the object form—repeat several more times, please.) The whomever clause in last example above developed in the following manner:

The king admired someone

Step 1: Change the NP to an interrogative word:

The king admired whomever

Step 2: Move the interrogative word to the front of the clause:

whomever the king admired

Step 3: Add the noun clause to the noun slot in the sentence:

Whomever the king admired became the court's poet laureate.

Here are some other examples of noun clauses (underlined) with "who" and "whom" in different sentence slots:

Subject: *Whoever argued for particular set of grammar rules often faced heated opposition from others during the seventeenth and eighteenth centuries.*

(*Whoever* as subject of noun clause; noun clause in subject slot of sentence)

Whomever Samuel Johnson consulted with helped create the most important dictionary of its time.

(*Whomever* as object of preposition *with* in noun clause; noun clause in subject slot of sentence)

Direct Object: *A common eighteenth-century debate concerned who should regulate English.*

(*who* as subject of the noun clause; noun clause in DO slot of sentence)

PN: *The reformers of the English language were whomever the intellectuals of the time deemed worthy of such an undertaking.*

(*whomever* as object of noun clause; noun clause in PN slot of sentence)

OP: *Scholars of the eighteenth century argued about who had the authority to regulate English.*

(*who* as subject of noun clause; noun clause as object of preposition *about* in sentence)

The court poet recited poetry to whomever the king invited to his royal gathering.

(*whomever* as object in noun clause; noun clause as object of preposition *to* in sentence)

Exercise 5.13 Getting a Grip on the Use of "Whoever" and "Whomever" in Noun Clauses

Fill in the blanks with "whoever" or "whomever."

1. _____ had been living in the eighteenth century would most likely have been oblivious to the language changes taking place.

2. _____ you talked to in eighteenth-century London spoke a different dialect of English from Londoners of the fifteenth century.

3. In the eighteenth century, London was a bustling, chaotic center of commerce and culture, so _____ was tired of living in the countryside could move to the city and try their luck there.

4. The wealthy Londoners could choose _____ they wanted to clean, cook, and shuttle them around town, as there were many poor people looking for work.

5. Because of nineteenth-century colonization, _____ took on the task of writing a dictionary had to add many new words that came from the languages of the colonies.

6 The British spread English to _____ they colonized.

7. In the new colonized countries, _____ wanted a job with the government had to speak English.

8. _____ resisted English in the new colonies in Asia and Africa faced consequences.

9. _____ lived during the Victorian era (1837–1901) most likely believed that women were inferior to and less intelligent than men.

10. Male scientists during this time period examined the brains of _____ had died and been left unclaimed in the morgue.

Exercise 5.14 Getting a Grip on "Wh– Type" Noun Clauses

Underline the "wh– type" noun clauses and indicate what slot each occupies in the sentences: subject (S), object (O), predicate nominative (PN), or object of preposition (OP). (Hint: One sentence does not have a noun clause.)

1. _____ Whoever uses formal grammar in casual conversations may be considered "odd."

2. _____ Many early grammarians were unsure about which Latin rules should be applied to English.

3. _____ Why Shakespeare's English might have offended some eighteenth-century grammarians most likely stems from his playful use of the language.

4. _____ What Samuel Johnson's dictionary accomplished was significant.

5. _____ The current arguments about language demonstrate how language issues are tied to concepts of identity.

6. _____ Language attitudes are revealed whenever there are moves to legislate language.

7. _____ Language debates indicate where there are immigration issues.

8. _____ The question is why do these language debates coincide with immigration debates?

9. _____   The Scottish people are examining what can be done to revive Scottish Gaelic.

10. _____   How the Scottish people feel about independence was revealed in a 2014 referendum.

Now that you've practiced identifying each type of noun clause individually, the next exercise will give you the opportunity to review both types together.

Exercise 5.15 Getting a Grip on "That Type" and "Wh– Type" Noun Clauses

Underline the one noun clause in each sentence below. Use the pronoun substitution test to help find the borders of the noun clause.

1. Your eighteenth-century English dialect indicated where you were from.

2. As in the past, you can often tell the social class of a person by how he or she speaks.

3. Whoever was called "fond" in eighteenth-century London was being called "foolish."

4. In the nineteenth century, England's fast advances in science, technology, and education were why the language changed as well.

5. Railways and new ways to communicate were what spurred interaction and language changes.

6. What really helped standardize English spelling was the availability of written materials for the masses.

7. Whoever receives an education from the best schools in England is expected to have a good command of the "Received Pronunciation," an upper-class dialect.

8. Why many American dialects sound different from each other is partially the result of different immigration patterns.

9. Examine where Britain established colonies, and you will hear English dialects that have taken on characteristics of the local languages.

10. People argue that English is responsible for the death of other languages in the former colonies.

Chapter Review

Exercise 5.16 Getting a Grip—Review of Adjective, Adverb, and Noun Clauses

Underline the dependent clauses in the sentences below and mark them as adjective (ADJ), adverb (ADV), or noun (N). There is only one dependent clause in each sentence.

1. _____ It is not surprising that words from African languages can be found in American English today.

2. _____ The thousands of slaves that were shipped to America brought with them hundreds of African languages.

3. _____ Colonization of the Americas and Africa impacted the indigenous people, who lost more than just their languages.

4. _____ In 1712, Jonathan Swift proposed an English academy whose job would be to "fix" the language.

5. _____ We can understand much of eighteenth-century English, even though our language is now quite different.

6. _____ Noah Webster understood that American English needed its own dictionary.

7. _____ The invention of the phonograph in the late 1800s provided historically important recordings of the English that was spoken at that time.

8. _____ Some linguists study the impact on Australian English of British convicts who were sent to Australia in the nineteenth century.

9. _____ Some former British colonies have maintained English as an official language because they believe it to be an asset in the global marketplace.

10. _____ India, where English is often used as the language of education, is a former British colony.

11. ADV African writers like Chinua Achebe write in English so that they can reach a broader readership.

12. ADJ Because language is part of identity, many areas, such as Scotland, are trying to revitalize their indigenous languages.

13. ADJ The official language of China, which is Putonghua (Mandarin), may become more widely studied by non-Chinese in the future.

14. _ADV_ If English continues in its role as the language for international communication, will it be responsible for wiping out lesser known languages?

15. _NCS_ Whether or not English will continue to be a world language is not certain.

[handwritten: ADV has to have comma (beg. sentence)]

[handwritten: ADV ,]

[handwritten: It]

[handwritten: can replace it & make sense]

Exercise 5.17 Getting a Grip—Review of Adjective, Adverb, and Noun Clauses

Find the five dependent clauses in the **Language Focus** box at the beginning of the chapter. Copy the dependent clauses, and mark them as adjective (ADJ), adverb (ADV), or noun (N).

Exercise 5.18 Getting a Grip—Review of Adjective, Adverb, and Noun Clauses

Read each sentence carefully and circle T (true) or F (false).

1. (T) F   Adjective, adverb, and noun clauses are all dependent clauses and cannot stand alone.

2. T (F)   Both adjective and noun clauses use the relative pronoun "that."

3. T (F)   The relative pronoun "which" can always be deleted in adjective clauses.

4. T (F)   The pronoun "whom" can only be used in the subject slot of a dependent clause.

5. T (F)   Adverb clauses of comparison ("than") are very movable in the sentence.

6. (T) F   An adjective clause that is essential for identifying the noun it is modifying does not get set off with commas.

7. (T) F   Adjective clauses begin with relative pronouns, but they can also begin with relative adverbs like "where."

8. (T) F   An adverb clause that begins a sentence is followed by a comma.

9. T (F)   A clause must have a subject, verb, and an object.

10. T (F)   The following is an adverb clause: "after seeing the book."

Answers to Exercises

Note that, for most of the exercises, only the first five answers are provided below. The rest of the answers are available at the publisher's website for adopting instructors.

Answers to Exercises in Chapter 1

Exercise 1.1 Getting a Grip on Nouns

1. The brain has a left hemisphere and a right hemisphere.
   Singular/plural test: brain/brains, hemisphere/hemispheres; determiner test: the brain, the hemisphere.

2. Some psycholinguists study the organization of the brain.
   Singular/plural test: psycholinguist/psycholinguists, organization/organizations, brain/brains; determiner test: the psycholinguists, the organization, the brain.

3. Researchers conduct fascinating experiments on people.
   Singular/plural test: researcher/researchers, experiment/experiments, person/people or people/peoples; determiner test: the researchers, the experiments, the people.

4. Brain scanners have facilitated psycholinguistic studies.
   Singular/plural test: scanner/scanners, study/studies; determiner test: the scanners, the studies.

5. Linguists may define language as a set of rules.
   Singular/plural test: linguist/linguists, language/languages, set/sets, rule/rules; determiner test: the linguists, the language, the set, the rules.

Exercise 1.2 Getting a Grip on Adjectives

1. Artificial intelligence **copies** human behavior.

2. New experimental designs **have emerged**.

3. Your left side **is regulated** by the right hemisphere.

4. Dysgraphia **is** a writing disorder.

5. Speech errors **provide** researchers with helpful information.

Exercise 1.3 Getting a Grip on Personal Pronouns Versus Adjectives

1. P (A)   Your brain has two hemispheres—the left and the right.

2. P (A)   Sentence context affects our language processing.

3. P (A)   Damage to specific regions of the brain can affect

         your language.

4. (P) A   Research on aging may help us in the future.

5. P (A)   Research labs are trying to map our neural structures.

Exercise 1.4 Getting a Grip on Personal, Reflexive, and Demonstrative Pronouns

   p   r   p

1. You cannot stop yourself from processing language. Your brain does it automatically.

        p   p

2. Have you ever had a word on the tip of your tongue, but you couldn't

   p

say it?

                                          p   p

3. Psycholinguists study this phenomenon. They call it a "word retrieval" problem.

                                        d

4. Dysgraphia is a writing disorder. This is also considered a processing disorder.

                                                          p

5. A study found that a patient with dysgraphia could spell words, but he could not spell nonwords, like "plarf."

Exercise 1.5 Getting a Grip on Indefinite Pronouns Versus Adjective Quantifiers

1. P   (A)   One study showed that one shot of alcohol increased some participants' ability to pronounce a foreign language more fluently.

2. (P) A   Most lost that ability after drinking a second shot of alcohol.

3. P   (A)   Why might some Southerners misunderstand the speech of Northerners (and vice versa)?

4. P   (A)   Many children have not been tested for dyslexia, even though they may be poor readers.

5. (P) A   How one learns to read may affect attitudes toward reading.

Exercise 1.6 Getting a Grip on Personal, Reflexive, Demonstrative, and Indefinite Pronouns

1. Nobody understands the brain completely.

2. How many meanings does "bank" have, and how do we choose the correct one?

3. Children first learn common words, and many of those can come from their storybooks.

4. Do babies teach themselves how to speak, or do they need our instruction?

5. Your brain processes ambiguous words more slowly than unambiguous ones.

Exercise 1.7 Getting a Grip on Identifying Pronouns

How many pronouns did you find? 6

Language Focus: Language and the Brain

Researchers in the fields of psycholinguistics and neurolinguistics investigate how languages are learned, lost, produced, understood, and stored in the brain. <u>Some</u> of the questions that these linguists ask include: How do <u>we</u> learn a first or second language? How do our short- and long-term memories affect language processing? What processes are involved in making the sounds that form words? Where do <u>we</u> store word meaning, and how do <u>we</u> access this information? How do <u>we</u> take a series of words and get meaning from <u>them</u>?

Exercise 1.8 Getting a Grip on Verb Forms

Base	Present Form	Past Form (Ved)	Infinitive Form (to V)	Present Participle Form (Ving)	Past Participle Form (Ven)
go	go(es)	went	to go	going	gone
beat	beat(s)	beat	to beat	beating	beaten
do	do(es)	did	to do	doing	done
ride	ride(s)	rode	to ride	riding	ridden

Exercise 1.9 Getting a Grip on Verb Tenses and Expanded Verb Forms

Past:	Our cultural background <u>affected</u> our way of thinking.
Present Perfect:	Our cultural background <u>has affected</u> our way of thinking.
Future Progressive:	Our cultural background <u>will be affecting</u> our way of thinking.
Past Perfect Progressive:	Our cultural background <u>had been affecting</u> our way of thinking.

Exercise 1.10 Getting a Grip on Verbs

One psycholinguistic experiment <u>is</u> the lexical decision task. In this task, participants <u>must decide</u> between words and nonwords on a screen. They <u>push</u> a "word button" for a real word and a "nonword button" for a nonword. For example, participants <u>should push</u> the "word button" for a string of letters like "brim," but not for "brif." Then the researcher <u>measures</u> the speed of word/nonword decisions. She also <u>records</u> the correctness of the decisions. This type of test <u>can inform</u> the experimenter about our mental dictionaries. Psycholinguists <u>have been using</u> such experiments to gather data about our brain functions.

Exercise 1.11 Getting a Grip on Adverbs

1. Y Ⓝ   The corpus callosum is a <u>bundle</u> of nerve fibers that connect the brain's two hemispheres.

2. Y Ⓝ   The corpus callosum allows <u>instant</u> communication between hemispheres.

3. Y Ⓝ   Some patients with epilepsy have the corpus callosum cut to relieve <u>epileptic</u> seizures.

4. Ⓨ N   After "split brain" surgery, the two hemispheres cannot communicate <u>anymore</u>.

5. Ⓨ N   Patients who undergo this surgery can <u>often</u> adapt to the situation with few problems.

Exercise 1.12 Getting a Grip on Adverbs Versus Adjectives

          ADV
The word "bank" is <u>very</u> ambiguous. (How many things can the word "bank"

          ADV ADV
represent?) Does it take <u>much</u> <u>longer</u> for our brains to process "bank" be-

cause of its multiple meanings? Studies show that the brain processes am-

          ADV   ADV
biguous and unambiguous words <u>differently</u>. The brain must work <u>harder</u> to

        ADJ
process <u>ambiguous</u> words.

Exercise 1.13 Getting a Grip on Prepositions

1. Ⓟ A   Our knowledge <u>about</u> brain functions is still limited.

2. Ⓟ A   Early researchers examined the brains <u>of</u> dead people.

3. P Ⓐ   They often went <u>out</u> and gathered brains from morgues.

4. Ⓟ A   In the 1800s, a man had a 43-inch iron rod blown <u>through</u> his head, and he survived.

5. P Ⓐ   The man, Phineas Gage, gave brain researchers a lot of information to work <u>with</u>.

Exercise 1.14 Getting a Grip on Coordinating and Correlative Conjunctions

                                CC

The brain has a right hemisphere <u>and</u> a left hemisphere. Much of language is processed in the left hemisphere. Aphasia is the loss of language due to brain damage to the left hemisphere. Two types of aphasia are Broca's

             C   CC

aphasia <u>and</u> Wernicke's aphasia. Broca's area is in front of the left ear <u>and</u> slightly above it. Patients with damage to Broca's area (Broca's aphasia)

                         COR

<u>not only</u> may have problems producing grammatically correct sentences <u>but also</u>

may have problems producing speech in general. Patients with Wernicke's

                                               CC

aphasia have damage to an area farther back from Broca's area <u>but</u> slightly higher above the left ear. Patients with damage to Wernicke's area sound

      CC

fluent <u>yet</u> oddly incoherent.

Exercise 1.15 Getting a Grip—Review of Word Classes

1. The <u>ethics</u> of research is <u>always</u> a sensitive issue.   <u>N</u>   <u>ADV</u>
2. Researchers are interested in how <u>children</u> learn <u>language</u>.   <u>N</u>   <u>N</u>
3. What about children who <u>never</u> <u>learn</u> language?   <u>ADV</u>   <u>V</u>
4. Research suggests a critical period for learning language, <u>and</u> children never achieve full language abilities if exposed to language <u>after</u> that time.   <u>C</u>   <u>P</u>
5. Researchers <u>have</u> not <u>agreed</u> on the exact time of the critical period, but <u>most</u> believe that the critical period ends at puberty at the latest.   <u>V</u>   <u>PRO</u>

Exercise 1.16 Getting a Grip—Review of Word Classes

   ADJ N   V ADJ ADJ   N
1. The doctor tested the baby's language.

   ADJ   N   V ADJ   N   P ADJ N
2. Some psycholinguists study the organization of the brain.

ADJ   ADJ   N   V ADJ   N
3. Many reading studies track eye movements.

    N   V   ADJ   N P N P ADJ N
4. Researchers examined Einstein's brain for "clues" to his intelligence.

ADJ   N   P ADJ ADJ   ADJ   N   V   ADJ
5. Male subjects with an attractive female experimenter made more
   ADJ   N
   speech errors.

Exercise 1.17 Getting a Grip—Review of Word Classes

1. T (F)   An adjective must modify an adverb.

2. T (F)   Correlative conjunctions can be remembered through the acronym FANBOYS.

3. T (F)   The most common slot for an adjective is immediately following the noun it modifies.

4. (T) F   A preposition exists in a prepositional phrase.

5. (T) F   There are three articles in English: a, an, and the.

Answers to Exercises in Chapter 2

Exercise 2.1 Getting a Grip on Noun Phrases with the Pronoun Substitution Test

Note: **There may be other pronouns** that can be substituted for the NPs. Below are examples.

1. (some vowels are rounded, and other vowels are considered
     some   others
  unrounded)

2. (Nasal consonants are produced through the nose. Try to hold your nose)
       they   it   it

3. (Vowels become nasalized when they are next to nasal consonants.)
   they   them

4. (You produce friction in your mouth to make sounds)
         it   it   them

5. (A sound produced with the lips is called a "labial")
      one   them   it

Exercise 2.2 Getting a Grip on Appositives

1. The International Phonetic Alphabet (IPA), a set of symbols, represents the sounds of languages.

2. The IPA symbol for the first sound in the word "unhappy" is called a schwa.

3. A common sound in English, the schwa is produced in unstressed syllables. The IPA symbol is /ⵝ/ and sounds like "uh" in "duh."

4. The word "California" is pronounced with two schwas in English. Can you find them?

5. English spelling, an outdated system, is not a good phonetic representation. For example, how many ways can /k/ (as in "kite") be spelled (e.g., cat, aqua, ache)?

Exercise 2.3 Getting a Grip on Prepositional Phrases

                                          P   NP
1. The sound /Ө/ ("th") is an uncommon sound in other languages.

   P   NP P   NP
2. In many parts of the country, "Mary," "merry," and "marry" are pronounced the same.

                      P   NP   P   NP
3. People who live in isolated areas speak with accents that differ
      P   NP
   from other accents.

                  P   NP   P   NP
4. For example, in Appalachian English, "fire" and "tire" rhyme with "car."

```
    P        NP                                    P    NP   P    NP
```
5. In Appalachian English, the "r" sound is inserted into words like "wash" ("warsh").

Exercise 2.4 Getting a Grip on Adjectival Prepositional Phrases

1. Y (N)   I studied click sounds in linguistics class.
             PST: I studied them in linguistics class.

2. (Y) N   My friend from South Texas pronounces "Dawn" and "Don" the same.
             PST: She pronounces "Dawn" and "Don" the same.

3. (Y) N   Writer Mark Twain provided examples of a rural Missouri dialect in his book *Huckleberry Finn*.
             PST: Writer Mark Twain provided them in his book *Huckleberry Finn*.

4. (Y) N   The migration patterns of settlers influenced local speech patterns.
             PST: They influenced local speech patterns.

5. (Y) N   Spanish has influenced the dialects of the Southwest.
             PST: Spanish has influenced them.

Exercise 2.5 Getting a Grip on Prepositional Phrases Used as Adjectives and Adverbs

1. ADJ   The bump behind your top teeth is called the alveolar ridge.
2. ADV   The sounds /t/, /d/, and /n/ are produced with the tongue hitting the alveolar ridge.
3. ADJ   The roof of your mouth is called the palate.
4. ADJ   An important organ for speech sounds is the larynx.
5. ADV   The vocal cords vibrate in your larynx.

Exercise 2.6 Getting a Grip on Prepositional Phrases Used as Adjectives and Adverbs

```
                                              ADJ
```
1. Our intonation can express feelings of happiness, sadness, etc.

```
                                         ADJ
```
2. Usually, we do not clearly enunciate each sound of a word.

ADJ
3. Intonation is the pattern of tones.

ADJ
4. Your tongue is a speech organ that produces a variety of sounds.

ADV
5. The IPA is used by linguists.

Exercise 2.7 Getting a Grip on Prepositional Phrases Used as Adjectives and Adverbs

ADJ
Language Focus: The Sounds of Language

ADJ
Phonology and phonetics are fields of linguistics that investigate the sound

ADJ   ADJ
systems of languages. Some of the questions that linguists ask include: How

ADV
do English sound patterns and articulations differ across dialects? How

ADJ
do the sound patterns of our language affect our ability to sound fluent

ADV   ADJ
in a second language? What is the inventory of speech sounds

ADV
across all languages? What factors influence the way we pronounce words?

Exercise 2.8 Getting a Grip on Prepositions and Particles

1. PP   She received a grant from the National Science Foundation.

2. PP   The participant had a video camera inside her mouth to film her vocal cords.

3. PV   The participant didn't come back to the lab.

4. PV   The researcher turned down the money for her book.

5. PV   The student came across two relevant journal articles.

Exercise 2.9 Getting a Grip on Active and Passive Voice

1. Passive: "Pin" and "pen" <u>are</u> pronounced the same by some people.

2. Passive: The "r" after vowels in words like "park" may not <u>be</u> pronounced by some Northeasterners.

3. Passive: The sounds "t" and "d" <u>might</u> be produced with the underside of the tongue rather than the tip of the tongue by speakers of Indian English.

4. Passive: A retroflex sound is <u>created</u> by the bottom of the tongue hitting the ridge behind the teeth.

5. Passive: Our pronunciation of a second language <u>can be</u> influenced by our first language.

Exercise 2.10 Getting a Grip on Active and Passive Voice

1.   <u>P</u>   The speech study was conducted by the graduate students.

2.   <u>A</u>   The speech sounds from our first language can give us an accent in our second language.

3.   <u>P</u>   In some dialects, "Dawn" may be pronounced as "Don."

4.   <u>P</u>   A Coca-Cola may be called "pop" in parts of the United States.

5.   <u>A</u>   In Vanuatu, the Lemerig language is dying.

Exercise 2.11 Getting a Grip on Conjunctive Adverbs and Coordinating Conjunctions

1. I learned French in Africa; as a result, my French is different from the French spoken in France.

2. British English is different from American English; we, nevertheless, can communicate.

3. The English spelling system can be difficult to learn; children, therefore, spend a great deal of time learning how to spell.

4. We often drop sounds in a word, and we sometimes add sounds as in real^{uh}tor.

5. "You and I" is often pronounced "You n I," but that does not cause a loss of understanding.

Exercise 2.12 Getting a Grip—Review of Noun Phrases

1. S   Some foreign language sounds may be difficult to pronounce even after a lot of practice.

2. A   /m/ and /n/, two nasal sounds, are produced in the nasal cavity.

3. S   In your larynx, your vocal cords vibrate to produce sound.

4. O   A head cold affects the sound of your voice.

5. A   Gullah, a dialect with African roots, is spoken along the Southeastern U.S. coast.

Exercise 2.13 Getting a Grip—Review of Prepositional Phrases

1. We may have difficulty pronouncing some foreign language sounds

       ADV   ADJ

even after months of practice.

                           ADV

2. /m/ and /n/, two nasal sounds, are produced in the nasal cavity.

   ADV

3. In your larynx, your vocal cords vibrate to produce sounds.

             ADJ   ADV

4. Gullah, a dialect with African roots, is spoken along the Southeastern U.S. coast.

          ADJ   ADV

5. My friend from East Texas often feels self-conscious about her accent.

Exercise 2.14 Getting a Grip—Review of Active and Passive Voice

1. A

2. P

3. A

4. A

5. P

Exercise 2.15 Getting a Grip—Review of Active and Passive Voice

1. The size of the vocal cords affects speech sounds →
   Speech sounds are affected by the size of the vocal cords.

2. Some teachers demand the use of active voice in papers. →
   The use of active voice in papers is demanded by some teachers.

3. The tip of the tongue produces sounds like /t/ and /d/. →
   Sounds like /t/ and /d/ are produced by the tip of the tongue.

4. English borrows words from other languages. →
   Words from other languages are borrowed by English.

5. According to some, English has killed other languages. →
   According to some, other languages have been killed by English.

Exercise 2.16 Getting a Grip—Review of Active and Passive Voice

1. Word meaning can be changed by tone. →
   Tone can change word meaning.

2. The sound of my voice was affected by a head cold. →
   A head cold affected the sound of my voice.

3. Spanish as a first language is spoken by almost 400 million people. →
   Almost 400 million people speak Spanish as a first language.

4. Possibilities are created by language. →
   Language creates possibilities.

5. My personal history is reflected by my dialect. →
   My dialect reflects my personal history.

Exercise 2.17 Getting a Grip—Review

1. (T) F   Following the terminology introduced in this chapter, a one-word noun is categorized as a noun phrase.

2. T (F) Prepositional phrases function as adjectives, verbs, and adverbs.

3. (T) F   Conjunctive adverbs only conjoin sentences, unlike coordinating conjunctions.

4. T (F)   Verbs in passive-voice sentences are recognized by a form of the verb "be" plus a present participle form (Ving) of the head verb.

5. T (F)   All passive-voice sentences must have a clear "doer" in a "by" phrase at the end of the sentence.

Answers to Exercises in Chapter 3

Exercise 3.1 Getting a Grip on "Be" Verbs

1. Today, gender is an important area of sociolinguistic research.

2. For my current research, I am very interested in gender issues.

3. Thirty years ago, gender was a biological construct and not a social factor in research.

4. Over the last decade, knowledge about the social dimensions of gender has been a pivotal factor in producing rich sociolinguistic research.

5. In the future, gender will be an essential factor in language studies.

Exercise 3.2 Getting a Grip on Linking Verbs

1. Y (N)   An official language bill is undergoing revisions in the Senate.

2. (Y) N   The Chinese writing system is different from English orthography.

3. Y (N)   I have a Chicago accent.

4. (Y) N   Spanish is a common second language in the United States.

5. (Y) N   French accents sound intriguing to many Americans. Why?

Exercise 3.3 Getting a Grip on Intransitive Verbs

1. Y (N)   Women generally use fewer swear words than men.

2. (Y) N   Do you <u>agree</u> with the sentence above?

3. Y (N)   Children <u>learn</u> gendered speech styles at a very young age.

4. Y (N)   Little girls <u>use</u> more inclusive speech, for example, "Let's do this."

5. (Y) N   Little boys often <u>speak</u> more directly, using commands like "Do this."

Exercise 3.4 Getting a Grip on Intransitive and Transitive Verbs

1. (IV) TV   Dialects <u>emerge</u> from immigration patterns.

2. IV (TV)   Everyone <u>has</u> an accent.

3. (IV) TV   My friend <u>switches</u> between Japanese and English in conversations.

4. IV (TV)   Writer Chinua Achebe <u>includes</u> Africanized English words in his novels.

5. IV (TV)   Some Japanese women <u>use</u> a language style different from men's.

Exercise 3.5 Getting a Grip on Linking, Intransitive, and Transitive Verbs

       LV
1. Sociolinguistics <u>is</u> the study of language in its social context.

   TV
2. It <u>covers</u> multiple areas of language research concerning language and identity.

Exercise 3.6 Getting a Grip on Sentence Patterns with Linking Verbs

1. ADV The second-language learners were <u>in the audience</u>.

2. PN   Spanish is <u>a common second language</u>.

3. PN   English is not <u>the official language of the U.S. government</u>.

4. PN   William Labov is <u>a famous sociolinguist</u>.

5. PN   Louisiana Cajun is <u>a mix of English, French, African, and Native American languages</u>.

Exercise 3.7 Getting a Grip on Sentence Patterns with Linking Verbs

Note that only selected sentences apply to the question posed.

2. The Chinese writing system is <u>different</u> from English orthography. *[PA]*

4. Spanish is <u>a common second language</u> in the United States. *[PN]*

5. French accents sound <u>intriguing</u> to many Americans. *[PA]*

6. My Chinese language skills grew <u>weak</u> from lack of practice. *[PA]*

9. Language has been <u>a controversial topic</u> in the United States. *[PN]*

10. Language is <u>part of your identity</u>. *[PN]*

Exercise 3.8 Getting a Grip on Sentence Patterns 4 and 5

1. <u>5</u> Children <u>learn</u> the dialect of their peers.

2. <u>5</u> Different regions of the United States <u>have</u> different words for soft drinks (e.g., soda, pop, Coke).

3. <u>5</u> I <u>recognized</u> her West Virginia accent.

4. <u>5</u> Students <u>have</u> varied cultural backgrounds.

5. <u>4</u> We all <u>speak</u> with an accent.

Exercise 3.9 Getting a Grip on Sentence Patterns 5, 6, and 7

1. <u>7</u> We <u>named</u> "gleek" the Word of the Year.

2. <u>6</u> Will Texas <u>give</u> the Spanish language official recognition?

3. <u>6</u> Your accent <u>gives</u> you a regional identity.

4. <u>5</u> Colonization <u>spread</u> the English language globally.

5. <u>7</u> Many people <u>consider</u> their native language a part of their identity.

Exercise 3.10 Getting a Grip on Sentence Patterns with Transitive Verbs

1. <u>DO</u> Society plays a <u>role</u> in language attitudes.

2. <u>DO</u>   The Mandarin language has <u>the largest number of speakers</u>.

3. <u>DO</u>   Many Texans speak <u>Spanish</u>.

4. <u>DO</u>   The Endangered Language Fund supports <u>the preservation of endangered languages</u>.

5. <u>IO</u>   Many linguists give <u>the Endangered Languages Fund</u> their support.

Exercise 3.11 Getting a Grip—Review of Terminology

LINKING VERB	TRANSITIVE VERBS
adverbial complement	direct object
predicate adjective	indirect object
predicate nominative	object complement
subject complement	

Exercise 3.12 Getting a Grip—Review of Verbs and Sentence Patterns

1. T (F)   Linking verbs can sometimes take direct objects.

2. T (F)   An object complement can refer back to the subject.

3. T (F)   A direct object is always a noun phrase or an adjective.

4. T (F)   An object complement can sometimes precede the direct object that it modifies.

5. T (F)   A transitive verb always has a predicate nominative after it.

Exercise 3.13 Getting a Grip—Review of Terminology

1. <u>DO</u>   Language conflicts have caused <u>wars</u> in the past.

2. <u>PN</u>   English is <u>an international language</u>.

3. <u>DO</u>   Your social group influences <u>your speech patterns</u>.

4. <u>IO</u>   The Swedish teacher gave <u>her students</u> vowel pronunciation worksheets.

5. <u>DO</u>   Some African languages have <u>clicks</u> for consonant sounds.

Exercise 3.14 Getting a Grip—Review of Terminology and Sentence Patterns

Note that the various patterns are identified below. Examples will vary.

Linking Verb Patterns:

Pattern 1 → Subject LV   <u>ADV</u>

Pattern 2 → Subject LV   <u>PA</u>

Pattern 3 → Subject LV   <u>PN</u>

Intransitive/Transitive Verb Patterns:

Pattern 4 → Subject IV   <u>no NP</u>

Pattern 5 → Subject TV   <u>DO</u>

Pattern 6 → Subject TV   <u>IO</u>   <u>DO</u>

Pattern 7 → Subject TV   <u>DO</u>   <u>OC</u>

Exercise 3.15 Getting a Grip—Review of Terminology and Sentence Patterns

Examples will vary.

Answers to Exercises in Chapter 4

Exercise 4.1 Getting a Grip on Gerunds with the Pronoun Substitution Test

Other pronouns such as "this" work in the pronoun substitution test as well.

1. <u>(Learning) a first language</u> seems to be an easy task.
            it

2. According to some linguists, <u>language (learning)</u> is a uniquely human endeavor.
                                      it

3. They believe that humans have a unique brain for <u>(learning) a language</u>.
                                                            it

4. <u>(Acquiring) a first language</u> means <u>(acquiring) social rules</u>.
            it   it

5. <u>(Learning) "please"</u> starts from an early age.
        it

Exercise 4.2 Getting a Grip on Identifying Gerunds with the Possessive Subject Test

Note: Answers may vary.

1. The parents were asking about <u>their/our using baby talk</u> with their four-<u>year-old</u>.

2. <u>The baby's language learning</u> is linked to the baby's cognitive development.

3. Little Jenny's way to communicate is by <u>her crying loudly</u>.

4. We enjoyed <u>our studying the stages of first-language acquisition</u>.

5. <u>Their producing words in a sequence</u> is a big step.

Exercise 4.3 Getting a Grip on Identifying Gerunds with the Verb Conjugation Test

1. <u>V</u>   Researchers are <u>discovering</u> the principles of language acquisition.

   Past Tense: Researchers discovered the principles of language acquisition.

   Future Tense: Researchers will discover the principles of language acquisition.

2. <u>G</u>   A child's goal is <u>communicating</u> with caretakers.

   Past Tense: A child's goal communicated with caretakers.

   Future Tense: A child's goal will communicate with caretakers.

3. <u>G</u>   One objective is <u>procuring</u> food from a caretaker.

   Past Tense: One objective procured food from a caretaker.

   Future Tense: One objective will procure food from a caretaker.

4. <u>V</u>   The child's cry is <u>indicating</u> a specific need.

   Past Tense: The child's cry indicated a specific need.

   Future Tense: The child's cry will indicate a specific need.

5. <u>V</u>   A child in the two-word stage is <u>using</u> two words as a complete sentence.

   Past Tense: A child in the two-word stage used two words as a complete sentence.

   Future Tense: A child in the two-word stage will use two words as a complete sentence.

Exercise 4.4 Getting a Grip on Gerunds

OP
1. Children overgeneralize rules during their language (learning).

OP
2. For example, a child may overgeneralize by (calling) all four-legged animals "doggie."

S
3. (Putting) "–ed" on all verbs is another way children overgeneralize, for example, "hitted."

DO
4. These overgeneralizations show a child's (learning) of rules.

S   DO
5. (Understanding) language precedes (producing) language.

Exercise 4.5 Getting a Grip on Participles

1. Learning two languages from birth, the child had many cognitive advantages.

2. Spanish, spoken as a first or second language by many Americans, is not allowed in some schools.

3. An older person learning a second language has unique challenges.

4. Those who speak two and three languages are often very

motivated learners.

5. Exposed to a second language at an early age, fluency was not a problem.

   ↑

   This sentence must be rewritten because there is no noun/pronoun to modify, for example:

   Exposed to a second language at an early age, fluency was not a problem for Sue.

Exercise 4.6 Getting a Grip on Participle Phrase Punctuation

1. Learning Hindi online, I had to look for opportunities to practice speaking it.

2. On the Internet, you can connect with other motivated people learning Hindi.

3. A language spoken by millions of people, Hindi is one of the official languages of India.

4. *Slumdog Millionaire*, filmed in India, had a bilingual cast.

5. To learn Hindi, I love watching any movie made in Bollywood.

Exercise 4.7 Getting a Grip on Participles

Linguists investigating first-language acquisition in children and second-language acquisition in children and adults pose a variety of challenging research questions. Second-language acquisition studies often focus on older language learners; however, interesting research is being conducted on young children's learning of two languages.

Exercise 4.8 Getting a Grip on Distinguishing Between Participles and Gerunds

1. G   Being isolated for almost fourteen years caused Genie to lose her ability to learn language.
   PST: It caused Genie to lose her ability to learn language.
   DEL: *caused Genie to lose her ability to learn language.

2. P   Being isolated for almost fourteen years, Genie was of interest to linguists and psychologists.
   PST: *It, Genie was of interest to linguists and psychologists.
   DEL: Genie was of interest to linguists and psychologists.

3. P   My mother, speaking loudly, asked my Japanese friend a question.
   PST: *My mother, it, asked my Japanese friend a question.
   DEL: My mother asked my Japanese friend a question.

4. <u>G</u>   My mother's style of "foreigner talk" is <u>speaking more loudly</u>.
   PST: My mother's style of "foreigner talk" is <u>it</u>.
   DEL: *My mother's style of "foreigner talk" is.

5. <u>G</u>   <u>Learning a second language</u> requires a number of strategies.
   PST: <u>It</u> requires a number of strategies.
   DEL: *requires a number of strategies.

Exercise 4.9 Getting a Grip on Participles

1. In the United States, a <u>growing</u> number of people speak Spanish.

2. School systems used to tell <u>Spanish-speaking</u> parents that Spanish would have a negative impact on their children.

3. <u>Losing their ability to speak Spanish</u>, many second-generation Latinos struggle to communicate with relatives.

4. Older high school students <u>trying to learn their heritage language</u> may find it difficult.

5. Linguists <u>researching second-language acquisition</u> know the challenges for adult language learners.

Exercise 4.10 Getting a Grip on Infinitives as Nouns

1. According to most research, children need <u>(to learn) a second language</u> earlier, not later.
                                                                    DO
                                                                    it

2. <u>(To learn) a second language after the age of ten</u> often means a lot more work for the learner.
                                            S
                                            it

3. In many American schools, children are not taught <u>(to speak) a second language</u> until high school.
                                                                    DO
                                                                    it

4. Many students are sent to language labs for developing their listening skills. ←No infinitive phrase

PN
5. The purpose of the study is for us (to investigate) complex language

it

processes.

Exercise 4.11 Getting a Grip on Infinitives as Adjectives

1. Her desire to learn about bonobos was almost as great as her

desire to learn from the bonobos.

2. Kanzi, an intelligent bonobo, has been a good primate for researchers
to study.

3. The quest to understand about bonobos, a genetically similar species
to humans, drives the research.

4. Kanzi learned to start a campfire, to peel an apple with a knife, and to

ask for something to eat.

5. Kanzi can indicate his desire to eat a banana using a computer.

Exercise 4.12 Getting a Grip on Infinitives as Adverbs

1. Bonobos are able to learn symbols for communication purposes.

2. Children learn a complicated system of symbols to communicate. Is it
the same?

3. Baby talk is easier for the child to understand.

4. Are some languages more difficult to learn?

5. Many researchers compare different languages to identify the universal
features of languages.

Exercise 4.13 Getting a Grip on Infinitives as Nouns, Adjectives, and Adverbs

                          ADJ   ADJ

1. One reason <u>to learn a foreign language</u> is the desire <u>to experience another culture.</u>

                    N

2. <u>To learn a second language</u> is a complex task.

                        ADJ

3. Our ability <u>to learn a first language</u> disappears by puberty, according to much research.

                                        ADV

4. After that critical period, a first language is most likely impossible <u>to learn.</u>

                    N

5. <u>To speak a foreign language fluently</u> shows a great deal of dedication to the task.

Exercise 4.14 Getting a Grip—Review of Verbals

1. <u>P</u>   Languages with different <u>writing</u> systems may be more difficult to learn.

2. <u>I-ADJ</u>   A language learner may have the desire <u>to assimilate into the new culture</u>, which can affect the rate of language acquisition.

3. <u>G</u>   For second-language learners, meaningful interaction is essential for <u>learning the language.</u>

4. <u>P</u>   "Communicative Language Teaching" is an approach that uses activities focusing on effective communication rather than activities <u>focusing on grammar.</u>

5. <u>P</u>   Learning to speak a second language fluently in a short period of time can be <u>challenging.</u>

Exercise 4.15 Getting a Grip—Review of Verbals

                                                          I-N

Many people are learning English, but their goals are <u>to communicate in a</u>

                                      I-N

<u>global world.</u> A person in Indonesia may need <u>to learn English</u> for global com-

                                          I-N
merce. Does he or she want <u>to sound</u> like someone from the United States?

                    P
Most English <u>spoken internationally</u> is by non-native English speakers

                    P
<u>communicating with other non-native speakers</u>; so why do many international

                                                        I-ADV
language schools hire only native English speakers <u>to teach English</u>? Do

you think that only native English speakers should teach English to second-

language learners?

Exercise 4.16 Getting a Grip—Review of Verbals

                                                                    P
Linguists <u>investigating first-language acquisition in children and second-</u>

                                                                    P
<u>language acquisition in children and adults</u> pose a variety of <u>challenging</u> re-

search questions. Second-language acquisition studies often focus on older

                                          P
language learners; however, <u>interesting</u> research is being conducted on

                    G
<u>young children's learning of two languages</u>. Additionally, studies of language

acquisition in primates have become quite controversial.

     Some of the questions that language researchers explore include:

How important is social interaction in language acquisition? In what order do

language learners acquire the different structures of language? How does

          G
<u>second-language learning</u> differ from first-language acquisition? How do

                                                        G
attitudes and motivation impact <u>learning a second language</u>? Can primates

                              I
or other animals learn <u>to use human language</u>?

Exercise 4.17 Getting a Grip—Review of Verbals

1. <u>F</u>   Gerunds function as nouns or adjectives.
          Gerunds only function as nouns.

2. <u>T</u>   Participles may have a Ving or Ven form.

3. <u>F</u>   Gerunds may modify the head verb of the sentence.
            As nouns, gerunds do not modify verbs.

4. <u>F</u>   Infinitives may use the form to + V or Ving.
            Infinitives do not use the Ving form.

5. <u>T</u>   When a participle phrase begins a sentence, it is followed by a
            comma.

Answers to Exercises in Chapter 5

Exercise 5.1 Getting a Grip on Phrases and Clauses

1. <u>P</u>   During the first century, the Celts <u>living in the British Isles</u> were
            invaded by Romans.

2. <u>P</u>   <u>With the fall of the Roman Empire</u>, Germanic tribes displaced
            the Romans.

3. <u>P</u>   The Germanic tribes moved into the British Isles, <u>forcing the
            Celts outward toward present-day Scotland, Ireland, and Wales.</u>

4. <u>C</u>   The Celtic language disappeared with the Celts <u>when they fled
            from the Germanic invaders</u>.

5. <u>P</u>   The three Germanic tribes—the Angles, Saxons, and Jutes—
            spoke languages <u>understood by each tribe</u>.

Exercise 5.2 Getting a Grip on Relative Pronouns "Which" and That"

1. The "Great Vowel Shift," <u>which affected the pronunciation of vowels in
    English</u>, occurred systematically over hundreds of years.

2. The first Bible <u>that was written in English</u> caused great controversy
    because of the use of the "heathen" language.

3. The King James version of the Bible, completed in 1611, shows that
    language changes. ←No ADJ clause

4. Languages <u>that change</u> have a better chance of survival.

5. Changes may occur in words <u>that are difficult to pronounce</u>. (We
    simplify them.)

Exercise 5.3 Getting a Grip on Relative Pronouns "Who," "Whom," and "Whose"

1. The Germanic tribes were first asked to come to Britain to defend it from the Picts and Scots <u>who</u> were trying to take control of Britain in the fifth century.

2. The Germanic tribes, <u>whom</u> the monk Gildes described as slaughtering tyrants, decided to stay in Britain.

3. The names of British towns provide information about the people <u>who</u> settled the areas.

4. Some British towns <u>whose</u> names come from pagan words were most likely established earlier than towns with Latin names.

5. Cynewulf, <u>who</u> was a poet in Britain, wrote religious poems around 800 C.E. in the local dialect, not Latin.

Exercise 5.4 Getting a Grip on Adjective Clauses Using "Which," "That," "Who," "Whom," and "Whose"

1. Combined: The Romans brought their language, which was Latin, to the British Isles during the first century.

2. Combined: The Romans also brought the Latin script, which was based on letters for consonants and vowels.

3. Combined: The Romans, whose rule lasted for more than 300 years, left Britain to take care of conflicts back home around 400 C.E.

4. Combined: Today, we would have trouble understanding Old English, which was formed from different West Germanic dialects.

5. Combined: Old English, which used prefixes and suffixes to extend its vocabulary, resembles German more than it does modern-day English.

Exercise 5.5 Getting a Grip on Adjective Clauses and Their Punctuation

1. Latin, <u>which was the language of Christianity</u>, never replaced English in Britain.

2. Old English, <u>which is very different from Modern English</u>, had complex word endings.

3. An Old English noun <u>that functioned as a subject</u> had a different ending from a noun <u>that was used as a direct object</u>.

4. "Fæder ure Þu Þe eart on heofonum" is Old English text <u>that means "our father who is in heaven."</u> ←Note that "who is in heaven" is also an adjective clause modifying "our father."

5. During the Norman occupation, Norman French, <u>which became the prestigious language in Britain</u>, was used for law and literature, and English remained the language <u>that the common folk spoke</u>.

Exercise 5.6 Getting a Grip on Adjective Clauses

1. The history of English is roughly divided into four time periods, <u>which are Old English, Middle English, Early Modern English, and Modern English</u>.

2. The division of English into Old, Middle, Early Modern, and Modern is mostly based on historical events <u>that influenced the language</u>.

3. The year 1066 is an important year in British history because it marks the conquest of England by the Normans, <u>who came from what is now northern France</u>.

4. The Norman Conquest of 1066, <u>which marked the beginning of the Middle English period</u>, started a decline in the use of English.

5. French, the language <u>the invaders brought to Britain</u>, was used by the elite class and kings.

Exercise 5.7 Getting a Grip on Adverb Clauses that Modify Verbs

1. The Norman invaders killed members of the British aristocracy <u>if they did not relinquish their lands</u>.

2. After the Norman Conquest, some common folk spoke a mixed French-English language. ←No adverb clause

3. <u>Although bilingualism (English/French) became more common among the ruling class</u>, most of the peasants spoke only English during the eleventh century.

4. Middle English borrowed from French vocabulary <u>because French was the language of the ruling elite in the eleventh century</u>.

5. During the twelfth century, Middle English started to evolve and become distinct from Old English. ←No adverb clause

Exercise 5.8 Getting a Grip on Adverb Clauses and Adjective Clauses with "That"

1. ADJ (ADV)   The pope was clear that English versions of the Bible would not be tolerated.

2. (ADJ) ADV   The English versions of the Bible that were available in the fourteenth century were handwritten.

3. (ADJ) ADV   During Shakespeare's time, there was great religious turmoil that pitted Catholics against Protestants (and others).

4. ADJ (ADV)   In some of Shakespeare's plays, it is clear that he was in love.

5. (ADJ) ADV   "Compare her face with some that I shall show, And I will make thee think thy swan a crow" is a quote from what play by Shakespeare? (*Romeo and Juliet*)

Exercise 5.9 Getting a Grip on Adverb Clauses with "That" and "Than"

1. In the mid-1300s, English started to be used in the courts more often than French was used.

2. The plague of 1350 killed millions of people; as a result, social changes for the surviving peasants came more quickly than they had before.

3. The Black Death that ravaged Britain was so horrendous that thousands of city dwellers died.

4. The Catholic Church was so devastated by the plague that many unqualified men were allowed to enter the clergy.

5. Lollards, who advocated church reform in the 1300s, wanted more Bibles translated into English, but they were considered so subversive that they had to go into hiding.

Exercise 5.10 Getting a Grip on All Types of Adverb Clauses

1. In the Early Middle English period, the plural noun marker "–s" became the standard, although the older form "–en" was often used for plural nouns in southern England.

2. Today, there are still vestiges of the "–en" plural marker in English, as you can see in the word "oxen."

3. During the Middle English period, Britain had many different dialects <u>because the areas had different settlement patterns and foreign occupation histories.</u>

4. <u>As England kept trade ties with other countries such as Germany and Holland,</u> Middle English became influenced by languages other than Latin and French.

5. Late Middle English spelling became more regularized <u>than Early Middle English spelling had been.</u>

Exercise 5.11 Getting a Grip on Identifying "That Type" Noun Clauses

1. <u>No NC</u>   Between Middle English and Early Modern English, vowels that Geoffrey Chaucer had used began to be pronounced differently.

2. <u>S</u>   <u>Whether or not people were aware of this vowel shift at the time</u> is uncertain.

3. <u>PN</u>   An example of another change during this time is (that) the "k," as in "knight," stopped being pronounced.

4. <u>S</u>   <u>That London was an important culture center in the fifteenth century</u> has been well documented.

5. <u>DO</u>   Historians know <u>that the patterns of migration into London helped form the London dialect.</u>

Exercise 5.12 Getting a Grip on Adjective, Adverb, and Noun Clauses Beginning with "That"

1. <u>N</u>   History shows <u>that the printing press helped make the London dialect the standard for England.</u>

2. <u>ADJ</u>   The man <u>that brought the printing press to England in 1472</u> was William Caxton.

3. <u>N</u>   We know <u>that Chaucer's English and Shakespeare's English did not sound the same.</u>

4. <u>N</u>   Do you believe <u>that Shakespeare is one of the greatest authors of the Early Modern English period?</u>

5. <u>ADJ</u>   The major vowel pronunciation change <u>that occurred in Middle and Early Modern English</u> is called the Great Vowel Shift.

Exercise 5.13 Getting a Grip on the Use of "Whoever" and "Whomever" in Noun Clauses

1. <u>Whoever</u> had been living in the eighteenth century would most likely have been oblivious to the language changes taking place.

2. <u>Whomever</u> you talked to in eighteenth-century London spoke a different dialect of English from Londoners of the fifteenth century.

3. In the eighteenth century, London was a bustling, chaotic center of commerce and culture, so <u>whoever</u> was tired of living in the countryside could move to the city and try their luck there.

4. The wealthy Londoners could choose <u>whomever</u> they wanted to clean, cook, and shuttle them around town, as there were many poor people looking for work.

5. Because of nineteenth-century colonization, <u>whoever</u> took on the task of writing a dictionary had to add many new words that came from the languages of the colonies.

Exercise 5.14 Getting a Grip on "Wh– Type" Noun Clauses

1. <u>S</u>   <u>Whoever uses formal grammar in casual conversations</u> may be considered "odd."

2. <u>OP</u>   Many early grammarians were unsure about <u>which Latin rules should be applied to English</u>.

3. <u>S</u>   <u>Why Shakespeare's English might have offended some eighteenth-century grammarians</u> most likely stems from his playful use of the language.

4. <u>S</u>   <u>What Samuel Johnson's dictionary accomplished</u> was significant.

5. <u>DO</u>   The current arguments about language demonstrate <u>how language issues are tied to concepts of identity</u>.

Exercise 5.15 Getting a Grip on "That Type" and "Wh– Type" Noun Clauses

1. Your eighteenth-century English dialect indicated <u>where you were from</u>.

2. As in the past, you can often tell the social class of a person by <u>how he or she speaks</u>.

3. <u>Whoever was called "fond" in eighteenth-century London</u> was being called "foolish."

4. In the nineteenth century, England's fast advances in science, technology, and education were <u>why the language changed as well</u>.

5. Railways and new ways to communicate were <u>what spurred interaction and language changes</u>.

Exercise 5.16 Getting a Grip—Review of Adjective, Adverb, and Noun Clauses

1. <u>ADV</u>   It is not surprising <u>that words from African languages can be found in American English today</u>.

2. <u>ADJ</u>   The thousands of slaves <u>that were shipped to America</u> brought with them hundreds of African languages.

3. <u>ADJ</u>   Colonization of the Americas and Africa impacted the indigenous people, <u>who lost more than just their languages</u>.

4. <u>ADJ</u>   In 1712, Jonathan Swift proposed an English academy <u>whose job would be to "fix" the language</u>.

5. <u>ADV</u>   We can understand much of eighteenth-century English, <u>even though our language is now quite different</u>.

Exercise 5.17 Getting a Grip—Review of Adjective, Adverb, and Noun Clauses

The English language spoken today developed from the many invaders
              ADJ
<u>who took turns ruling the British Isles</u>.

Each invading group brought along its own culture and language, contributing
              N
to <u>what is now called Modern English</u>.

Remnants of the Latin, German, French, and Scandinavian languages
                        ADJ
<u>that were spoken by such conquerors hundreds of years ago</u> are still part of
                        ADJ
the English language <u>we speak today</u>.

ADJ

Among the questions <u>that linguistic historians ask</u> are:

Exercise 5.18 Getting a Grip—Review of Adjective, Adverb, and Noun Clauses

1. (T) F   Adjective, adverb, and noun clauses are all dependent clauses and cannot stand alone.

2. T (F)   Both adjective and noun clauses use the relative pronoun "that."

3. T (F)   The relative pronoun "which" can always be deleted in adjective clauses.

4. T (F)   The pronoun "whom" can only be used in the subject slot of a dependent clause.

5. T (F)   Adverb clauses of comparison ("than") are very movable in the sentence.

Hyperlinks

Chapter 1

YouTube.com, "Bruno Mars—When I Was Your Man [Official Video]." February 5, 2013. www.youtube.com/watch?v=ekzHIouo8Q4

YouTube.com, "Genie (Secret of the Wild Child)." August 29, 2012. www.youtube.com/watch?v=hmdycJQi4QAr

YouTube.com, "Genie Wiley—TLC Documentary (2003)." January 18, 2013. www.youtube.com/watch?v=VjZolHCrC8E

YouTube.com, "Language of Truth and Lies: I-Words." August 1, 2011. www.youtube.com/watch?v=Vc073RIC7_M

Chapter 2

Phonetics.ucla.edu, "The Vibrating Vocal Folds." www.phonetics.ucla.edu/vowels/chapter2/vibrating%20cords/vibrating.html

YouTube.com, "How English Sounds to Non-English Speakers." October 8, 2011. www.youtube.com/watch?v=Vt4Dfa4fOEY

YouTube.com, "Xhosa Lesson 2. How to Say 'Click' Sounds." January 11, 2009. www.youtube.com/watch?v=31zzMb3U0iY

Chapter 3

AmericanDialect.org, "Words of the Year." www.americandialect.org/woty

CBSNews.com, "Faith Salie on Speaking with 'Vocal Fry.'" September 12, 2013. www.cbsnews.com/video/watch/?id=50154925n

Chapter 4

Koko.org, "The Gorilla Foundation." www.koko.org

TED.com, "Susan Savage-Rumbaugh: The Gentle Genius of Bonobos." April 2007. www.ted.com/talks/susan_savage_rumbaugh_on_apes_that_write.html

YouTube.com, "Genie (Secret of the Wild Child)." August 29, 2012. www.you tube.com/watch?v=hmdycJQi4QA

YouTube.com, "Koko the Gorilla Cries over the Loss of a Kitten." February 14, 2013. www.youtube.com/watch?v=AJglyBAqBBU

Chapter 5

YouTube.com, "The Canterbury Tales Rap (General Prologue)—In Middle English." December 8, 2010. www.youtube.com/watch?v=4E-0PaK4RtI

YouTube.com, "The History of English in 10 Minutes." November 26, 2011. www.youtube.com/watch?v=rexKqvgPVuA

YouTube.com, "Shakespeare: Original Pronunciation." October 17, 2011. www.youtube.com/watch?v=gPlpphT7n9s

Glossary

action verb. A term in traditional grammar identifying a verb that is transitive or intransitive; it is also used to refer to all verbs that are not linking verbs. *See also* intransitive verb and transitive verb.

active voice. *See* voice.

adjectival. A word or group of words functioning as an adjective.

adjectival prepositional phrase. *See* prepositional phrase.

adjective. A word that describes or qualifies a noun or pronoun. It adds to, changes, enriches, or expands the meaning of the noun or pronoun that it modifies and often describes its attributes, quantity, or quality. Examples: *Brains are com-plex.* (*Complex* modifies *brains.*) *Recent research is focusing on brains.* (*Recent* modifies *research.*)

adjective clause. A dependent clause that modifies a noun or pronoun most often located in an independent clause. It usually begins with a relative pronoun (who, whose, whom, which, that) or a relative adverb (when, where, why). Example: *Linguists who study the role of language in society are called sociolinguists.* (The underlined adjective clause modifies *Linguists.*)

adjective phrase. A word or phrase (with head word) that functions as an adjective. Example: *The invaders were very cruel.* (The adjective phrase with the head adjective *cruel* modifies *invaders.*)

adjective quantifier. A word or phrase that answers either the question "how much?" or "how many?" of the noun or pronoun it modifies (e.g., all, both, more, enough, some). Example: *Many children are raised speaking two languages.*

adverb. A word that modifies or qualifies another adverb, verb, or adjective. It conveys information about its time, place, manner, purpose, frequency, or degree. It tells when, where how, why, how often, or to what extent. Example: *I really want to see the exhibit.*

adverb clause. A dependent clause that functions as an adverb and starts with a subordinating conjunction (e.g., although, because, if, than, that, until, when). It modifies or qualifies a verb, adverb, or adjective usually located in the independent clause. Example: *Because early invaders brought French to England, English incorporated many French words*. (The underlined adverb clause modifies the verb *incorporated* and answers the adverb question "why?")

adverb of degree. An adverb that increases or decreases the effect of the verb. Examples: *I absolutely agree with you. I somewhat agree with you.*

adverb of frequency. An adverb that modifies a verb and answers the question "how often?" Example: *Dyslexia often goes undiagnosed for years.*

adverb of manner. An adverb that modifies a verb and answers the question "how?" Such adverbs generally are derived from adjectives by the addition of "–ly" (e.g., rapid, rapidly; quick, quickly) and are often movable in the sentence. Examples: *Carlos finished the exam rapidly. Carlos rapidly finished the exam. Rapidly, Carlos finished the exam.*

adverb of place. An adverb that answers the question "where?" Example: *Sanae went home.*

adverb of purpose. An adverb that answers the question "why?" often as prepositional phrase or adverb clause. Example: *She was concerned about their learning because of their low test scores*. (Prepositional phrase answering why she was concerned.) *Because they had low test scores, the teacher was concerned.* (Adverb clause also answering the question "why?")

adverb of time. An adverb that situates the action in time. Often movable within the sentence, it answers the question "when?" Example: *Felix left yesterday.*

adverb phrase. A word or phrase (with head word) that functions as an adverb. Example: *The ashes of the English Bible drifted upward.*

adverbial. A word or group of words that functions as an adverb.

adverbial prepositional phrase. *See* prepositional phrase.

adverbial subject complement. A phrase or clause that follows a linking verb and describes or modifies the subject. Examples: *The exam is tomorrow. He is in Japan.*

antecedent. A pronoun must agree with the noun that it refers to, which is called its antecedent. Example: *John gave his time to work with the student.* (*John* is the antecedent of *his*.)

appositive. A noun or pronoun, often with modifiers, that is set beside another noun or pronoun to explain or identify it. Example: *Your friend Roger studied Khmer.* (*Roger* is an appositive that identifies *Your friend*.)

article. Words (a, an, the) that are placed before nouns or pronouns and function as adjectives. Classified as definite (the) when referring to a specific noun or pronoun and indefinite (a, an) when referring to a nonspecific noun or pronoun. Examples: *The young boy speaks four languages. I know a young woman who studied the languages of Tibet.*

aspect. The time of an event, indicated by the use of the perfect (e.g., *I have studied*), progressive (e.g., *I am studying*), or perfect progressive verb forms (e.g., *I have been studying for an hour*).

auxiliary verb. A form of the verb "be," "do," or "have" or a modal (e.g., can, may, should) that expands the three basic verb tenses. Example: *I may study Chinese next semester*.

BE substitution test. A test used to identify linking verbs. If a form of the verb "be" can substitute for a "suspected" linking verb, then it functions as a linking verb. Example: *The bonobos seem intelligent*. BE substitution test applied: *The bonobos are intelligent*. (With the linking verb *are* substituted for *seem*, the sentence retains its meaning.)

"be" verb. The most irregular verb in English (e.g., am, are, is, was, were, have been, are being). Can be used as a linking verb (e.g., *Eduardo is Venezuelan*) or a helping verb (e.g., *Eduardo is studying*).

clause. A string of words containing a subject and a verb. May be dependent (cannot stand alone; e.g., *after I studied*) or independent (can stand alone; e.g., *I went to school*). *See* dependent clause *and* independent clause.

common noun. A noun that refers to a person, idea, or thing and typically is not capitalized. The word "language" is a common noun, but "Gaelic" is a particular language, so it is a proper noun. *See also* proper noun.

complement. A word or group of words that follow and complete the verb. These may also complete the subject (with linking verbs). Examples: *She is a student*. (*student* is a subject complement.) *She is studying Swahili*. (*Swahili* is a direct object.) *See also* subject complement, object complement, *and* verb phrase.

complete predicate. A traditional grammar term identifying the main verb along with all of its modifiers. Example: *The students learned the Spanish song quickly*. *See also* simple predicate.

complete subject. A traditional grammar term identifying all of the words relating to the subject of the sentence. It is referred to as the subject noun phrase in contemporary grammar. Example: *The first participants in the brain study were re-examined ten years later*. *See also* simple subject.

conjunction. Words that conjoin similar words, phrases, or sentences. *See also* coordinating conjunction, correlative conjunction, *and* subordinating conjunction.

conjunctive adverb. A word that joins two independent clauses or sentences and signals the relationship between the two (e.g., also, anyway, besides, certainly, likewise, moreover, nevertheless, therefore). Example: *Not many people speak Scottish Gaelic; nevertheless, it has cultural value in Scotland*.

coordinating conjunction. A word that joins words, phrases, or clauses of grammatically similar categories (nouns, adjectives, etc.). Best remembered by the acronym FANBOYS: for, and, nor, but, or, yet, so. Example: *The brain was damaged in the right and left hemispheres.*

copular verb. *See* linking verb.

correlative conjunction. A pair of conjunctions (e.g., both/and, not only/but also, either/or, neither/nor) that joins grammatically similar words, phrases, and clauses that are not adjacent to each other. Example: *The crying baby was neither hungry nor thirsty.*

count noun. A noun that can be divided by numerical units (e.g., clocks, computers, flags, desks, chairs). Example: *There are 15 computers in the classroom.* *See also* noncount noun.

dangling participle. A participle that is left "hanging" because the participle (adjective) does not logically modify a noun in the clause. Example: *Arriving at the airport early, the rain blew wildly.* Could be rewritten with the pronoun "I": *Arriving at the airport early, I felt the rain blow wildly. See also* participle.

definite article. *See* article.

demonstrative adjective. A word (this, these, that, those) that identifies a noun or pronoun. Example: *This language is very interesting.* (*This* modifies the noun *language.*) *See also* demonstrative pronoun.

demonstrative pronoun. A word (this, these, that, those) that functions as a pronoun. Example: *This is quite challenging.* (Demonstrative pronoun functions as subject of sentence.) Often confused with demonstrative adjective, which must modify a noun or pronoun: *This language is quite challenging.* (Demonstrative adjective modifies *language.*) *See also* demonstrative adjective.

dependent clause (subordinate clause): A clause (contains a subject and a verb) that cannot stand alone as a full sentence. It can function as a noun, adjective, or adverb. Example: *People that speak two languages have many cognitive advantages.* (The adjective clause modifies *People* in the independent clause.) *See also* independent clause.

descriptive adjective. An adjective that assigns an attribute to its noun. Example: *Kanto is an endangered language.* (Descriptive adjective *endangered* modifies *language.*)

descriptive grammar. An approach to grammar based on the usage of native speakers. *See also* prescriptive grammar.

determiner. A word that restricts or helps define the meaning of a noun phrase. Includes articles (e.g., *The language died*), demonstratives (e.g., *That language is endangered*), quantifiers (e.g., *Most languages change over time*), and possessives (e.g., *My native language is Afrikaans*).

direct object. A noun or pronoun that follows a transitive verb and answers the question "what?" or "whom? Example: *He learned Swahili.* (He learned what?)

double modal. A series of two modals, such as "might could." Considered non-standard usage but practiced in dialects primarily in the Southern United States. Example: *We might could attend the seminar.*

function. The property of a word based on what that word is doing in a specific context. For example, the word "student" may function as a noun in one context but as an adjective in another: *The student studies brain waves.* (Functions as the subject noun.) *The student's research focused on brain waves.* (Functions as an adjective modifying the noun *research.*)

future perfect progressive verb form. A verb aspect indicating a continuous action that will finish at some time in the future. It is formed by adding "will have been" to the present participle of the verb. Example: *Next month, I will have been studying Russian for two years.*

future perfect verb form. A verb aspect indicating action that will finish at some time in the future. It is formed by adding "will have" to the past participle of the verb. Example: *A child will have learned approximately fifty words by the time she is twelve months old.*

future progressive verb form. A verb aspect indicating a continuous action that will take place over a period of time in the future. It is formed by adding "will be" to the present participle of the verb. Example: *I will be studying Hindi in India next year.*

future tense. A verb describing action that will occur in the future. Usually, it is formed by placing the auxiliary verb "will" in front of the head verb. Example: *They will finish their brain research next year.*

gerund. A noun (e.g., subject, direct object, indirect object, or predicate nominative) that is formed with the present participle of a verb (verb plus "–ing"). Example: *Practicing is important.* (*Practicing* is the subject of the sentence.)

gerund phrase. A gerund plus its complements from its "past life" as a verb. Example: *Studying Khmer in Cambodia will be an interesting experience.* (The gerund *studying* is the head noun in the gerund phrase.) *See also* head noun.

gradable. An adjective that shows different degrees (e.g., hot/hotter/hottest, cold/colder/coldest, scared/more scared/most scared).

grammar. A term that has a variety of definitions and may include structural patterns, word formation patterns, sound systems, etc.

grammatical. A sentence or phrase that conforms to standard language usage.

head noun. The main noun or pronoun in a noun phrase. Example: *My research study examines language attitudes.* (*Study* is the head noun in the subject noun phrase and is modified by the adjectives *my* and *research*; *attitudes* is the head noun in the object noun phrase and is modified by the adjective *language.*)

head verb. The main verb in a verb phrase. Example: *The students have been observing a dual-language classroom.* (*Observing* is the head verb in the verb phrase *have been observing a dual-language classroom.*) *See also* verb phrase.

indefinite article. *See* article.

indefinite pronoun. A pronoun that has no specific antecedent (e.g., anyone, someone, some, any, each, everyone, all, none, several).

independent clause (main clause). A group of words made up of a subject and verb that can stand alone as a complete sentence. Example: *I must review earlier studies before I start my new research.* (*I must review earlier studies* is an independent clause and can stand alone, whereas *before I start my new research* is a dependent clause and is not a complete sentence.) *See also* dependent clause.

indirect object. A noun, pronoun, or noun phrase that follows a transitive verb and identifies to or for whom (or what) the action of the verb is performed. Must be followed by a direct object. Example: *The researcher gave the participants twenty dollars.* (The indirect object, *the participants*, is followed by the direct object, *twenty dollars.*) *See also* direct object *and* IO movement test.

infinitive. A verbal consisting of the word "to" plus the base form of a verb (e.g., to go, to sit, to stop) that functions as a noun, adverb, or adjective. Example: *Tomoko wanted to go.* (Infinitive used as a noun.)

infinitive phrase. The infinitive form of a verb (e.g., to stop, to finish) and its complements used together as a noun, adjective, or adverb. Example: *The group wanted to study Hebrew.* (The infinitive phrase includes the infinitive *to study* and the complement *Hebrew.*)

intensifier. An adverb that modifies an adjective or an adverb and stresses the quality of the word. "Very" is a commonly used intensifier, along with "quite," "completely," "rather," "greatly," and so on. Example: *The brain is quite complex.*

interjection. An exclamatory word that is not grammatically part of the sentence. An interjection is added to provide emphasis or to express sudden or strong emotion (e.g., yikes, what the heck, great).

intransitive verb. A verb that does not have a direct object: Example: *The English language developed from the languages of the early invaders.* (The verb *developed* is followed by a prepositional phrase, not an object.) *See also* transitive verb.

IO movement test. A test used to determine whether a noun phrase functions as an indirect object (IO). Move the suspected IO to the end of the sentence and insert "to" or "for" in front of it. If the sentence retains its meaning and is still grammatically correct, then the noun phrase is an indirect object. Example: *Kodjo gave me French lessons.* IO movement test applied: *Kodjo gave French lessons to me.* (Test proves that *me* is an indirect object; be sure to move it back to its original position before the direct object.)

linking verb. A verb that links the complement back to the subject. The verb "be" is the most common linking verb (e.g., is, am, are, was, were, be, being, been, and become). Other verbs may also be used as linking verbs, particularly verbs of sense (e.g., smell, seem, appear). Examples: *The brain seemed normal. The brain is normal.* (*Seemed* and *is* both link *normal* to the subject *brain*.) *See also* BE substitution test.

main clause. *See* independent clause.

main verb. *See* head verb.

mass noun. *See* noncount noun.

modal. A type of auxiliary verb that indicates modality or attitude, that is, likelihood, ability, permission, or obligation (e.g., can/could, may/might, must, will/would, shall/should). Example: *We must visit the National Museum to see the runes.*

modifier. A word or phrase that qualifies the meaning of another word or phrase. Example: *Psycholinguists conduct interesting experiments.* (The adjective *interesting* modifies the noun *experiment.*)

noncount noun (mass noun). A noun that cannot be counted because it is regarded as a whole and not able to be divided into parts (e.g., cloth, ice, water, sugar). It is usually expressed as a measurement (e.g., gallon, liter, pound). Example: *I bought three pounds of coffee.* Some nouns can be either a noncount or a count noun depending on context (e.g., *Two coffees, please*). *See also* count noun.

noun. Traditionally defined as a word that refers to a person, place, idea, or thing. Nouns fill specific slots in a sentence, such as the subject, object, or object of preposition. They commonly have both singular and plural forms (language/languages) and can be preceded by a determiner (a, an, or the) or a number (one, two, three, etc.). Example: *The two languages are commonly spoken in Togo.* (The plural noun *languages* is modified by a determiner, *the*, and a number, *two*. The proper noun *Togo*, does not have either, though it is still a noun.)

noun clause. A dependent clause that functions as a noun in a sentence (e.g., subject, object). Usually begins with a subordinating conjunction (e.g., that, who, whoever, whom, why, what, whatever, when, where, whether, if, how). Example: *Whether there was one mother language or many separate languages is a topic that is hotly debated.* (The underlined noun clause is the subject of the sentence.)

noun phrase. A noun, pronoun, or a group of words containing a head noun that fills a noun slot, such as the subject or object of a verb. Example: *The doctor knew the best options.* (The subject noun phrase has a head noun *doctor*; the direct object noun phrase has the head noun *options.*)

object complement. A noun, pronoun, or adjective phrase or clause that completes the direct object. Example: *They named the bonobo Kanzi.* (*Kanzi* describes the direct object *bonobo.*)

object of preposition. *See* prepositional phrase.

participle. A present or past participle verb form that can be used in a verb or can function as an adjective or a noun. The present participle consists of the verb plus "–ing" (walking, talking, eating). The past participle form is often the same as the past tense of the verb; however, there are many irregular past participle forms (e.g., eat/eaten, go/ gone, speak/spoken). *See also* gerund and participle phrase.

participle phrase. An adjective phrase that contains a participle and its complements from its previous life as a verb. Example: *A child learning her first language often overgeneralizes word meanings.* (The underlined participle phrase modifies the noun *child*.) *See also* dangling participle.

particle. A word that looks like a preposition but functions differently, completing a phrasal verb. The phrasal verb generally cannot be understood from its parts; it forms an idiomatic expression. Example: *She turned down (refused) the scholarship.*

parts of speech. *See* word classes.

passive voice. *See* voice.

past perfect progressive verb form. A verb aspect that indicates a continuous action that was completed in the past. It is formed by adding "had been" to the present participle of the verb. Example: *She had been studying French for two years when she moved there.*

past perfect verb form. A verb aspect that indicates an action was completed at some time in the past but is relevant now or in the past. It is formed by adding the auxiliary verb "had" to the past participle of the verb. Example: *I had studied Arabic for six months before I felt comfortable speaking it.*

past progressive verb form. A verb aspect that indicates a continuous action that was completed in the past. It is formed by adding the past tense form of "be" (was or were) to the present participle form of the verb. Example: *I was studying the structure of Farsi.*

past tense. A verb indicating action that occurred in the past. Example: *My friend taught me Gaelic.*

personal pronoun. A word used to refer to a person or thing. These consist of first-person personal pronouns (e.g., I, we, me, us, mine, ours), second-person personal pronouns (you, yours), third-person personal pronouns (she, he, it, they, her, him, them), and possessive (mine, ours, yours, hers, his, its, theirs).

phrasal verb. *See* particle.

phrase. Traditionally defined as a group of words that function together as a noun, adjective, adverb, or verb. In contemporary grammar, one word or a group of words (with a head word) can serve as a phrase. *See also* adjective phrase, adverb phrase, noun phrase, *and* verb phrase.

possessive adjective. An adjective used with nouns to show possession (e.g., my, our, your, his, its, their, Fred's, brother's). Examples: *In the thirteenth century, people in the British Isles had to hide their English Bibles. Little of Bede's manuscripts from the first century have survived.*

possessive pronoun. *See* personal pronouns.

possessive subject test. A test used to identify gerunds. If the present participle form of the verb (e.g., walking, talking) can be modified by a possessive noun or pronoun, the present participle is functioning as a gerund. Example: *Crying is a form of communication*. Possessive subject test applied: *A baby's crying is a form of communication*. (Confirmation that *Crying* functions as a gerund.)

predicate. In traditional grammar terminology, one of the two main parts of a sentence; the other is the subject. The predicate is a word or phrase that follows the subject to complete the meaning and contains the verb and any complements. In contemporary grammar, the predicate is called the verb phrase. Example: *The corpus callosum is a bundle of nerve fibers*. *See also* simple predicate *and* complete predicate.

predicate adjective. An adjective that follows a linking verb and modifies the subject of the sentence; also referred to as a subject complement. Example: *The language seemed difficult*. (The predicate adjective *difficult* modifies the subject *language*.)

predicate nominative (predicate noun). A noun that follows a linking verb and refers back to the subject of the sentence; also referred to as a subject complement. Example: *The most challenging language was Finnish*. (The predicate nominative *Finnish* refers back to the subject *language*.)

preposition. A word (or words) that situates a noun or pronoun in time or space (e.g., in, on, above, below, along, before, at) or indicates manner, reason, or purpose (e.g., without, for, because of). The preposition is always part of a prepositional phrase, which consists of a preposition and a noun phrase (called the object of preposition). *See also* prepositional phrase.

prepositional phrase. A phrase that begins with a preposition and ends with a noun phrase (object of preposition). It functions as an adjective or an adverb. Example: *The mouse's brain was removed for analysis*. (The underlined prepositional phrase functions as an adverb in the sentences answering the question "Why was it removed?")

prescriptive grammar. An approach to grammar based on the rules found in handbooks, often described in terms of right and wrong (e.g., never end a sentence with a preposition). *See also* descriptive grammar.

present perfect progressive verb form. A verb aspect that emphasizes an ongoing action or the duration of an action that occurred in the past and may continue in the present. It is formed with the auxiliaries "have" and "be." The auxiliary "have" reflects the verb tense, and "be" is always in the past participle form, "been." Examples: *They have been studying bonobos for thirty years. She has been living in Togo for ten years.*

present perfect verb form. A verb aspect that expresses an action that happened or was completed in the (usually recent) past and may occur again. It is formed by adding the auxiliary "have" (or "has") to the past participle form of the head verb. Examples: *Researchers have documented old Norse runes (alphabet) from the first century. One of these researchers has written an article on the runes.*

present progressive verb form. A verb aspect indicating an action that is occurring in the present and is ongoing. It is formed with the auxiliary verb "be" and the present participle form of the head verb. Example: *Archaeologists are excavating Neolithic buildings in Scotland.*

present tense. A verb form indicating a present state, a habitual action in the present, or a continuous action. Can also refer to a future action. Example: *After the mouse dies, the researcher places its brain in a special fluid.*

pronoun. A word that replaces a noun or a group of words used as a noun. Includes personal pronouns (e.g., you, he, she), reflexive pronouns (e.g., yourself, himself, ourselves), demonstrative pronouns (this, that, these, those), and indefinite pronouns (e.g., some, few, many).

pronoun substitution test (PST). A test used to identify a noun phrase. If the suspected noun, noun phrase, or noun clause can be replaced with a pronoun, it is most likely a noun. Example: *Second-language learners often learn formulaic expressions.* PST applied: *They often learn them.* (Identifies *second-language learners* and *formulaic expressions* as noun phrases.

proper noun. The name of a person, place, or institution that is capitalized (e.g., Barack Obama, Brooklyn, the Smithsonian Institution). *See also* common noun

punctuation. Conventional marks (e.g., period, comma, semicolon) used to help a reader follow a text.

quantifier. A word or phrase that complements a noun by expressing its quantity (e.g., some, much, many, few, little, a lot, half). Example: *Few women were literate in fourteenth-century England.*

reflexive pronoun. A pronoun (myself, ourselves, yourself, yourselves himself, herself, itself, themselves) that refers to its antecedent within the same sentence. Example: *During the sixteenth century in England, priests often had special priest holes in castles to hide themselves from "priest hunters."*

relative adverb. An adverb (where, when, why) that introduces an adjective clause. Example: *They explained the reason why languages die.* (The adjective clause *why languages die* is introduced by the relative adverb *why*.) *See also* adjective clause.

relative pronoun. A pronoun (that, which, who, whom, whose) that introduces an adjective clause and refers to an antecedent outside the adjective clause. Example: *The Normans who invaded England in 1066 brought their French language with them.* (The relative pronoun *who* introduces the adjective clause *who invaded England in 1066,* which modifies *Normans.*) *See also* adjective clause.

sentence structure. The grammatical arrangement of words in sentences.

simple predicate. Traditional terminology for the verb of the sentence without its complements. Example: *She studied Latin. See also* complete predicate.

simple subject. Traditional terminology for the noun or pronoun that indicates the person or thing that is often the doer of the action (verb). Does not include any modifiers. Example: *The left hemisphere of the brain controls many language functions. See also* complete subject.

Standard English. The dialect spoken by educated speakers of the language, which is not the same for all English-speaking countries (e.g., British Standard English, American Standard English).

subject. *See* simple subject *and* complete subject.

subject complement. A noun, pronoun, adjective, or adverb phrase or clause that follows a linking verb and refers back to the subject of the sentence. Examples: *The research is complex. The speaker is Noam Chomsky.*

subordinate clause. *See* dependent clause.

subordinating conjunction. A conjunction (e.g., after, because, if, as soon as, than) that introduces an adverb or a noun clause. Example: *The English language has a rich vocabulary because the early invaders brought new languages to the British Isles.* (The underlined conjunction introduces the adverb clause *because the early invaders brought new languages to the British Isles.*) *See also* adverb clause and noun clause.

transitive verb. A verb that requires at least one object noun phrase or clause complement. Example: *The Vikings brought their Norse language to Britain.* (*their Norse language* is the direct object.)

verb. A word that describes an action or an occurrence or indicates a state of being (e.g., run, think, discuss, talk, live, be, stay, sit, have, multiply).

verb conjugation test (VCT). A test to identify verbs. Only verbs can be conjugated (i.e., changed to present, past, or future tense). If a word cannot be conjugated, then it is not a verb. This test helps determine whether a present participle form is functioning as a verb, gerund, or participle. Example: *An early stage of language development is babbling.* VCT applied: *An early stage of language development babbled.* (The VCT shows that *babbling* is not a verb—it is a gerund.)

verb phrase. A phrase consisting of the verb along with the complements (e.g., subject complement, objects). Referred to as the complete predicate in traditional terminology. Example: *Caretakers provide linguistic input to children*.

verb tense. A form that expresses the time at which an action takes place. There are three basic verb tenses in English: present (e.g., take), past (e.g., took), and future (e.g., will take). *See also* aspect.

verbal. A verb form that functions as a gerund (noun), participle (adjective), or infinitive (noun, adjective, adverb). May be used alone or in a phrase. Example: *Practicing the second language is important*. (Underlined is a gerund phrase; *practicing* is the gerund.) *See also* gerund, participle, *and* infinitive.

"very" test. A test used to identify many adjectives and adverbs. If a word can be intensified with the adverb "very," it is functioning as an adjective or an adverb. Example: *The research is interesting*. Very test applied: *The research is very interesting*. (Proves that *interesting* is an adjective or an adverb.)

voice. A subject-verb relationship that influences the structure of a sentence. When a sentence is active, the subject performs the action. When a sentence is passive, the subject is the receiver or the target of the action. Voice not only influences sentence structure but also the form of the verb. Examples: *Felix produced a strange sound* (active). *A strange sound was produced by Felix* (passive).

word classes. Traditionally called parts of speech. There are eight major word classes covered in Chapter 1 in the following order: noun, adjective, pronoun, verb, adverb, preposition, conjunction, and interjection.

Index

Note: Italic page numbers with *t* indicate tables.

A

Abbreviations, xxi
Action verbs, 71, 72, 207
   See also Intransitive verbs; Transitive verbs
Active voice, 59–64, 218
   exercise(s), 62, 64, 69–70
Adjectival prepositional phrases, 51–54, 207
   exercise(s), 55–57
Adjective clauses, 132–149, 207
   as dependent, 130, 132
   exercise(s), 148–149, 163, 169–170
   noun phrases and, 133–135, 137–139, 141
   punctuation, 135–136, 143–145
      exercise(s), 145
   quirks, 146–149
      adjective clauses with relative adverbs, 148
      exercise(s), 148–149
      relative pronoun deletion, 146–149
   relative pronouns, 132–143
      antecedents, 132
      definition, 216–217
      deletion, 146–149, 154
      exercise(s), 136, 141–143, 155, 163
      "that," 135–136, 142–143, 153–155, 162, 163
      "which," 133–135, 142–143

"who," 137–138, 141–143
"whom," 137, 138–140, 141–143
"whose," 137, 140–143
Adjective phrases, 207
Adjective quantifiers, 7, 9–10, 19–20, 207, 216
Adjectives, 7–12
   articles, 7, 9, 208
   comparative, 11, 156
   definition, 7, 207
   demonstrative, 7, 9, 16, 210
   descriptive, 7, 11–12, 210
   determiners, 7, 9–11, 210
   exercise(s), 12
   function of, 119
   gradable, 11, 211
   versus indefinite pronouns, 19–20
   infinitives as, 119–121
      exercise(s), 120–121
   modified by adverb clauses, 152–158
      exercise(s), 155, 157
      introduced by "than," 156–157
      introduced by "that," 152–155, 157, 162, 163
   modified by adverbs, 29–31
   numbers, 7, 10
   versus personal pronouns, 14–15
   possessives, 7, 10, 14, 215
   quantifiers, 7, 9–10, 19–20, 207, 216
   slots, 7–8, 72
   superlative, 11
   "very" test, 11, 218
   See also Participles; Predicate adjectives

219

Adverb clauses, 149–158, 207–208
  as dependent, 130
  exercise(s), 157–158, 163, 169–170
  modifying adjectives and adverbs,
      152–158
    exercise(s), 155, 157
    introduced by "than," 156–157
    introduced by "that," 152–155, 157,
        162, 163
  modifying verbs, 150–152
    exercise(s), 152
    punctuation, 151
  movability, 150
  punctuation, 151
  subordinating conjunctions, 149–150
Adverb clauses of degree, 152, 156
Adverbial prepositional phrases, 54–57
  exercise(s), 55–57
Adverbial subject complement, 80, 81, 82,
    208
  exercise(s), 83, 92–93
Adverbs, 26–31
  conjunctive, 41, 65–67, 65t
    exercise(s), 67
  definition, 26–27, 207
  of degree, 27, 29–30, 208
    exercise(s), 30, 31
  infinitives as, 121–124
    exercise(s), 122–123
    modifying adjectives, 122
    modifying verbs, 121–122
  intensifiers, 29, 212
  of manner, 27–28, 208
  modified by adverb clauses, 153, 156
  modified by adverbs, 29–31
  modifying adjectives and adverbs,
      29–31
  modifying verbs, 27–28
  movability, 27–28, 30, 43, 53, 66,
      121–122
  versus prepositions, 32
  relative, 148, 216
  as subject complement, 80, 81, 82
  superlative, 28
  of time, place, and frequency, 28, 81,
      208
Adverbs of degree, 27, 29–30, 208

Adverbs of manner, 27–28, 208
Adverbs of place, 28, 81, 208
American Dialect Society, 89
Antecedents, 13, 132, 208
Appositives
  definition, 208
  gerund phrase, 99
  gerunds as, 97, 98
  infinitive as, 118
  noun clauses as, 159
  noun phrases as, 46–48
  punctuation of, 47, 111
Articles, 7, 9, 208
Aspects of verbs, 23–25, 209
Auxiliary (helping) verbs, 21, 23–25, 209
  active and passive voice, 61
  versus linking verbs, 74
  perfect aspect, 23–24, 209
  perfect progressive aspect, 24, 209
  progressive aspect, 24, 61, 209

B
BE substitution test, 73–74, 78–79, 209
"Be" verb
  as auxiliary verb, 23–24, 74, 209
  definition, 8, 209
  as irregular, 22, 75
  as linking verb, 72–75
  in passive voice, 59–64
  verb forms, 21t
  See also BE substitution test
Bonobos, 105
Brain
  contralateral wiring, 36
  language and, 3

C
Canterbury Tales (Chaucer), 146
Chaucer, Geoffrey, 146
Clauses, 129–170
  definition, 129–131, 209
  dependent, 130
  independent, 130, 212
  versus phrases, 129, 130–131
  See also different types of clauses
Commas. See Punctuation
Common nouns, 5, 209

Comparative adjectives, 11, 156
Comparative adverbs, 28
Complements
    definition, 72, 209
    in linking verb sentence patterns,
        80–83
    See also Subject complement
Complete predicate, 4, 209
Complete subject, 4, 209
Conjunctions, 33–35
    conjunctive adverbs, 41, 65–67, *65t*,
        209
        exercise(s), 67
    coordinating conjunctions, 33–34, 66,
        209–210
        exercise(s), 67
    correlative conjunctions, 34–35, 210
    definition, 33, 209
    exercise(s), 35
    punctuation, 34, 66
    subordinating, 149–150, 160–163,
        217
Conjunctive adverbs, 41, 65–67, *65t*, 209
Coordinating conjunctions, 33–34, 66, 67,
        209–210
Copular verbs. *See* Linking verbs
Correlative conjunctions, 34–35, 210
Count nouns, 5, 10, 210

D
Dangling participles, 108–109, 210
Definite articles, 9, 208
Deletion test, 114–115
Demonstrative adjectives, 7, 9, 16, 210
Demonstrative pronouns, 16, 210
Dependent clauses, 130, 160, 210
    See also Adjective clauses; Adverb
        clauses; Noun clauses
Descriptive adjectives, 7, 11–12, 210
Descriptive grammar, xvi, 210
Determiner test, 5–6
Determiners (adjectives), 7, 9–11, 210
Direct objects (DOs)
    definition, 210
    gerund phrases, 99
    gerunds as, 97, 98
    infinitives as, 118

in transitive verb patterns, 84–89
    exercise(s), 92–93
Double modals, 26, 211

E
Eccleston, Karl, 48
English language
    history, 129, 131, 164
    Nonstandard English, xvi
    sound of, 48
    Standard English, xvi, 217
Essential adjective clauses, 146–149
Essential clauses, 135, 143–145

F
Fairbairn, Brian, 48
First-language acquisition. *See* Language
        and languages
Function versus form analysis, 4, 211

G
Genie (girl), xviii, 39
Gerund phrases, 96–97, 99, 211
Gerunds, 96–104
    as appositives, 97, 98
    definition, 211
    as direct objects, 97, 98
    exercise(s), 99–100, 101, 103, 104
    form, function, example, *96t*
    identifying, 96–98
    as object complements, 97, 98
    as object of preposition, 97, 98
    versus participles, 114–116
        exercise(s), 115–116
    as predicate nominative, 96, 97, 98,
        102–103
    as subjects, 96, 97, 98
    tests for, 98–104
        deletion test, 114–115
        exercise(s), 99–100, 101, 103
        possessive subject test, 100–101, 215
        pronoun substitution test (PST),
            98–100, 114–115
        verb conjugation test (VCT),
            101–103, 217
Glossary, 207–218
Gradable adjectives, 11, 211

H

Head noun, 4, 42, 211
Head verb, 4, 23, 42, 212
Helping verbs. *See* Auxiliary verbs
Hyperlinks, 205
    See also specific subjects

I

Indefinite articles, 9, 208
Indefinite pronouns, 18–19, *18t*, 212
Independent clauses (main clauses), 130, 212
Indirect objects (IOs)
    definition, 212
    gerund as, 97, 98
    gerund phrase, 99
    in transitive verb sentence patterns, 85–86
        exercise(s), 92–93
Infinitive phrases, 117
    definition, 212
    exercise(s), 122–124
    identifying, 117–118
    versus prepositional phrases, 50
Infinitives, 116–124
    as adjectives, 119–121
        exercise(s), 120–121
    as adverbs, 121–124
        exercise(s), 122–123
        modifying adjectives, 122
        modifying verbs, 121–122
    as appositives, 118
    definition, 212
    exercise(s), 122–124
    form, function, example, *96t*
    identifying, 117–118
    as nouns, 118–119
        exercise(s), 119
    versus prepositional phrases, 50
    splitting, 123
    as subjects, 118
    verb forms, *21t*, 22
Intensifiers (adverbs), 29, 212
Interjections, 36, 212
International Phonetic Alphabet (IPA), 41
Interrogative type noun clauses. *See* "Wh-type" noun clauses

Intransitive verbs (IVs), 76–77
    definition, 212
    versus linking verbs, 78–79
    sentence patterns, 83–84, *90t*, *91t*
        exercise(s), 84–85
    See also Action verbs
(In)transitive verbs. *See* Intransitive verbs; Transitive verbs
IO. *See* Indirect objects
IO (indirect object) movement test, 85–86, 87, 212
IPA (International Phonetic Alphabet), 41
Irregular verbs, 22, 75
IV. *See* Intransitive verbs

K

Koko (gorilla), 110

L

Language and languages
    acquisition, 39, 95
        primates, 105, 110
    brain and, 3
    click sounds, 58
    English language
        history, 129, 131, 164
        sound of, 48
    new words, 89
    sociolinguistics, 71
    speech sounds, 41, 45, 48
    vocal fry, 80
Larynx, 45
Lexigrams, 105
Linguistics, 3, 41
Linking adverbials. *See* Conjunctive adverbs
Linking verbs (LVs), 8, 71, 72–76
    versus auxiliary (helping) verbs, 74
    BE substitution test, 73–74, 209
    definition, 212
    exercise(s), 75–76
    versus (in)transitive verbs, 78–79
    purpose, 72, 74
    sentence patterns, 80–83, *90t*
LV. *See* Linking verbs
Lying, use of "I," 13

M

Main (independent) clauses, 130, 212
Main verb. *See* Head verb
Mars, Bruno, 22
Mass nouns. *See* Noncount nouns
Modals, 25–26, 61, 211, 213

N

Neurolinguistics, 3
Non-be verb. *See* BE substitution test
Noncount nouns, 5, 10, 213
Nonessential adjective clauses, 146, 147
Nonstandard English, xvi
Noun clause slots, 158–160
Noun clauses, 158–168
    as appositive, 159
    definition, 213
    exercise(s), 169–170
    as predicate nominative, 159
    pronoun substitution test (PST),
        158–159, 160, 163, 216
    slots, 158–160
    "that type" noun clauses, 160–163
        exercise(s), 161–162, 163
    "wh– type" noun clauses, 160, 164–168
        exercise(s), 166–168
Noun phrase appositives, 46–48
Noun phrases (NPs)
    adjective clauses and, 133–135,
        137–139, 141
    as appositives, 46–48
    definition, 213
    exercise(s), 67–68
    gerunds in noun slots, 97–98
    identification, 43–45
    as object of preposition, 49–53
    as objects, 43–44
    pronoun substitution test (PST), 43–45,
        216
    as subjects, 4, 42–43
    in transitive verb phrases, 77–78, 85–89
Nouns, 4–6, 42–48
    common nouns, 5, 209
    count nouns, 5, 10, 210
    definition, 4, 213
    exercise(s), 5–6, 44–45
    head noun, 4, 42, 211

identification, 4–5
    determiner test, 5–6
    singular/plural test, 5–6
infinitives as, 118–119
    exercise(s), 119
noncount nouns, 5, 10, 213
noun phrase appositives, 46–48
pronoun substitution test (PST), 43–45,
    216
proper nouns, 5, 216
slots, 6
as subject complement, 82
as subjects, 6, 42
See also Gerunds
NP. *See* Noun phrases
Numbers, as adjectives, 7, 10

O

Object complement (OC)
    definition, 213
    gerund as, 97, 98
    gerund phrase, 99
    in transitive verb sentence patterns,
        86–89
    exercise(s), 92–93
Object of preposition
    gerund as, 97, 98
    gerund phrase, 99
    noun phrase as, 49–53
Objects
    noun phrases as, 43–44
    See also Direct objects; Indirect objects
OC. *See* Object complement
Open University, 131

P

PA. *See* Predicate adjectives
Participle phrases
    definition, 214
    essential versus nonessential, 111–113
    exercise(s), 110–111, 113, 116
    participles in, 106
    placement, 107–108
    punctuation, 110–113
Participles, 105–116
    dangling, 108–109, 210
    definition, 214

Participles *(continued)*
    exercise(s), 110–111, 113, 114
    form, function, example, *96t*
    versus gerunds, 114–116
        deletion test, 114–115
        exercise(s), 115–116
        pronoun substitution test (PST),
            114–115
    identifying, 107–109
    past participle, 105
    present participle, 105
    punctuation, 110–113
        exercise(s), 113
    Ven, 105–106
    Ving, 105–106
Particles, in phrasal verbs, 57–58
Parts of speech. *See* Word classes
Passive voice, 59–64, 218
    avoidance, 64
    exercise(s), 62, 64, 69–70
Past participle, *21t*, 22, 105
Pennebaker, James W., 13
Perfect (verb aspect), 23–24, 209
Perfect progressive (verb aspect), 24, 209
Personal pronouns, 13, 14–15, *14t*, 214
Phonetics, 41
Phonology, 41
Phrasal prepositions, 31
Phrasal verbs, 57–58
Phrases, 214, 130–131
    versus clauses, 129, 130–131
    See also different types of phrases
Possessive adjectives, 7, 10, 14, 215
Possessive subject test, 100–101, 215
PP. *See* Prepositional phrases
Predicate adjectives (PAs), 81–82
    definition, 215
    exercise(s), 83, 92–93
    modified by adverb clauses, 152–153,
        156
    modified by adverbial prepositional
        phrases, 55
    as subject complement, 55, 80, 81–82
        exercise(s), 92–93
Predicate nominative (PN)
    definition, 215
    exercise(s), 83, 92–93

gerund as, 96, 97, 98, 102–103
noun clauses as, 159
as subject complement, 80, 82
    exercise(s), 83, 92–93
Predicate noun. *See* Predicate nominative
Predicates, 3–4, 215
Prepositional phrases (PPs), 49–58
    adjectival, 51–54
        exercise(s), 55–57
    adverbial, 54–57
        exercise(s), 55–57
    definition, 31–32, 215
    determining function of, 51
    exercise(s), 50–51, 55–57, 68–69
    versus infinitives, 50
    object of preposition
        gerund as, 97, 98
        gerund phrase, 99
        noun phrase as, 49–53
    versus phrasal verbs, 57–58
Prepositions, 31–32, *31t*, 215
    exercise(s), 32
Prescriptive grammar, xvi, 215
Present participle, *21t*, 22, 105
Primate Learning Sanctuary, 105
Primates, language acquisition, 105, 110
Progressive (verb aspect), 24, 61, 209
Pronoun substitution test (PST)
    for adjectival prepositional phrases,
        52–54
    for adverbial prepositional phrases,
        54–55
    definition, 216
    for gerunds, 98–100
    for noun clauses, 158–159, 160, 163
    for noun phrases, 43–45, 216
Pronouns, 13–20, *14t*
    antecedents, 13, 132, 208
    definition, 13, 216
    demonstrative, 16, 210
    exercise(s), 15, 17, 19–20
    indefinite, 18–19, *18t*, 212
    personal, 13, 14–15, *14t*
    reflexive, *14t*, 15, 216
    relative
        adjective clauses, 132–143
        exercise(s), 136, 141–143

Pronouns, relative *(contiinued)*
  "that," 135–136, 142–143, 162
  "which," 133–135, 142–143
  "who," 137–138, 141–143
  "whom," 137, 138–140,
    141–143
  "whose," 137, 140–143
  antecedents, 132
  definition, 216–217
slots, 13
Proper nouns, 5, 216
PST. *See* Pronoun substitution test
Psycholinguistics, 3
Punctuation
  adjective clauses, 135–136, 143–145
    exercise(s), 145
  adverb clauses, 151
  appositives, 47, 111
  conjunctions, 34
  conjunctive adverbs, 66
  coordinating conjunctions, 66
  definition, 216
  participles, 110–113
    exercise(s), 113
  verbs modified by adverb clauses,
    151

Q

Quantifiers (adjectives), 7, 9–10, 19–20,
  207, 216

R

Reflexive pronouns, *14t*, 15, 216
Relative adverbs, 148, 216
Relative clauses. *See* Adjective clauses
Relative pronouns
  adjective clauses, 132–143
    antecedents, 132
  exercise(s), 136, 141–143, 155, 163
  "that," 135–136, 142–143, 153–155,
    162, 163
  "which," 133–135, 142–143
  "who," 137–138, 141–143
  "whom," 137, 138–140, 141–143
  "whose," 137, 140–143
  definition, 216–217
  deletion, 146–149, 154

  "who" versus "whom," 133, 137, 140,
    165–166
Restrictive clauses. *See* Essential clauses

S

Savage-Rumbaugh, Susan, 105
Second-language acquisition. *See*
  Language and languages
Sentence patterns, 71–94
  intransitive verbs, 83–84, *90t*, *91t*
    exercise(s), 84–85
  linking verbs, 80–83, *90t*
  transitive verbs, 84–90, *90t*, *91t*
    exercise(s), 84–85, 89–90, 92–93
Shakespeare, William, 164
Sign language, 110
Simple predicate, 4, 217
Simple subject, 4, 217
Singular/plural test, 5–6
Social media, additions to vocabulary, 6
Sociolinguistics, 71
Speech, parts of. *See* Word classes
Speech patterns, 80
Split infinitives, 123
Spooner, William Archibald, 18
Spoonerisms, 18
Standard English, xvi, 217
Subject complement
  adverbial subject complement, 80, 81,
    82, 208
  definition, 80, 217
  exercise(s), 83
  infinitive as, 118
  nouns as, 82
  predicate adjectives as, 55, 80,
    81–82
    exercise(s), 92–93
  predicate nominative as, 80, 82
    exercise(s), 83, 92–93
Subject noun phrases, 4, 42–43
Subjects
  definition, 217
  gerunds as, 96, 97, 98
  infinitives as, 118
  noun phrases as, 4, 42–43
  nouns as, 6, 42
  traditional terminology, 3–4

Subordinate clauses. *See* Dependent clauses
Subordinating conjunctions, 149–150, 217
  in noun clauses, 160–163
Superlative adjectives, 11
Superlative adverbs, 28

T
"Than" (subordinating conjunction), 156–157
"That" (relative pronoun)
  adjective clauses, 135–136, 142–143, 153–155, 162, 163
    exercise(s), 136, 142–143, 155, 163
    relative pronoun deletion, 146–148, 154
  usage, 133
"That" (subordinating conjunction)
  introducing adverb clauses, 152–155, 157, 162, 163
  in noun clauses, 160–163
"That type" noun clauses, 160–163
  exercise(s), 161–162, 163
Transitive verbs (TVs), 76, 77–79
  definition, 217
  versus linking verbs, 78–79
  sentence patterns, 84–90, *90t, 91t*
    exercise(s), 84–85, 89–90, 92–93
  See also Action verbs

V
VCT. *See* Verb conjugation test
Verb classes, 71, 72–79
  action verbs, 71, 72, 207
  exercise(s), 75–76, 77, 78, 79
  See also Intransitive verbs; Linking verbs; Transitive verbs
Verb conjugation test (VCT), 101–103, 217
Verb forms, 21–23, *21t*, 211, 214, 215–216
  See also Infinitives; Participles
Verb phrases (VPs), 4, 34, 42–43, 71, 218
Verbals, 95–127
  definition, 95, 218
  types, *96t*
  See also Gerunds; Infinitives; Participles

Verbs, 21–26
  active and passive voice, 59–64
    exercise(s), 62, 64, 69–70
  aspects, 23–25, 209
  auxiliary (helping) verbs, 21, 23–25, 209
    active and passive voice, 61
    versus linking verbs, 74
    perfect aspect, 23–24, 209
    perfect progressive aspect, 24, 209
    progressive aspect, 24, 61, 209
  complements, 72
  definition, 21, 217
  exercise(s), 22, 24–25, 26
  head verb, 4, 23, 42, 212
  irregular, 22, 75
  modals, 25–26, 61, 211, 213
  modified by adverb clauses, 150–152
    exercise(s), 152
    punctuation, 151
  modified by adverbs, 27–28
    adverbs of manner, 27–28, 208
    adverbs of time, place, and frequency, 28, 81, 208
  phrasal verbs, 57–58
  tenses, 21, 23, 211, 214, 216, 218
  See also Action verbs; Intransitive verbs; Linking verbs; Sentence patterns; Transitive verbs
"Very" test, 11, 218
Vocal cords, 45
Vocal fry, 80
Voice, active and passive, 59–64, 218
  exercise(s), 62, 64, 69–70
VP. *See* Verb phrases

W
Weiner, Anthony, 13
"Wh– type" noun clauses, 160, 164–168
  exercise(s), 166–168
"When" (relative adverb), 148
"Where" (relative adverb), 148
"Which" (relative pronoun)
  adjective clauses, 133–135, 142–143
    exercise(s), 136, 142–143
    relative pronoun deletion, 146, 147
  usage, 133

"Who" (relative pronoun)
   adjective clauses, 137–138, 141–143
      exercise(s), 141–143
   usage, 133, 137, 140, 165–166
"Whom" (relative pronoun)
   adjective clauses, 137, 138–140,
         141–143
      exercise(s), 141–143
   relative pronoun deletion, 147
   usage, 133, 138, 140, 165–166
"Whose" (relative pronoun)
   adjective clauses, 137, 140–143
      exercise(s), 141–143
   usage, 133
"Why" (relative adverb), 148
Wiley, Genie, 39
Word classes, 3–39, 218
   See also Adjectives; Adverbs;
         Conjunctions; Interjections;
         Nouns; Prepositions; Pronouns;
         Verbs

X
Xhosa (language), 58

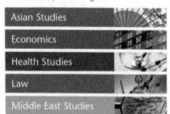